CURRICULUM IN EARLY CHILDHOOD EDUCATION

Curriculum in Early Childhood Education: Re-examined, Reclaimed, Renewed critically and thoroughly examines key questions, aims, and approaches in early childhood curricula.

Designed to provide a theoretical and philosophical foundation for examining teaching and learning in the early years, this fully updated and timely second edition provokes discussion and analysis among all readers. What influences operate (both historically and currently) to impact what happens in young children's classrooms? Whose perspectives are dominant and whose are ignored? What values are explicit and implicit? Each chapter gives readers a starting point for re-examining key topics, encourages a rich exchange of ideas in the university classroom, and provides a valuable resource for professionals. This second edition has been fully revised to reflect the current complexities and tensions inherent in curricular decision-making and features attention to policy, standardization, play, and diversity, providing readers with historical context, current theories, and new perspectives for the field.

Curriculum in Early Childhood Education is essential reading for those seeking to examine curriculum in early childhood and develop a stronger understanding of how theories and philosophies intersect with the issues that accompany the creation and implementation of learning experiences.

Jennifer J. Mueller is Dean of the School of Education at St. Cloud State University, USA.

Nancy File is Kellner Professor of Early Childhood Education at University of Wisconsin-Milwaukee, USA.

CURRICULUM IN EARLY CHILDHOOD EDUCATION

Re-examined, Reclaimed, Renewed

Second edition

Edited by Jennifer J. Mueller and Nancy File

NEW YORK AND LONDON

Second edition published 2020
by Routledge
52 Vanderbilt Avenue, New York, NY 10017

and by Routledge
2 Park Square, Milton Park, Abingdon, Oxon OX14 4RN

Routledge is an imprint of the Taylor & Francis Group, an informa business

© 2020 Taylor & Francis

The right of Jennifer J. Mueller and Nancy File to be identified as the authors of the editorial material, and of the authors for their individual chapters, has been asserted in accordance with sections 77 and 78 of the Copyright, Designs and Patents Act 1988.

All rights reserved. No part of this book may be reprinted or reproduced or utilised in any form or by any electronic, mechanical, or other means, now known or hereafter invented, including photocopying and recording, or in any information storage or retrieval system, without permission in writing from the publishers.

Trademark notice: Product or corporate names may be trademarks or registered trademarks, and are used only for identification and explanation without intent to infringe.

First edition published by Routledge 2012

Library of Congress Cataloging-in-Publication Data
A catalog record has been requested for this book

ISBN: 978-1-138-10300-9 (hbk)
ISBN: 978-1-138-10301-6 (pbk)
ISBN: 978-1-315-10331-0 (ebk)

Typeset in Bembo
by Taylor & Francis Books

Printed in Canada

CONTENTS

Preface   *vii*

1 Curriculum and Research: What Are the Gaps We Ought to Mind, Redux   1
   Nancy File

2 Public Policy and Early Childhood Curriculum in the United States   17
   Christopher P. Brown and David P. Barry

3 Standards, Correlations, and Questions: Examining the Impact of the Accountability Regime on Early Childhood Curriculum   34
   Jennifer J. Mueller and Nancy File

4 From Theory to Curriculum: Developmental Theory and Its Relationship to Curriculum and Instruction in Early Childhood Education   51
   J. Amos Hatch

5 The Curriculum Theory Lens on Early Childhood: Moving Thought into Action   64
   Jennifer J. Mueller and Kristin L. Whyte

6 Engaging with Critical Theories and the Early Childhood Curriculum   80
   Mindy Blaise and Sharon Ryan

7 Infant-Toddler Curriculum: Reconsider, Refresh, and
   Reinforce   96
   Diane M. Horm, Kyong-Ah Kwon, and Deborah E. Laurin

8 Unpacking the Tensions in Open-ended Preschool
   Curriculum: Teacher Agency, Standardization, and English
   Learners in Creative Curriculum and High/Scope   114
   Sara Michael-Luna, Lucinda G. Heimer, and Leslee Grey

9 Re-examining Play in the Early Childhood Curriculum   129
   John A. Sutterby and Deepti Kharod

10 A Story about Story: The Promise of Multilingual Children
   and Teachers and a Framework for Integrated Curriculum   144
   Elizabeth P. Quintero

11 Changing the Discourse: The Capability Approach and Early
   Childhood Education   161
   Cary A. Buzzelli

12 Countering the Essentialized Discourse of Curriculum:
   Opening Spaces for Complicated Conversations   177
   *Andrew J. Stremmel, James P. Burns, Christine Nganga, and
   Katherine Bertolini*

13 A Vision of Early Childhood Curriculum Built on Strong
   Foundations   193
   Katherine K. Delaney, Kristin L. Whyte, and M. Elizabeth Graue

14 Reclaiming and Rediscovering in Early Childhood
   Curriculum: Possibility and Promise   209
   Nancy File and Jennifer J. Mueller

Contributor Biographies   216

Index   221

PREFACE

May we live in interesting times. . .

This is a volume of chapters that engages around critical and timely questions of curriculum in the field of early childhood. We were honored and excited to have the publishers of this volume find the work compelling and relevant enough to ask us to continue this crucial dialogue in a second edition of the book. Our conversations about and our work related to early childhood curriculum had certainly continued, developed, and progressed over the seven years between editions. Scholars in the field have continued to grapple with what has come to be in the area of early childhood curriculum. In that time (thankfully) we grew and changed as teachers, scholars, and human beings. And, of course, the teachers, students, and children with whom we continued to work supported an emergent and generative context for deepening understanding of and connection with what young children need and have the right to expect from us as curriculum actors.

However, we were also appreciative of the wisdom in seeing the crucial necessity of both supporting and pushing this type of critical engagement about curriculum in our beloved field, which is currently suffering from yet another existential crisis, to define for ourselves what is important, "good," and fundamental for our youngest learners. Many of the warnings that were professed in the first edition have seemingly come to be as we navigate a context of what Kilderry (2015) terms "the intensification of performativity in early childhood education" (p. 633), where she notes that "early years practitioners increasingly have to wrestle with demands for accountability, performativity and standardized approaches to their practice" (p. 634). This has grave impacts on how we view children and their capabilities; on whose knowledge is deemed important and worthwhile; on how we understand knowledge and learning in the first place for and with young children; on how we see our jobs as educators in this context; and how we understand our place in the conversation.

As Michael Apple (2018) reminds us – indeed beseeches us – it is an especially important time for educators to take an explicitly activist role. He notes the necessity for us to

> engage as public intellectuals – bearing witness to negativity – telling the truth about what is happening in education and the larger society; showing spaces of possibility where critically democratic practices might flourish; and acting as critical secretaries of the actual realities.
>
> (p. 4)

It is a time in early childhood education, we argue, where the endeavor no longer needs to focus on establishing our importance as a field of study, justifying our rigor in our research, or staking our place in the educational trajectory. We have taken seriously our work for this volume in the act of *reclaiming* the direction our curriculum studies, enactments, and embodiments must take in early childhood in order to support rich and deep democratic participation (Cochran-Smith et al., 2016). Toward this we have renamed this second edition in order to highlight that "reclaiming" that we believe to be so important. In the first edition we re-examined, rediscovered, and renewed. Here we again re-examine, and in that re-examining, we are reclaiming the direction of our field in order to rediscover possibility and new ways of thinking and engaging – perhaps even the "not yet thought" (Young, 2013, p. 107).

We are incredibly grateful for the group of scholars who joined (or rejoined) us in this project. We again have engaged a group of educators deriving from a broad range of perspectives within the field of early childhood education. This range of perspective is key as the issues we face are complex, and (as we hopefully have learned) resolutions and new thinking will not emerge from a single story. Rather, it is the collaboration and the opportunity for new connections that will help us to do what is right and good for children – realizing that this is an evolving and ever-changing set of ideas. Later in this volume, Elizabeth Quintero engages with Bhabha's conceptions of "third space" where schools of thought can converge and hybrid ideas can emerge, setting us on new paths of understanding that were not possible without the integrative connections. We believe that the ideas, concepts, and approaches presented in these chapters help us push the discussions about early childhood curriculum into that third space, which is generative and life-giving.

We viewed the second edition as an opportunity to do something more than update the first edition. To that end, we took account of the contexts for early childhood curriculum that exist today and brainstormed the topics that we felt were important for the field to consider and reconsider at this uncertain time. As a result, some chapter topics are entirely new, and we invited some new scholars to join the conversation. We were also able to take advantage of the fact that our scholarly colleagues were exploring different interests and new approaches to their work. Thus, readers familiar with the first edition will find some familiar names writing from new perspectives. Rather than just revising our previous conversation, we are creating new platforms and possibilities.

Thus, again, we did not provide a common definition of curriculum to our contributors, nor did we work from one ourselves. However, we do believe that, overall, this volume takes a more activist, urgent stance – less about defining curriculum in multiple ways and more about curriculum as the lived experiences of children and teachers, what knowledge children are entitled to within these experiences, and how we must draw from multiple sources in order to theorize, create, and enact curriculum. This all has connection to the social justice-oriented and rich democratic participatory approaches that we need to disrupt the current contexts of radical standardization, marketization, commodification, accountability, and curriculum as a product that shape teaching and learning in the current political context. With young children always at the center of our work, we hope that this conversation pushes us to take seriously our obligation to honor who they are – their ways of thinking and knowing – to create and work within a curriculum that provides them the access to all of the knowledge to which they are entitled (Young, 2013).

Turning to the chapters, while not specifically delineated into sections, they are ordered in a way to invite readers to think about early childhood curriculum beginning with the larger social and educational contexts shaping our work. Then the chapters address particular theoretical schools of thought and the impacts that these have had on our thinking about and understanding of early childhood curriculum. The chapters then move into examinations of more specific curricular approaches considering infants/toddlers, play-based, open-ended, and story-based/integrated curriculum approaches. The book finishes out with three chapters devoted to critique of our current situation in early childhood curriculum development, but also, importantly that offer renewed ways of approaching, "re-understanding," and carrying out our work with teachers, families, and children.

The role of Chapter 1 is to provide a review of the research-based ways of knowing about curriculum. Nancy File explores the questions pursued through scholarly inquiry related to curriculum in early childhood. Recognizing the overwhelming presence of questions of "what works" in research about curriculum, File critiques the capacity of current approaches to provide answers crucial to determining how children might be best served.

Chapter 2 takes us into the larger policy contexts that shape and influence early childhood curriculum. Christopher Brown and David Barry explore these contexts, both historical and current. They examine how the standards-based accountability reforms, deriving from a particular approach to curriculum and learning based in standardization and efficiency, have impacted teachers' practice and our ability to enact curriculum that serves all children well.

In Chapter 3, File joins co-author Jennifer Mueller to examine further how the standards and accountability movement has evolved, examining the national disciplinary content standards, state-level early learning standards, and standards for developmentally appropriate practice. They examine this context in relation to early childhood curriculum, exploring key packaged and commercially available curriculum products. They also explore what this means for how teachers view and can engage in their work in classrooms.

The role of Chapter 4 is to help the reader to understand the connections between developmental theory and the evolution of curriculum and instruction in early childhood classrooms. This is the one chapter from the first edition offered again in the second. The author, Amos Hatch, was retiring as we began this work, and we still wanted to include this important essay. Hatch contends in his chapter that developmental theory is insufficient to define the content of early learning. Drawing upon Vygotskian theory, he illustrates potential approaches in math and science learning.

The book moves from here in Chapter 5, authored by Jennifer Mueller and Kristin Whyte, to explore the contributions that curriculum theory might offer the work being undertaken in early childhood. They explore the field of curriculum theory historically and then focus in on recent work related to democratic participation. The discussion looks at enduring tensions between theory and practice and argues that early childhood can progress through the struggle of reimagining and enacting curriculum that embodies authentic, collective participation.

In Chapter 6, Mindy Blaise and Sharon Ryan hone in on critical theory, providing an overview of what this as a field of study has contributed to our thinking about early childhood curriculum. They suggest ways that critical theory might evolve and further diversify in order to continue to disrupt and dismantle the logic of dualisms inherent in Western thought that influence our understandings and enactments of early childhood curriculum. They conclude with the reassertion of the importance of critical theory as a lens for contemporary early childhood practice.

In Chapter 7, authored by Diane Horm, Kyong-Ah Kwon, and Deborah Laurin, the reader is re-introduced to curricula offered for infants and toddlers, with updates regarding the major curricula available to this age group. The authors explore two major issues in the field, a definition of curriculum and the current focus on preparing children for what comes next (i.e., readiness), now addressed by recent scholarship addressing the youngest children.

Chapter 8, by Sara Michael-Luna, Lucinda Heimer, and Leslee Grey, examines how two common open-ended, early childhood curriculum approaches (Creative Curriculum and High Scope) have changed and shifted in light of the context of heightened standardization and accountability. They discuss the tensions for teachers as they try to meet the accountability demands whilst continuing to stay true to child-centered approaches to teaching. They illustrate the promises and pitfalls of open-ended curricula in this context, including the harm that can ensue when cultural context is used in superficial, inauthentic ways.

Chapter 9 focuses on the very important component of play in early childhood curriculum. John Sutterby and Deepti Kharod remind us of the tensions inherent as a focus on skills and academics in programming for young children continues to proliferate. They reiterate the importance of play and highlight the multitude of spaces where play can occur and be the conduit for learning for young children. They also discuss new venues for play that may serve to reshape our understandings of play-based learning.

In Chapter 10, Elizabeth Quintero pushes us to think about how we authentically include in the official curriculum the ways of knowing and understanding of the wide diversity of children and students that engage with us in classroom settings. Focusing specifically on multilingualism, she suggests that story should serve as the basis of curriculum development and as the foundation for an integrated curriculum that connects to the content areas and reflects the assets that children from all communities bring to the table. She shares a lifetime of research with multilingual children and student teachers in "third space" learning, providing rich examples of the ways that story can support and create new/hybrid opportunities and engagement.

Cary Buzzelli brings us Chapter 11 where he introduces readers to the major tenets of the Capability Approach. He contends that it provides a moral foundation for addressing teaching and learning. His exploration of what this approach can offer the field is framed around a series of "what if" questions. As this approach is just beginning to take hold within the field, we view the discussion as an important point of "possibility" to take hold of in ECE.

In Chapter 12, Andrew Stremmel, James Burns, Christine Nganga, and Katherine Bertolini provide critique of the standardization context, arguing that this has brought us to an "essentialized audit culture" in early childhood education. In response to this, they engage readers in discussion to help us re-understand learning in early childhood from a humanizing perspective where relationship building and the space for complicated conversations can be supported.

This brings us to Chapter 13, where Katherine Delaney, Kristin Whyte, and Elizabeth Graue bring us back to early childhood curriculum in context. They argue for a site in which early childhood curriculum is focused first and foremost upon children, their questions, their interests, and their capabilities. This is best realized, they contend, when teachers are able to both honor the ways in which young children learn and make meaning and respond with a willingness to explore content in depth, an approach that is perhaps most difficult, yet most reflects the idea of serving young children well.

The volume ends, in Chapter 14, with a discussion of key points and overarching themes that connect the work of our contributors. As was our goal for the volume, we believe that this set of chapters has provided both critique and direction forward. We hope that it will engender dialogue within the field; what appears here is a beginning point, not an end.

At the same time, this act of writing represents an end point for our work, and before moving on, we must acknowledge those who have contributed to it. First and foremost, we are grateful to our contributors, all of whom eagerly took on the work of offering up their thinking. As editors, we performed the expected tasks of assisting in shaping the arguments and tweaking the writing. Yet also, we were incredibly enriched ourselves by our engagement with the ideas offered by our contributors – thank you for stimulating our ongoing growth. We are also grateful to our colleagues who have helped us move to this point, the teacher education students with whom we have engaged, resulting in reciprocal growth; our fellow early childhood teachers, faculty, and researchers for the long conversations held with them; and the children we have known, who have always been at the center of why it all matters.

Individually, Jennifer must thank her family for all the love, support, and patience they could muster throughout this process – which included a job change and an across-state-lines move. I also thank my teacher education and early childhood colleagues – now from two institutions – who are always willing to jump into the work with passion and enthusiasm, and that ever-important focus on "the babies." And I thank our teachers and teacher candidates who constantly help me to "keep it real" and push my thinking in really important and expansive ways.

Nancy acknowledges the support of her family, for their interest, cheering, and willingness to tolerate the "I don't want to talk about it" reply when stress was the deepest. After decades (!) in the field, I am so grateful to all those friends in the profession, some of them contributors to the volume, and some who have overlapped with my work in other venues. They had a large role in shaping my thoughts and supporting me personally, a mix that is incredibly generative and a true gift.

References

Apple, M. (2018). *The struggle for democracy in education: Lessons from social realities*. New York, NY: Routledge.

Cochran-Smith, M., Stern, R., Sánchez, J.G., Miller, A., Keefe, E. S., Fernández, M.B., Chang, W., Carney, M.C., Burton, S., & Baker, M. (2016). *Holding teacher preparation accountable: A review of claims and evidence*. Boulder, CO: National Education Policy Center. Retrieved from http://nepc.colorado.edu/publication/teacher-prep

Kilderry, A. (2015). The intensification of performativity in early childhood education. *Journal of Curriculum Studies*, 47(5), 633–652.

Young, M. (2013). Overcoming the crisis in curriculum theory: A knowledge-based approach. *Journal of Curriculum Studies*, 45(2), 101–118.

1

CURRICULUM AND RESEARCH

What Are the Gaps We Ought to Mind, Redux

Nancy File

Research is inextricably tied to the topic of curriculum in early childhood education (ECE). The field has long embraced children's development as the source for approaching professional work with children, culminating in the publication of the guidelines reflected in *Developmentally Appropriate Practice* (Copple & Bredekamp, 2009, the most recent edition). Over the three iterations of its publication, the conceptual framework of Developmentally Appropriate Practice (DAP) has been increasingly tied to research findings about children's development and learning across domains. As well, with the advancement of the standards and accountability era, there is an emphasis on curriculum being research- or evidence-based and reflective of early learning standards. Finally, in a field that is viewed, in part, as funded by discretion or choice, there is a long-standing reliance on research to demonstrate the effectiveness of ECE, which includes an emphasis on the teaching and learning taking place in classrooms.

In this chapter, I discuss trends and issues in research efforts focused on early childhood curricula in the United States. In spite of decades of study in this area, I contended in the first edition of this book that it was still prudent for the field to heed the infamous caution from the London Underground system to "mind the gap." In the case of the Underground, the gap is used to denote the space between the platform and the car, where people can misstep and fall. It still seems an apt metaphor for examining the relationship between research and ECE curriculum. Where are the gaps between what we know and what we need to know? What gaps are evident in how the research is typically approached? Where is the potential for misstep, here realized as failing to serve young children well?

Initially I examine research from two perspectives of study, noting gaps in general. This will offer both a summary from the previous edition and will include more recently published research. The first perspective is questions framed as "what works" – inquiry I will refer to as "*if*" curricula work. The second perspective is questions of "*how*" curriculum works. My discussion is unavoidably brief and thus, not comprehensive. From there I discuss gaps that exist within the specific aspects of the research.

The relationship between curriculum and research is necessarily multi-faceted. As noted previously, ECE has embraced children's development as being at the heart of practice. DAP is "not based on what we think might be true or what we want to believe about young children" but is "informed by what we know from theory and literature about how children develop and learn" (Copple & Bredekamp, 2009, p. 10). Furthermore, carrying out the curriculum "includes following the predictable sequences in which children acquire specific concepts, skills, and abilities" (p. 18). This knowledge is established through research. It is drawn upon in order for curriculum developers to claim a curriculum is research- or evidence-based. Operating in another direction, it is important to consider how research *about* curriculum provides information about what curricula do – or fail to do – for young children. In this chapter, I will focus on the latter influence, research about curriculum.

How Sufficient Is Our Research Knowledge?

In this section I utilize the concept of gap to consider the question of how well what we know about curriculum matches what we need to know. Two approaches taken to this problem include questions related to curriculum effectiveness and curriculum processes.

Does Curriculum Work?

A question that has formed the base for much of the research has been that of effectiveness, or does a curriculum accomplish its stated purposes? Studies of early childhood curriculum effectiveness initially flourished in the 1960s as researchers implemented preschool interventions intended to prepare children for school. The Consortium for Longitudinal Studies concluded, "It appears that a variety of curricula are equally effective in preparing children for school and that any of the tested curricula is better than no preschool program at all" (Consortium for Longitudinal Studies, 1983, p. 442). Powell (1987) later countered, after reviewing a wider set of the early literature, that the type of preschool curriculum "does matter" (p. 205). He concluded that the research base provided both cautious suggestions and, ultimately, further questions.

In the early 2000s, preschool curriculum effectiveness was the purpose of the Preschool Curriculum Evaluation Research (PCER) initiative, an ambitious multi-site examination of 14 preschool curricula in comparison to teachers implementing practice as usual, in randomly assigned classrooms. Based upon examining the patterns of findings across child outcome data, the report offered the conclusion that only two of the curricula were more effective than the control for achievement outcomes over the preschool (pre-kindergarten) year (Preschool Curriculum Evaluation Research Consortium, 2008). An impact on math measures was found for a researcher-developed math curriculum, supplemented by DLM Early Childhood Express math software. Impacts across early literacy and language measures were found for a relatively prescriptive curriculum package, DLM Early Childhood Express with Open Court Reading. This particular curriculum continued to show effectiveness on similar academic measures at the end of kindergarten. Positive effects at the end of kindergarten on academic outcomes were noted also for a researcher-developed language curriculum (language effects) and for a relatively scripted curriculum developed by Success for All (reading effects). Overall, the lack of positive achievement effects across most of the curricula at both times of assessment was notable (Preschool Curriculum Evaluation Research Consortium, 2008). Future research efforts have tended to be much less on the grand-scale that was envisioned with PCER, perhaps in response to the largely null findings.

Concurrently with the implementation of PCER, the question of "does a curriculum work" was taken up via the What Works Clearinghouse, an initiative of the U.S. Department of Education. Groups of researchers assessed the available evidence for a curriculum, determining if studies met conditions set for methodological rigor and then considering the findings. To this day, upon examining the early childhood curriculum reviews, it does not take long to reach two conclusions. First, there is a dearth of research that meets the conditions set for consideration of the data, experimental or quasi-experimental studies. Second, there are few conclusions established thus far regarding a curriculum found to "work," although practice guides for early math and reading instruction were released.

A variation of this basic question has been for researchers to examine the effectiveness of a curriculum relative to differences among children – what works for whom – with a tendency to focus on child characteristics that are common demographic measures. The investigators from independent projects who made up the Consortium for Longitudinal Studies pooled their analyses to examine family structure (presence or not of a father), maternal education, child's sex, and child's "ethnic background" (which we would currently refer to as race, as samples were largely African American). In the pooled analyses, which admittedly may have masked differential effects of curricula in conditions where multiple curricula were being implemented, there were no significant effects of these variables in regression analyses predicting child outcomes such as IQ scores, achievement test scores, placement in special education, and grade retention (Lazar & Darlington, 1982).

On the other hand, some individual-site project investigators who pursued early curriculum comparison studies did report differential effects relative to these demographic variables. Miller and Bizzell (1983) reported that in middle school, boys who had been enrolled in non-didactic preschool models scored higher on reading and math achievement tests than boys who had enrolled in didactic models. These differences were larger and more consistent than the differences found in the subsample of girls, as well as being in a different direction (Miller & Bizzell, 1983).

A contrasting approach to analysis was taken by the Preschool Curriculum Evaluation Research initiative. In the report released about cross-site analyses, child demographic variables, including race/ethnicity, sex, and maternal education, were treated as co-variates and controlled. Potential interactions of these variables with curricula were not examined (Preschool Curriculum Evaluation Research Consortium, 2008).

As noted previously, more recent investigations about *if* curriculum works have been smaller-scale. Researchers have tended to investigate more focused and/or supplementary curricula and approaches toward specific goals, rather than comprehensive approaches designed to provide the sum of the classroom experiences. For example, Wang, Firmender, Power, and Byrnes (2016) offered a meta-analysis of studies of mathematics curricula in pre-kindergarten and kindergarten. They noted that these focused curricula showed moderate to large effect sizes for children's learning in 29 studies, with effect sizes being larger when instruction was offered for 120–150 minutes per week compared to 23–90 minutes. Thus, it appears that clear and careful intent in curriculum design, in an area as highly researched as early mathematics learning, coupled with a critical mass of instructional time, did matter to children's learning.

Interestingly, the dataset from the PCER study has been recently re-analyzed with new queries. Nguyen, Jenkins, and Whitaker (2018) separated what they termed the "whole child" curricula (Creative Curriculum and High Scope – designed to be comprehensive approaches) and the curricula focused on either mathematics or language/literacy for comparisons at the end of pre-kindergarten. They also examined if implementation of these curricula in a Head Start versus a public-school pre-kindergarten program mattered. They found that program auspice did not impact child outcomes, while the targeted curricula impacted outcomes in the targeted domains. In conclusion, they deemed the targeted approaches more successful.

In another analysis of the PCER dataset, Jenkins et al. (2018) reported that literacy-focused curricula resulted in higher literacy-related outcomes at the end of pre-kindergarten compared to Creative Curriculum and High Scope (considered together), though with a modest effect size; a more substantial effect size was found when literacy-focused curricula were compared to the locally-developed curricula that served as control conditions. There was no significant difference between the Creative Curriculum and High Scope compared to the locally developed curricula. Similarly, the math-focused curricula resulted in both higher math and academic outcomes at the end of pre-kindergarten compared to Creative Curriculum and High Scope. In spite of the lack of impact on child outcomes, Creative Curriculum and High Scope classrooms evidenced higher scores on classroom process measures (e.g., Early Childhood Environment Rating Scale) compared to the locally developed curricula. Based on the results of these re-analyses, members of the research team have concluded that "while it is conceivable that some kind of effective global, whole-child curriculum will be developed, there is currently no strong evidence to support these curricula as they currently exist" and "it may be best to focus more attention on assessing and implementing proven skill-focused curricula and move away from the comparatively ineffective whole-child approach" (Jenkins & Duncan, 2017, p. 42).

Prior to moving forward, it bears noting that the PCER study was conducted in the early 2000s; these data are now almost 15 years old. The context that drives curriculum development has changed, with early learning standards ubiquitously entrenched and now in second or later renditions in most states. Both the Creative Curriculum and High Scope groups have continued to develop their approaches and resources for teachers. For example, the fourth edition of Creative Curriculum was published in 2002. In 2016, the sixth edition was made available, with widely expanded teacher materials and resources. What was once contained within a book is now an extensive set of materials. While the age of the dataset is mentioned previously as a limitation of the study by Nguyen et al. (2018), the recommendation by Jenkins and Duncan (2017) just is not accurate in referring to these curriculum models "as they currently exist" (p. 42) being the status of the comparisons made by this research group. The gap in the edition of the curricula under study is indeed a pertinent methodological question for any conclusions being drawn.

While the question of "what works" appears to be fairly straightforward, the evidence in the literature is not robust. This reflects a significant gap indeed. But is the question entirely straightforward? Why are the answers we have long sought so elusive? I take up these questions again later in the chapter.

How Does Curriculum Work?

The research interests explored in this section are focused on the workings of curriculum. What might make curriculum effective or not? What processes operating within a curriculum are important? What do children experience within curriculum? In contrast to the previous section, in addition to quantitative designs, qualitative methods have been employed here.

In an early investigation, Stallings (1975) examined first- and third-grade classrooms utilizing a range of curriculum models in Project Follow Through (intended to extend the benefits of Head Start approaches for low-income children). A large number of variables that captured teaching processes in the classrooms were included in the analyses, and they illustrate some of the complexity of curriculum and teaching. For example, Stallings noted that higher reading and math scores were associated with small group instruction in first grade but large group instruction in third grade. Systematic instructional patterns, with the introduction of information, followed by questioning and immediate feedback, were also associated with higher reading and math scores. On the other hand, Stallings concluded that children scored higher on a problem-solving measure when they were in classrooms with more flexibility, marked by things such as a variety of materials and activities and some child choice in grouping and seating during the day. The extensive report from Stallings reflects how dense an examination of the workings of curriculum can be.

More recently, Early and her colleagues (2010) detailed the experiences of children in preschool programs across several states. While they did not utilize the notion of curriculum in describing their work, they coded via observation the types of experience variations that occur within the curriculum. Overall, they found that on average children spent slightly more time in teacher-assigned activities (37 percent) than in meals and routines (34 percent) or than in free choice activities (29 percent). Perhaps not surprisingly, regarding the nature of the activity, various language and literacy activities (17 percent – categories were non-exclusive) were coded as comprising the content of children's activities more frequently than science (11 percent) or math (8 percent), but only slightly more than social studies and art (15 percent each).

The Early et al. (2010) study included an examination of classroom differences relative to race and income. In classrooms where children were relatively better off financially, there was more free choice time and less time spent as "no coded learning activity." When classrooms enrolled more African American children, there was more time spent in teacher-assigned settings, as well as in meals/routines. Classrooms with more Latino/a children were found to have higher proportions of time spent in teacher-assigned activities and more time spent in language/literacy activities.

These studies indicate that there may be systematic differences in the experiences children have in classrooms. In some cases differences may be the result of curricular emphases, but without more in-depth examination, it isn't possible to understand the relationship of these research findings to curriculum.

A closer examination of the experiences of individual children within the curriculum is provided by qualitative researchers. For example, Quintero (2015) reported on a multi-year project focused on building integrated curriculum that was strongly related to children's local contexts (e.g., family, community) and that allowed children's learning potential to be highlighted in the creation of the curriculum. Those operating as teacher-researchers have particular power underlying their examinations of curriculum. For example, Gallas (1995) detailed in book form the connections between her approach to science curriculum, conducting "science talks" and children's construction of thinking. The analysis of classroom discourse provided unique insights into the complexity of curriculum in action, illustrating the theories children developed and questions emanating from their sense of wonder at the world. Ballenger (1999) reflected upon her approaches to teaching alphabet knowledge in relation to the ways children made use of their alphabetic knowledge to think about their own identities and their relationships with others. Mardell (1999) explained units he developed with preschoolers that led to deep explorations of topics others might have found unusual, including exploring music via an initial focus on the Beatles and an astronomy unit. Finally, the contributions of Paley are unparalleled in this area. For example, her description of a curriculum built around Leo Lionni's children's books reflects both the potential intellectual challenges for children and a profound understanding of children (Paley, 1998). With their base in classrooms, qualitative studies provide an understanding of the *how* of curriculum that is unique in its contribution to our knowledge. Yet, the work remains at a distance from the canon of the field defined as research-based because it is considered localized (thus not generalizable) and is non-peer-reviewed in its publication. In addition, these researchers are more interested in understanding emergent forms of curricula than in approaches to be adopted and replicated at scale.

In summary, questions regarding *how* curriculum works have generally received less attention than questions of *if* a curriculum works. The gaps here between what we know and what we need to know are great. The quantitative observational research has typically involved complex coding schemes with answers that are elusive and partial. Qualitative research has illuminated the tip of the iceberg that is curriculum enactment. There is much to learn about how teachers and children interact within the curriculum and how the curriculum supports learning and development.

Gaps in Theorizing and Designing Research

In this section I will consider how gaps have operated in the tasks of the theorizing that underlies the research endeavor as well as in the tasks of designing the research. Farran (2011) declared that the ECE field needs a better "theory of change" (p. 6). She was writing to the topic of curricula focused on a "readiness" agenda. She noted that if readiness for kindergarten achievement was a goal (while also elucidating various approaches to defining this concept), that there should be a well-theorized progression (similar to a logic model, widely used in research and evaluation today) that specified the experiences provided to children, which led to the skills they would learn, and then the outcomes expected. While not adopting this type of linear progression in thinking, I want to draw upon the idea of theorizing about children's learning in relation to curricula and how it does and should work, something that is not widely discussed in the research literature.

What Is Curriculum and What Is Important in It?

This question, perhaps sounding commonsensical, has been under-theorized in much of the research literature. As noted by Powell (1987) in reflection on earlier efforts to conduct research on curriculum, the work was marked by "the confounding of content, activities, and materials with teaching techniques" (p. 194). In other words, while content and instruction may be separable at the theoretical level, it is more difficult to recognize these aspects of the endeavor as research is conducted to understand curriculum. And, currently, as curricula are more highly engineered, the curriculum has become a package of goals, content, teaching strategies, and materials. This sets the stage for how complex the topic of curriculum is in actuality.

The definition of curriculum and identification of important elements has often been undertaken implicitly by researchers or theorized in reference to research findings (hence, apart from any form of curriculum theory). Within the quantitative paradigm, curriculum typically represents a package of content and methods, as authored by an entity. Here, curriculum is akin to an intervention – an outcome is desired and curriculum is a means to that outcome. It is, in effect, an independent variable. In much of the "*if*"-focused research, the curriculum is largely a black box, unexamined in detail, considered a replicable independent variable.

Control of variables is important in this paradigm. Thus, an important feature of curriculum is that researchers can assess the fidelity with which a curriculum is implemented. The more tightly engineered the curriculum, the easier to create measures of fidelity to the content and methods used in the classroom. The potential gap here is the connection of fidelity to a curriculum to the actual learning that takes place in a classroom – is it crucial to follow the scripted activities and expectations or is learning better supported by more flexibility? To what extent has the question of what is important in curriculum been addressed not by theoretical dialogue, but by methodological commitments to measurability?

An alternate approach to theorizing is evident in mathematics-based curriculum research. Working from the highly researched area of the development of young children's mathematical thinking, Clements and Sarama (2016) described the process of designing instructional activities focused on the learning trajectories reflected in this research. The theoretical base of the curricula is more clearly in sight here, as informed by what is known about learning. Yet, as noted by Farran (2011), young children's learning is most often not a clear and linear process whereby we can predict when children's skills might advance. In this case, mathematics-focused curricula appear to be an exception, not the norm. While in the opening of the chapter I noted that DAP is established upon the notion of developmental sequences, the question remains of whether our knowledge about early learning is strong enough (or learning itself is linear enough) to support the design of curricula that "include carefully sequenced lessons that support, build on, and can be adapted to each stage in a child's learning progression" (Phillips et al., 2017, p. 24). When the assumption underlying curriculum design is that this is possible to do and has been accomplished in a curricula, in effect the curriculum begins to assert a version of developmental progression that becomes "developmental reality."

In a recent summary of research about pre-kindergarten, Phillips et al. (2017) provided the following regarding curriculum and what is important:

> Effective curricula provide engaging activities focused on skills and concepts that are ripe for learning by young children and that provide an essential foundation for more demanding, conceptually rich learning opportunities to follow. There is growing evidence that stronger achievement outcomes occur when teachers rely on curricula that focus on a given skill area such as language/literacy, math and self-regulation as distinct from curricula that

attempt to address and incorporate all domains of development simultaneously, sometimes referred to as "global" curricula.

(pp. 23–24)

Here, what is important in curriculum is defined in relation to findings about achievement from earlier research. It is a post-hoc definition, absent of theorizing about what young children need and why they need it, except that it appears to work toward this end of achievement outcomes. At the same time, what this statement provides about curriculum is frustratingly general in nature toward the task of curriculum development.

On the other hand, qualitative researchers are more likely to regard curriculum as lived experiences in the teaching/learning process, with a package (if it is included) to be only a part of the phenomenon. Here curriculum is not theorized as *the* input in an input-output model because it will be lived out differently in all classrooms, in the messy and localized process of individual children learning together in a group, nested within a larger group of classrooms, nested within a particular community.

The task for qualitative researchers is to be clear about their theorizing regarding what curriculum includes and how children's lived experiences connect to this phenomenon of education. For qualitative researchers the issue is not related to control; their goal is understanding. Well-designed qualitative research can examine the question of what is important in curriculum from a variety of perspectives, but the work depends upon the clarity and coherency with which researchers approach the task of understanding.

So, what are the gaps here and what might be the missteps in how children are served by curriculum? When the phenomenon being researched is under-theorized, we risk that findings are impacted by questions that are based upon what we have been finding, without recognition of how that matters. For example, are achievement scores all we want to impact via curriculum? Is a "whole child" approach ineffective because it is not adequate for children or because of how we have implicitly come to think about what curriculum means and what should be important in it? Is a search for effective curricula leading the early childhood field away from the notions of integrated learning that have traditionally defined our understanding of how young children make meaning? If so, is that a misstep or a step forward for children?

What Parts Do Teachers and Children Play in the Curriculum?

For qualitative researchers, curriculum is a lived experience; thus, teachers and children are essential to the equation of understanding the processes of teaching and learning. This should be evident, if we think back to the examples described earlier about how researchers operating within this paradigm have explored how curriculum works. These actors are essential to the theorizing that takes place in high-quality qualitative research. For example, Mihai, Butera, and Friesen (2017) explored differences in teachers' take-up of a newly-supplied curriculum set, illustrating the complexities of curriculum enactment. They detailed many impacts on this, including teachers' personal circumstances, judgments about the curriculum's fit for the children, perspectives about being able to effect change with children, and the involvement of their teaching teammates within the classroom. Other recent research provides the possibility of visioning the work of the teacher as impossible to script within curriculum manuals, instead being dependent upon the teacher's foundation of knowledge and skills in teaching practices, deep content knowledge, and understanding of children's home cultures (Graue, Whyte, & Delaney, 2014). Graue and colleagues framed this teacher work around the metaphor of improvisation, and it provides a vision of teachers as more than implementers of a pre-planned curriculum.

However, in quantitative research, because curriculum is most often conceptualized as an entity in itself, teachers may be considered as separate from it. Even with tightly scripted curricula, teachers may verge from script, and they certainly differ amongst each other on personal style. For example, Pence, Justice, and Wiggins (2008) found variations in teacher fidelity to the curriculum both across time and across different aspects of the curriculum model they were evaluating. Powell et al. (2008) made it clear that teachers are not blank slates, and their implementation of curriculum is related to their understanding of the content being taught as well as their own beliefs about appropriate learning goals and teaching strategies. Baker and her colleagues (Baker, Kupersmidt, Voegler-Lee, Arnold, & Willoughby, 2010) found that teacher implementation of an intervention curriculum was significantly related to their context, center-level variables. Among their findings, they noted that teachers who rated their work environments as more collegial, supportive, and fair implemented more activities from the intervention curriculum. More recently, in surveys with teachers who were largely educated at the bachelor's and master's level, findings revealed that teachers' self-efficacy related to teaching literacy, science, and math varied across these domains, with self-efficacy decreasing in the order in which these domains are listed (Gerde, Pierce, Lee, & Van Egeren, 2018).

In response to findings such as these, emphasis has been placed upon professional development (Phillips et al., 2017). The type of professional development offered to teachers based upon Graue et al.'s (2014) improvisation theorizing would be very different from a program developed to address gaps in knowledge or informed by issues of fidelity of implementation. However it remains to be seen how similar teachers can be propelled to be, what it is important that they do similarly, and, indeed, what this means for a curriculum to be responsive to all children. There are still many gaps in our knowledge about how teachers, coming with their own beliefs about curriculum and learning, work/personal situations, knowledge and skills, and sense of their capacities, work within the curriculum on a day-to-day basis.

Regarding the role of children in the curriculum, again qualitative researchers are able to focus upon how children engage with activities. For example, Sutterby (2005) documented how children in an early childhood classroom subverted the goals of the teacher and curriculum, in one case using the Montessori practical life materials to represent cosmetics.

Our nascent knowledge from quantitative research in how children experience curriculum is thus far based on variables related to demographic definitions of their identities. For example, Miller, Bugbee, and Hybertson (1985) found that during language lessons, more individual instruction was given to boys who were off-task, in comparison to girls, who were more often reprimanded when off-task. Boys who volunteered more often and offered opinions more often were given a higher ratio of positive-to-negative validation by their teachers. Conversely, girls who volunteered more often and asked more questions were given a higher ratio of negative-to-positive reinforcement by their teachers. Results such as these should be a concern; unfortunately, this has not been a thriving area of curriculum research.

So, there is much left to learn about children's individual processes involved in the activities of teaching and learning. Within the area of "what works" research, the emphasis is the attainment of goals – children's achievement scores. Children represent individuals, yes, but the research focus is dependent upon aggregated scores and group averages. The control of variables related to children "gets rid of the noise" so to speak, but also results in the erasure of individual differences among children and families and their contexts.

Farran (2011) noted that the readiness concept is often related to the notion of "fixing" children. The deficit perspective has long influenced curriculum researchers. More recently, this perspective has been recast to one of *differences* that arise from the contexts in which children are reared (Dray & Wisneski, 2011). Regardless, a primary driver behind curriculum research has been to learn how to move children living in poverty closer to the developmental profiles of children who are not. What assets children may bring to the equation is not theorized. Without this, curriculum has proceeded to be developed and researched with implicitly agreed upon goals and hidden biases. In addition, the individual learning processes of children are subsumed within a standardized intervention designed to address a problem.

The gap between this research/theoretical paradigm and other possibilities impacts children and families to the extent that we have short-circuited theorizing about the child within the curriculum. Offering another perspective, Colegrove and Adair (2014) documented children's emerging agency as learners in a classroom when the curriculum provided these opportunities, the teachers moving toward responding to children to stretch their understanding rather than planning based upon their standardized benchmark scores. (Note: This research was theorized using the Capability Approach; see Chapter 11 in this volume by Buzzelli.) The potential impact of differences in how children and teachers are theorized within the curricula, and the dearth of research about day-to-day teaching and learning are important gaps to note.

How Should We Assess Outcomes of Curriculum?

An outcomes-focus for curriculum research is centered in quantitative approaches. It is important to consider whether our outcome measures have been adequately theorized and whether we have measures sufficient to the research that must be designed. If measures are matched appropriately to the curriculum, one expects positive results if the curriculum is indeed effective. For example, Neuman, Pinkham, and Kaefer (2015) found that a supplementary set of curriculum materials was effective for children's learning of the vocabulary words included in the teaching. The intervention did not, however, result in increases in scores on the standardized Peabody Picture Vocabulary Test.

However, the question of matching intent to outcome is fraught with difficulty. Do we have valid assessments of all aspects of learning? To what degree and in what specific areas does any particular standardized assessment narrow our conceptions of children's learning and experiences, as contended by Graue (1998)? What values and cultural ways of knowing have impacted the development of these assessments, making this a definitively non-neutral process? Graue argued that standardized assessments act to create impressions that development – or learning – is a singular process with universal paths.

A typical assessment battery is often shared across recent studies, consisting of perhaps the Peabody Picture Vocabulary Test, measures of early literacy focused on phonological awareness, and portions of the Woodcock-Johnson battery for literacy/language and mathematics. More recently, measures of executive functioning have gained in interest among researchers. These assessments represent what is available, as well as what can be accomplished most readily in a context that calls for individual child assessment. A further consideration of researchers is instruments that cover a sufficient age span.

This assessment paradigm has been conceptualized as representing a small set of academic skills (Farran, 2017). Farran noted the lack of deeper learning skills evident within the standard assessment battery. Snow and Matthews (2016) critiqued literacy assessments as being too tied to constrained skills (e.g., alphabetic knowledge) which are directly teachable and not reflecting enough unconstrained skills (e.g., vocabulary), which are more difficult to influence, as well as assess. In both of these critiques, it is clear that researchers perceive an important gap. Methodologically, research has moved forward based upon available assessments. Theoretically, it follows, that either there is a gap between the intent of the curriculum and assessment, or, alarmingly, curricula have been narrowed to meet what we currently measure. The need for more varied measures is clear throughout the research field, including, for example, "more easy-to-use measures of skills like critical thinking, creativity, and problem solving" (Weiland, 2018, p. 190).

In summary, there are many ways in which gaps emerge in the research about curriculum in early childhood. When curriculum is treated as a black box, we end up knowing little about the processes involved for children and teachers.

Tightly engineered curricula are more amenable to effectiveness research questions, but perhaps not strongly theorized with an eye toward the messy contexts of real learning. Too often curriculum is researched as a "thing" rather than an enactment of teaching and learning processes that involve people. And, finally, we are stuck in a paradigm of effectiveness and accountability that is driven more by what *can* be measured than what it matters to measure. This paradigm renews itself as a measure, shows predictability for future learning, and then the content of that measure becomes the "first stage of what is to be learned."

Conclusion 3 gaps.

I conclude that there remain significant gaps between what we know about curriculum in early childhood and what we need to know. For the reasons mentioned at the start of the chapter (i.e., the standards/accountability era, the need to prove the return on investment for discretionary programs in early childhood), the focus has remained on *if* what we do in the classroom works. It is difficult to design a rigorous evaluation of curriculum that does not fail in some ways to account for what is involved in the highly contextualized processes of education. Our lack of answers may not be attributable to poor science, but instead the inadequacies of our assumptions, models, and tools in relation to questions that are only simple on the surface. We must consider whether the answers we believe can be found are illusory or, indeed, would prove ultimately helpful in the form in which they can be addressed. Where can research most effectively interact with practice?

Another gap exists between the *if* and *how* questions. They remain separate in part because the quantitative paradigm is the only available method for answering the former. Questions of *how* allow the possibility of alternative paradigms and a greater focus on local context. Furthermore, we still need to find places for the scholarship contributed from those who employ critical approaches to examine the meanings of curriculum (for example, Cannella, 1997). Crossing the gap found among vastly different epistemologies and methods remains a challenge but doing so would allow for more interaction among the questions of what we need to know, how we need to know it, and why it matters to young children and their families.

Finally, gaps exist within the work of theorizing. Too little research is based upon theories of curriculum. This is an issue for curriculum developers as well. The gaps between the citations of research findings typically provided in the theoretical rationales underlying a curriculum and the particular experiences provided within the curriculum are often uncomfortably wide. If the research is not powerful enough to tell us "do it this way" (and most often is not), then we need to construct a strong understanding of *why* we would do it this way. The approach espoused in DAP is accompanied by claims that a research-based understanding of child development provides "much clearer guidance for programming decisions than do other, more value laden philosophies" (Bredekamp, 1991, pp. 202–203). Yet, curriculum is inherently value-laden. Who do we want our children to be, and why? Is curriculum an intervention for a young child, or is it about living the early years of life? How much control do we need to exert over what and how a child learns, and how does that control look at various stages of life? Who determines what needs to be "accomplished" during the pre-kindergarten year or what is important for infants/toddlers? By taking hold of questions such as these, the field will be better situated to provide curricula that are responsive to young children in their home, community, and larger contexts. Essential research about curriculum is based upon a strong theoretical understanding of what must be necessarily considered in curriculum.

References

Baker, C.N., Kupersmidt, J.B., Voegler-Lee, M.E., Arnold, D.H., & Willoughby, M.T. (2010). Predicting teacher participation in a classroom-based, integrated preventive intervention for preschoolers. *Early Childhood Research Quarterly*, 25, 270–283.

Ballenger, C. (1999). *Teaching other people's children: Literacy and learning in a bilingual classroom*. New York: Teachers College Press.

Bredekamp, S. (1991). Redeveloping early childhood education: A response to Kessler. *Early Childhood Research Quarterly*, 6, 199–209.

Cannella, G.S. (1997). *Deconstructing early childhood education: Social justice & revolution*. New York: Peter Lang.

Clements, D.H., & Sarama, J. (2016). Math, science and technology in the early grades. *The Future of Children*, 26(2), 75–94.

Colegrove, K.S., & Adair, J.K. (2014). Countering deficit thinking: Agency, capabilities and the early learning experiences of children of Latina/o immigrants. *Contemporary Issues in Early Childhood*, 15, 122–135.

Consortium for Longitudinal Studies (1983). *As the twig is bent. . . Lasting effects of preschool programs*. Hillsdale, NJ: Lawrence Erlbaum.

Copple, C., & Bredekamp, S. (2009). *Developmentally appropriate practice in early childhood programs* (3rd ed.). Washington, DC: National Association for the Education of Young Children.

Dray, B.J., & Wisneski, D.B. (2011). Mindful reflection as a process for developing culturally responsive practices. *Teaching Exceptional Children*, 44(1), 28–26.

Early, D.M., Iruka, I.U., Ritchie, S., Barbarin, O.A., Winn, D.C., Crawford, G.M., . . . & Pianta, R.C. (2010). How do pre-kindergarteners spend their time? Gender, ethnicity, and incomes as predictors of experiences in pre-kindergarten classrooms. *Early Childhood Research Quarterly*, 25, 177–193.

Farran, D.C. (2011). Rethinking school readiness. *Exceptionality Education International*, 21(2), 5–15.

Farran, D.C. (2017). Characteristics of pre-kindergarten programs that drive positive outcomes. In *The current state of scientific knowledge on pre-kindergarten effects* (pp. 45–49). Center for Child and Family Policy, Duke University. ERIC Document Reproduction Service No. ED574393.

Gallas, K. (1995). *Talking their way into science: Hearing children's questions and theories, responding with curriculum*. New York: Teachers College Press.

Gerde, H.K., Pierce, S.J., Lee, K., & Van Egeren, L.A. (2018). Early childhood educators' self-efficacy in science, math, and literacy instruction and science practice in the classroom. *Early Education and Development, 29*, 70–90. doi:10.1080/10409289.2017.1360127

Graue, E., Whyte, K., & Delaney, K.K. (2014). Fostering culturally and developmentally responsive teaching through improvisational practice. *Journal of Early Childhood Teacher Education, 35*, 297–317. doi:10.1080/10901027.2014.968296

Graue, M.E. (1998). Through a small window: Knowing children and research through standardized tests. In B. Spodek, O.N. Saracho, & A.D. Pellegrini (Eds.), *Issues in early childhood educational research* (pp. 30–48). New York: Teachers College Press.

Jenkins, J.M., & Duncan, G.J. (2017). Do pre-kindergarten curricula matter? In *The current state of scientific knowledge on pre-kindergarten effects* (pp. 37–43). Center for Child and Family Policy, Duke University. ERIC Document Reproduction Service No. ED574393.

Jenkins, J.M., Duncan, G.J., Auger, A., Bitler, M., Domina, T., & Burchinal, M. (2018). Boosting school readiness: Should preschool teachers target skills or the whole child? *Economics of Education Review, 65*, 107–125,

Lazar, I., & Darlington, R. (1982). Lasting effects of early education: A report from the consortium for longitudinal studies. *Monographs of the Society for Research in Child Development, 47*(2–3, Serial No. 195).

Mardell, B. (1999). *From basketball to the Beatles: In search of compelling early childhood curriculum*. Portsmouth, NH: Heinemann.

Mihai, A., Butera, G., & Friesen, A. (2017). Examining the use of curriculum to support early literacy instruction: A multiple case study of Head Start teachers. *Early Education and Development, 28*, 323–342.

Miller, L.B., & Bizzell, R.P. (1983). Long-term effects of four preschool programs: Sixth, seventh, and eighth grades. *Child Development, 54*, 727–741.

Miller, L.B., Bugbee, M.R., & Hybertson, D.W. (1985). Dimensions of preschool: The effects of individual experience. In I.E. Sigel (Ed.), *Advances in applied developmental psychology, Vol. 1* (pp. 25–90). Norwood, NJ: Ablex.

Neuman, S.B., Pinkham, A., & Kaefer, T. (2015). Supporting vocabulary teaching and learning in prekindergarten: The role of educative curriculum materials. *Early Education and Development, 26*, 988–1011.

Nguyen, T., Jenkins, J.M., & Whitaker, A.A. (2018). Are content-specific curricula differentially effective in Head Start or state prekindergarten classrooms? *AERA Open, 4*(2), 1–17.

Paley, V.G. (1998). *The girl with the brown crayon*. Cambridge, MA: Harvard University Press.

Pence, K.L., Justice, L.M., & Wiggins, A.K. (2008). Preschool teachers' fidelity in implementing a comprehensive language-rich curriculum. *Language, Speech, and Hearing Services in Schools, 39*, 329–341.

Phillips, D.A., Lipsey, M.W., Dodge, K.A., Haskins, R., Bassok, D., . . . & Weiland, C. (2017). Puzzling it out: The current state of scientific knowledge on pre-kindergarten effects: A consensus statement. In *The current state of scientific knowledge on pre-kindergarten effects* (pp. 19–30). Center for Child and Family Policy, Duke University. ERIC Document Reproduction Service No. ED574393.

Powell, D.R. (1987). Comparing preschool curricula and practices: The state of the research. In S.L. Kagan & E.F. Zigler (Eds.), *Early schooling: The national debate* (pp. 190–211). New Haven, CT: Yale University Press.

Powell, D.R., Diamond, K.E., Bojczyk, K.E., & Gerde, H.K. (2008). Head Start teachers' perspectives on early literacy. *Journal of Literacy Research, 40*, 422–460.

Preschool Curriculum Evaluation Research Consortium (2008). *Effects of preschool curriculum programs on school readiness (NCER 2008–2009)*. National Center for Education Research, Institute of Education Sciences, U.S. Department of Education. Washington, DC: U.S. Government Printing Office.

Quintero, E.P. (2015). *Storying learning in early childhood: When children lead participatory curriculum design, implementation, and assessment*. New York: Peter Lang. doi:10.3726/978-1-4539-1566-0.

Snow, C.E., & Matthews, T.J. (2016). Reading and language in the early grades. *The Future of Children*, 26(2), 57–74.

Stallings, J. (1975). Implementation and child effects of teaching practices in Follow Through classrooms. *Monographs of the Society for Research in Child Development*, 40(7–8, Serial No. 163).

Sutterby, J.A. (2005). "I wish we could do whatever we want!": Children subverting scaffolding in the preschool classroom. *Journal of Early Childhood Teacher Education*, 25, 349–357.

Wang, A.H., Firmender, J.M., Power, J.R., & Byrnes, J.P. (2016). Understanding the program effectiveness of early mathematics interventions for prekindergarten and kindergarten environments: A meta-analytic review. *Early Education and Development*, 27, 692–713. http://dx.doi.org/10.1080/10409289.2016.1116343

Weiland, C. (2018). Commentary: Pivoting to the "how": Moving preschool policy, practice, and research forward. *Early Childhood Research Quarterly*, 45, 188–192.

2

PUBLIC POLICY AND EARLY CHILDHOOD CURRICULUM IN THE UNITED STATES

Christopher P. Brown and David P. Barry

Introduction

Public policies are formulated and implemented to attend to societal problems, and what is seen as a "problem" depends on both the place and time in which the issue is being studied or addressed. Historically, the public care and education of children in the United States, particularly for children under the age of 5, has been contentious. The normalizing narrative of the nuclear family has dominated much of this history (Rose, 1990), and thus, policies to address issues surrounding the early care and education of young children have been slow to emerge and take hold. For the education of children ages 5 to 8, policymakers have typically focused on issues of school readiness and academic achievement, primarily as it relates to the subjects of reading and mathematics. Still, for all children participating in ECE programs, it was not until recently that "what" was being taught to them on a day-to-day basis became the focus of policymakers.

We begin this chapter by providing a brief history of the evolution of policymakers' focus on early childhood education (ECE) before and after the implementation of NCLB, the No Child Left Behind Act (2002). We do so to contextualize how the field has arrived at this point, where policymakers are mandating the use of specific curricula in ECE programs. We then investigate how policymakers' demands affect teachers' practice and briefly examine who curricular policies serve and what knowledge policymakers deem being most worthy. We end this chapter by discussing how the impact of policy on curriculum affects those who work within the field of ECE, whether that work happens with children on a day-to-day basis, with teachers in professional development trainings or workshops, or if that work is ECE research, and we consider the future directions of curriculum in ECE.

The Evolution of ECE Curriculum and Its Connection to Policy

When examining the history of ECE curriculum, the implementation of NCLB in the US in 2001 significantly altered conversations about curriculum and what policy levers policymakers might pull to control the day-to-day practices of early educators working in the public schools. For instance, Part B, Subpart 1 under Title 1 of NCLB, known as the Reading First initiative, which funded state-grant reading programs, mandated the use of scientifically research-based kindergarten through third grade reading curricula. Meaning, policymakers deemed only "certain" curricula could be used to teach reading when participating in this program. Because of this and other changes mandated by NCLB, we divided this brief examination in the history of ECE policy and its impact on programs and their curricula prior to and after the implementation of NCLB.

To be clear, this history is incomplete and focuses only on those programs to which we could make clear curricular connections. For example, we do not discuss the history of day nurseries or the establishment of state-based licensure programs/ requirements for private or non-profit child care providers, and we also avoid examining such national policies as the establishment of the Children's Bureau in 1912 by President Taft and the Lanham Act that emerged during World War II (cf., Gomez & Rendon, 2019).

Pre-NCLB

Kindergarten

Kindergarten was one of the first ECE programs to draw the attention of policymakers to the education of young children in the US. In 1854, Margarethe Meyer Schurz founded the first kindergarten in Watertown, WI, and the first US public kindergarten emerged in the 1870s through the work of individuals such as Susan Blow in St. Louis and spread across numerous urban cities (Beatty, 1995). There were many political arguments put forward for these programs to become a part of public schooling. For example, some supporters saw these programs as a form of "child rescue"; others saw it as means to Americanize the influx of immigrants that were arriving in the US, and many viewed these programs as a form of preparation for elementary school (Beatty, 1995). In terms of curricula, many of the early programs attempted to offer children learning experiences that mimicked Froebel's vision of kindergarten, which was rooted in his gifts and occupations designed to foster the development of the whole child (Brosterman, 1997). Such practices often contradicted the teacher-directed content-focused instruction commonly found in the primary grades at this time.

Dombkowski (2001) noted that kindergarten teachers in the public schools at the beginning of the 20th century "(backed by kindergarten advocacy organizations) took on the mission of trying to influence their primary-grades colleagues in order to correct the shortcomings and abuses they saw in traditional, teacher-centered primary education," (p. 529). However, pressure from school administrators, primary school teachers, and families themselves to ensure children were ready for elementary school created a tension that still exists today between beliefs about what types of learning experiences children should have in kindergarten and how different those experiences and curricula should be from what occurs in the elementary grades (Beatty, 1995; Dombkowski, 2001). Nevertheless, the Great Depression in the 1930s stalled the expansion of kindergarten, and in some instances, these programs were completely eliminated from local communities and did not re-emerge until the baby-boom post World War II (Brewer, Gasko, & Miller, 2011).

Nursery Schools

G. Stanley Hall (1900), one of the early scholars taking an interest in the development of children, began his child study experiments in Pauline Shaw's charity kindergartens in Boston. Hall's studies led him, as well as many other psychologists, such as Gesell, Freud, and Piaget, to question what types of experiences should be taking place in kindergarten as well as in the home to prepare children for a successful life. Academically, this increased interest in understanding child development led to a growing child study movement among universities (Beatty, 1995). For instance, the Laura Spelman Rockefeller Memorial Foundation awarded significant sums of money to several colleges and universities to establish child study institutes. The institutes' lab schools began the nursery school movement, and middle-class families became attracted to the notion that science could enhance their child's development.

Politically, as these model programs were expanding across the US, the onset of the Great Depression led to the Federal Emergency Relief Administration (FERA) starting federally funded nursery school programs in 1933 as a means to employ school teachers and school staff. The care of children was a secondary goal. The program was incorporated into the Works Progress Administration (WPA) in 1934 when FERA was terminated. Nevertheless, the WPA funded almost 1500 nursery schools, and two-thirds were a part of public school systems (Dombkowski, 2001). Although federal support for these programs did not last long, both the university nursery schools and those funded by the WPA had a significant impact on how the education of young children was viewed. Their "emphasis on the physiological and hygienic needs of young children led to widespread changes in the kindergarten, including an emphasis on proper nutrition, napping, and activities to encourage muscular development without overtaxing fine motor skills" (Dombkowski, 2001, p. 533). This expanded view of learning continued to add to the conflict between early childhood educators and their elementary school colleagues as these programs expanded across the US.

Project Head Start

Project Head Start emerged in 1965 under the Economic Opportunity Act and the Elementary and Secondary Education Act (ESEA) as a part of the Johnson Administration's War on Poverty. This legislation is significant because federal policymakers defined the role of the federal government in ECE as a provider of intervention services that could alter the academic trajectory of particular populations of children, meaning publicly funded ECE in the US was framed as a tool for intervention that is to provide children with a specific set of knowledge and skills to be ready for school rather than as a basic right for all children. Moreover, these policies identified the root cause of academic failure, which leads to economic failure, in the child's home environment. Whereby, this legislation established a system of education in which the children who participated in it were deemed "at-risk" for school success, and these children primarily came from low-income and non-White families.

Issues of Accountability

As soon as the federal government took on these roles in ECE and K-12 education, controversy arose. For instance, the Nixon administration responded to Johnson's Great Society education policies by creating the National Institute of Education, which investigated the return that society received for its investment in education.[1] Such legislation further entwined the issue of accountability with governmental funding of ECE programs. Additionally, studies such as the Westinghouse Learning Corporation's (1969) evaluation of Head Start suggested that the IQs of students in the program quickly faded, which raised concerns over the effectiveness of these government-funded programs (Cuban, 1998).

Researchers responded to these critiques of Head Start by arguing that while increases in IQ might not be sustainable, students who participated in such programs were more successful academically and socially as they continued through school than those students who did not receive these services (e.g., Schweinhart & Weikart, 1980). This work spawned the neoliberal "return on investment" argument (e.g., Reynolds, Temple, Robertson, & Mann, 2002), or what the Nobel-laureate economist James Heckman (2000) has termed human capital theory, that underlies the current push for ECE reform. This argument shifts the premise for funding ECE programs from breaking the cycle of poverty for others to saving the taxpayer money.

This history of ECE programs that serve children 0 to 5 prior to the implementation of NCLB demonstrates that policymakers were not focused on issues of curricula. Rather, the dominant policy conversations circulated around issues of funding, custodial care, and generally defined school readiness. In response to these reforms, ECE advocates focused on demonstrating that these programs mattered and that the practice of teaching young children needed to be different from what was typically found in the elementary schools. For children in the public school system, the implementation of ESEA by the Johnson administration began a wave of reforms that led to the current standards-based accountability movement, which emphasizes standardization, academic achievement, and accountability.

Elementary School and Standards-based Accountability Reform

The first two waves of reform that led to the current framing of public education in the US were the National Commission on Excellence in Education's (NCEE) publication of *A Nation at Risk* (1983) and the nation's governors' pursuit of education reform initiatives[2] (e.g., National Governors' Association, 1986). Through these initiatives, educational stakeholders promoted a decentralized system of education that emphasized the development of educational goals naming the content and skills students are to learn while assessing their performance in relation to that content. These shifts in education policy escalated the curricular expectations for students in the early grades (Freeman & Hatch, 1989) and led to the increased use of readiness tests for kindergarten and first grade entry (Shepard & Smith, 1988; Meisels, 1989).

Professional organizations, such as the National Association for the Education of Young Children (NAEYC) and the Association for Childhood Education International (ACEI), responded to this emphasis on accountability and formal academic instruction in ECE by publishing organizational responses for what they termed appropriate practices for young children (e.g., Solley, 2007). Documents, such as NAEYC's *Developmentally Appropriate Practice in Early Childhood Programs Serving Children Birth through Age 8* (Bredekamp, 1987), sparked a series of research-based organizational responses for selecting appropriate types of curricula and assessments to use with young children (e.g., Bredekamp & Rosengrant, 1995). Furthermore, empirically based studies supported these organizations' works by identifying the effects of inappropriate assessments and curricula on young children (e.g., Bryant, Clifford, & Peisner, 1991).

In the early 1990s, the standards-based accountability movement, the third wave of reform, emerged from the Clinton Administration's Goals 2000 legislation,[3] which made its first goal that every child in the US would start school ready to learn (National Education Goals Panel, 1997). Many within the field of ECE (e.g., Meisels, 1992) worried this goal would promote such inappropriate practices as the use of assessments to determine kindergarten entry (e.g., Gnezda & Bolig, 1988). These gateway exams, if used to deny children entry to kindergarten programs, would exclude "children from participating in the school curriculum" necessary to succeed in elementary school (Shepard, 1994, p. 207).

Shortly after the Goals 2000 legislation, the federal government reauthorized the ESEA in 1994, titled the Improving American Schools Act (IASA). IASA ushered in the era of standards-based accountability (SBA) reform, which are policies that enact a theory of action (Argyris & Schon, 1974) that defines the goals, and in turn, the practices toward which an entire education system including administrators, teachers, students, and their families work. Under this reform process, the goal for each of the stakeholders in the education system is to ensure that all students are taught the mandated knowledge and skills (content standards), are tested on their mastery of the content (performance standards), and reach the specified level of achievement they must attain on the tests (proficiency standards) (O'Day, 2002). If students do not meet the proficiency standards, consequences, or what is commonly referred to as "high-stakes," can be put in place to hold them, their teachers, school, and/or district accountable. While these high-stakes assessments typically do not begin until the third grade, many states and school districts in the US began to put in place instructional expectations on ECE teachers and a series of assessment measures across the early grades to ensure children are on a trajectory for success by the time they take their state's high-stakes assessments (Brown, 2007a).

Thus, at the beginning of the 21st century, the groundwork of the implementation of NCLB was laid. Moreover, the purpose of publicly funded ECE programs was clearly defined by policymakers as school readiness programs that were to increase students' academic skills and knowledge so that they were prepared to attain high levels of academic performance as they entered elementary school. Yet, how ECE programs accomplished this goal was not the central focus of policymakers or of their education reforms.

Post-NCLB

Kindergarten and Elementary School

The implementation of NCLB in 2002 by the federal government increased demands for SBA reform in the United States. Under NCLB, if school personnel failed to improve the adequate yearly progress (AYP) of their students on their state's tests, the consequences were an opening for market-based interventions. Families had the opportunity to transfer out of failing schools or access tutorial services, which can be run by private companies. Persistent failure by schools could result in their reconstitution. This focus on the AYP of students in reading, math, and science led to stakeholders paying further attention to what types of learning experiences children had prior to the mandatory third grade tests (Brown, 2007b) – in other words, do they possess the skills the state assessments demand they have? Moreover, as noted previously, the Reading First initiative under Title 1 further expanded the reach of policymakers over what types of instructional experiences children were having on a day-to-day basis in their classrooms.

Furthermore, such a focus on the AYP of elementary school students led to what Hatch (2002) termed "accountability shovedown" (p. 462) in the early childhood years, which means that content and performance expectations, as well as the didactic instructional practices of older grades, have been shoved down by administrators and others into younger-grade classrooms. This shovedown frames learning as a lock-step process where student outcomes demonstrate the effectiveness of teachers.

Head Start and Publicly Funded Preschool

Following the implementation of NCLB, the Bush Administration implemented the Good Start, Grow Smart (GSGS) initiative targeted to students ages 3–5 in government supported programs. GSGS required the Head Start program to increase its focus on students' academic achievement. As well, it mandated that states receiving federal monies supporting preschool programs formulate early learning standards in pre-reading, language, and mathematics that aligned with their K-12 counterparts (e.g., Scott-Little, Kagan, & Frelow, 2006). Together, these federal initiatives ensured that SBA reforms would continue to define the policies and practices for publicly funded ECE programs (Brown, 2007a).

Pre-K Reform

Shortly after the implementation of NCLB and the implementation of GSGS, states across the US began to expand access to publicly supported Pre-K programs (Barnett et al., 2016). The theory of action behind the expansion of Pre-K is evidence showing these programs "enhance children's capacity to learn, which might improve their later elementary school performance" (Burger, 2010, p. 160). Empirical research continues to emerge demonstrating the positive effect public Pre-K programs have on children's social and academic development (e.g., Magnuson, Ruhm, & Waldfogel, 2007), and it appears that the key factor in improving children's academic and social achievement is dependent upon the intentionality of interactions that teachers have with their students (e.g., Howes et al., 2008) rather than the type of curriculum being implemented in the ECE classroom (e.g., Graue, Clements, Reynolds, & Niles, 2004).

Race to the Top

NCLB solidified the notion that policies addressing the field of ECE must attend to issues of school readiness, academic performance, and accountability. Such initiatives were furthered by the Obama Administration's *Race to the Top – Early Learning Challenge Grant* (RTT-ELC) in 2013. This grant required applicants to demonstrate that any federal dollars they received for ECE offered children access to high-quality integrated early learning programs that used assessments to document improved student achievement while holding ECE programs accountable. It also further exemplifies how policymakers continue to focus on issues of school readiness, academic performance, and accountability when implementing ECE reforms.

Quality Rating Improvement Systems

One aspect of the RTT-ELC grant that we have not discussed in this chapter is that of quality. Researchers have consistently shown that high-quality early learning experiences can improve children's language, academic, and social skills (e.g., Burchinal, Kainz, & Yaping, 2011). However, a substantial number of children attending ECE programs in the US do not have access to such programs (Barnett et al., 2016). Policymakers have sought to improve the quality of ECE programs through the establishment of a Quality Rating Improvement System (QRIS), which expanded rapidly due to the RTT-ELC grant. Almost every state in the US is now developing or implementing a QRIS (Tout et al., 2010). QRIS is an accountability system that scores ECE programs on a range of quality measures, which include such criteria as licensing compliance, staff qualifications, research-based curricula, teacher-to-child ratios, and even assessment measures of children's varying developmental domains, that are then converted into an overall rating of quality at the program level (Zellman & Fiene, 2012). This rating is designed to inform families and the community about the quality of specific ECE programs, and the score also gives the programs information relevant to improving their quality in relation to the items scored on the QRIS (Zellman & Fiene, 2012). So far, the impact of these programs on children's academic and social development is mixed at best (e.g., Burchinal et al., 2011; Sabol & Pianta, 2012). Yet, in many instances, these QRIS programs continue to dictate what it is early educators are supposed to do within their daily practices with young children.

ECE Policy and Curriculum Today

In recent years, such state initiatives as the Common Core or the passage of Every Student Succeeds Act in 2015, which replaced NCLB, continue to demonstrate that policymakers frame ECE as a programmatic response to the problems of school readiness and academic achievement, and they continue to put in place systems of accountability to ensure these programs are meeting the goals of these policies. In brief, this framing reflects the global shift towards neoliberalism, which frames governance through economic rather than democratic terms (Brown, 2018). Meaning, policymakers frame ECE as a governmental investment in children, and as such, the programs must produce successful learners who become earners and consumers that will repay the state for these initial costs by requiring less governmental support and paying taxes through employment in later life (Ailwood, 2008).

This neoliberal framing positions early educators as technicians who are to teach all children the same sets of knowledge and skills needed to succeed in elementary school and later in life (Apple, 2001). Such an understanding of ECE creates a range of challenges for practitioners. First, by prioritizing what and when children are to learn, policymakers' reforms have brushed aside a core belief within the history of ECE that curricular decisions should be based on the individual personal, sociocultural, linguistic, and developmental capabilities of children (Brown, 2009a). Second, these policies emphasize academic achievement, which means not only do early educators need to demonstrate their worth through their ability to produce students who achieve high on test scores but must also become "salespeople for their own pedagogical performances" or be replaced, which can also lead to competition among teachers within a school community (De Lissovoy, 2014, p. 428). Lastly, the purpose of early education is no longer viewed as a journey that is to provide children with learning experiences that are to prepare them to become active and engaged members of the larger democratic society. Rather, early childhood teachers and programs are to "focus on readiness in the now"; meaning they are to enact a standardized vision of schooling that prepares children for a constant barrage of assessments that begin as soon as they enter public schooling and continuously grow in expectations as they progress from one grade level to the next (Brown, 2013, p. 570).

The Impact of Policy on Teachers' Curricular Decision-making

The impact of these neoliberal ECE reforms on early educators' practices is well documented (e.g., Nxumalo, Pacini-Ketchabaw, & Rowan, 2011). For instance, Bassok, Latham, and Rorem (2016) analyzed data from two kindergarten cohorts that participated in the Early Childhood Longitudinal Study (ECLS-K:1998 and ECLS-K:2011) and found a large increase from 1998 and 2010 in the time kindergarten teachers spent on academic skills instruction as well as greater use of standardized assessments, while both kindergarten and first grade teachers spent less time on child-selected activities, music, and art. In another instance, Alford, Rollins, Padrón, and Waxman (2016) investigated a total of 91 pre-kindergarten (Pre-K), kindergarten, first grade, and second grade classrooms across 21 elementary schools in a large south-central city in the US and found that regardless of grade level, teachers "consistently utilized whole class, didactic, teacher-centered instructional practices in their classrooms – regardless of the sex and/or ethnic make-up of their students" (p. 629).

Even prior to entering elementary school, policy documents, such as Head Start's Early Learning Outcomes Framework (Administration for Children and Families, 2015), Pre-K operating guidelines that mandate the implementation of specific curricula (e.g., Georgia Department of Early Care and Learning, 2018), or state mandated early learning standards (e.g., Scott-Little et al., 2006), demonstrate how policymakers' SBA reforms have been shoved down into the early years. For example, the Head Start framework presents specific age-based achievement goals children are expected to attain across several developmental domains (approaches to learning; social emotional development; language and literacy; cognition; perceptual, motor, and physical development) from 0 to age 5. Bullough Jr., Hall-Kenyon, MacKay, and Marshall (2014) found that the implementation of these reforms, that require the increased use of student and teacher assessments within Head Start, overwhelmed classroom teachers and forced them to engage in practices that conflict "with what they believe most needs to be done for the children" (p. 63).

Combined, these studies demonstrate that children in ECE classrooms are more likely to be learning (and tested on) literacy and math skills and are less likely to be engaged in learning centers that encompass a variety of disciplines (e.g., art, music, science, etc.) and sensory experiences (e.g., sand and water tables) than they were before NCLB. Essentially, these policies create an ECE context in which "learning becomes nothing more than a means to an end"; its "inherent value is lost" and children never get "the chance to experience the exhilaration of learning as an inherently valuable human activity" (Hatch, 2015, p. 115).

Who and What Policy Leaves Out

Policymakers' focus on readiness in the now, standardization, and academic achievement not only privileges certain types of knowledge and silences others (Brown & Brown, 2010; Pérez & Saavedra, 2017), but their reforms also often "suggest that a small group of students are educationally and economically vulnerable" and need "to be isolated and fixed" (Fine, 1988, p. 16). Combined, these issues illuminate the significance in early educators questioning what it is they are expected to do with young children (Pacini-Ketchabaw, 2014) as well as how policymakers' reforms are shaping their conceptions of teaching young children, particularly children who may possess varying cultural, linguistic, and socioeconomic resources that go unnoticed by policymakers' reforms (Adair, 2014; Brown, Weber, & Yoon, 2015).

These policies that privilege some and silence others is not a new phenomenon in the US. Historically, education policies have been used as a means to control the social, economic, and political participation of those who have been "othered" in the US. For example, 19th-century immigrants "as ardent Americanizers saw it, not only had to learn new skills but also had to shed an old culture" (Tyack, 1974, p. 235). Examples of this historical discrimination still appear today in ECE. For example, Adair, Colegrove, & McManus (2017) documented how Latinx children can be denied opportunities to participate in what are considered best practices in ECE that offer them choice and voice in their learning because education stakeholders, such as superintendents, administrators, teachers, parents, and even young children, believed, via the perpetuation of the myth of Hart and Risley's (1995) word gap, they lacked the vocabulary needed to do so. Additionally, Lee (2017) has shown how teachers can latch on to such dominant discourses as school readiness and ADHD to not only view young children through a deficit perspective, which in her study were two African-American pre-kindergarteners, but early educators can also use these discourses to control children's bodies and actions while ignoring the strengths and interests they bring to the classroom that should be incorporated into the curriculum.

As Brown and Lan (2015) noted, the past five decades of SBA reform in the US have fortified "a White, middle-class conception of school readiness" that has "pushed out any sort of space" within the ECE process, be it curriculum or instructional practices, that considers what Yosso (2005) termed the "cultural wealth" of children and their families, and as such, these reforms have "the potential to further disengage and/or disempower children and their families as they progress through school" (p. 10). To move forward, Nxumalo and Cedillo (2017) contend that members of the ECE community must question their over-reliance on Euro-Western knowledges and neoliberal conceptions of ECE so that they can begin to consider how implementing anti-racist (e.g., Doucet & Adair, 2013), decolonial (e.g., Pérez & Saavedra, 2017), and non-anthropocentric approaches (e.g., Taylor & Pacini-Ketchabaw, 2015) to ECE curricula may enable the field to respond to and move beyond policymakers' demands for standardization and increased academic achievement.

The Impact of Curricular Policies on Young Children

The history of ECE reform has and continues to impact what it is ECE stakeholders do with young children no matter their role in the field. For practitioners, it is critical to continue to question how policymakers' neoliberal reforms position early educators as well as frame the goals early educators must achieve with children and families (Brown, 2018). Meier (2000) noted that teachers need to become "agents of democracy" (p. 17) who advocate for democratic practices and policies throughout the education system that support the education of all children. Loh and Hu (2014) added early educators need to develop a "neoliberal literacy" (p. 20) so that they can read and interpret the current governing and political discourses shaping ECE. One way to do this is to become familiar with examples of how teachers in the US (e.g., Brown & Mowry, 2017) and abroad (e.g., Gupta, 2015) are responding to and countering policymakers' push for standardization and academic achievement.

For researchers, it is important to recognize how policies, such as NCLB, have impacted, and in many cases narrowed, both funded and published educational research around issues of what works either in terms of improving early educators' practices or the performance of their students (Brown & Lee, 2012; Erickson, 2014; Lincoln & Cannella, 2004). Such questioning may provide researchers opportunities to begin to ask "fundamental questions about curriculum, teachers' roles, and the ends as well as the means of schooling," (Cochran-Smith & Lytle, 1999, p. 274) as well as question how these reforms do or do not take into account the "funds of knowledge (Moll, Amanti, Neff, & González, 1992) that exist among the teachers, school, children, their families, and the local community within each early learning environment" (Brown & Englehardt, 2016, p. 236).

For teacher educators, it is important to examine how other teacher educators are addressing these issues in their own teacher education programs (e.g., Pérez, Ruiz Guerrero, & Mora, 2016; Souto-Manning, Cahnmann-Taylor, Dice, &

Wooten, 2008). Moreover, there appears to be a need for teacher educators to work with pre/in-service teachers to navigate as well as mitigate the impact of these reforms on both pre/in-service teachers' instructional decision-making and their interactions with children and their families on a day-to-day basis (Brown, 2010). To do this, teacher educators could/should work with pre/in-service teachers to learn to work on what Dahlberg, Moss, and Pence (1999) term the "two legs" of teaching (p. 139), the practical leg and the critical leg (Brown, 2009b). Practically speaking, teacher educators should work with their students to question what knowledge they are drawing upon in their instructional decision-making and how they are using that knowledge to instruct the children in their classrooms; essentially, questioning whether they are making curricular and instructional decisions based off of the learning needs of the children in their classrooms or through policymakers' demands. To assist pre/in-service teachers in walking on their critical leg, similar to practicing teachers, teacher educators should help pre/in-service teachers recognize that they are not alone in the process by sharing examples of how practicing teachers are responding to and countering these reforms so that they can "discern the complexity of this reform process as well as imagine possibilities for resisting or countering these policies in their classrooms, schools, and local communities" (Brown, 2009b, p. 254).

Lastly, all groups should seek out ways to form alliances and build communities within schools across stakeholder groups, such as teachers, administrators, families, community members outside of the school (Apple, 2001). This work requires early educators to recognize that there are "multiple perspectives" in understanding and enacting policymakers' reforms, and by doing so, it can help them "trouble social issues and normative perceptions in a critically conscious manner, positioning themselves as agents of change in their classrooms and beyond" (Souto-Manning, 2017, p. 96). Whereby, by being inclusive of multiple perspectives on how neoliberal education policies impact the lives of different stakeholders, this could deepen early educators' understanding of and empathy across groups, potentially leading to greater unity among all stakeholders.

The Future of Policy and ECE Curriculum

Public policy will continue to affect the field of ECE in numerous ways. When considering issues of curriculum and instruction, how policymakers continue to frame the issues of access, readiness, standardization, and accountability will impact what types of curricular decisions teachers can make and how they view the learning and development of the children they work with on a daily basis. This chapter presented a brief history of ECE reform in the US to provide insight as to how the field has arrived at its current framing by policymakers as a vehicle intended to ready children for academic and life success through standardized practices that privilege particular forms of knowledge and skills and silence others.

Going forward, it is important to remember a few points the history of education reform has taught us. At the state and local level, policymakers tend to emphasize cheap reforms that do not challenge local control (Brown, 2008). At the national level, any new initiative that includes funding will be tied to issues of accountability. In either case, systemic reforms that alter any field of education, be it Head Start or Pre-K-12 public education systems, are rarely passed, and instead, reform tends to be evolutionary rather than revolutionary (Majone, 1989), meaning change in policy that supports the education of young children is a slow and difficult process. Nevertheless, policymakers will not stop implementing new educational reforms, and thus, all those working within the field of ECE must recognize that what is expected to be taught and how it must be taught will always be a contentious issue.

Notes

1 At this same time, Nixon vetoed the Comprehensive Child Development Act of 1971, which was to expand the federal government's funding of childcare and education while creating a framework for child services (Beatty, 1995, p. 198).
2 The governors' initiatives traded a decrease in state policymakers' governance over school districts and other academic issues for an increase in the role of academic accountability in ensuring improved student performance.
3 Goals 2000 developed out of the President H. W. Bush's failed America 2000 legislation, the reform proposal that emerged from the 1989 Education Summit in Charlottesville, VA.

References

Adair, J.K. (2014). Examining whiteness as an obstacle to positively approaching immigrant families in US early childhood educational settings. *Race, Ethnicity, and Education*, 17, 643–666.
Adair, J.K., Colegrove, K.S.S., & McManus, M.E. (2017). How the word gap argument negatively impacts young children of Latinx immigrants' conceptualizations of learning. *Harvard Educational Review*, 87, 309–334.
Administration for Children and Families (2015). *Head Start early learning outcomes framework: Ages birth to five*. Washington, DC: Department of Health and Human Services.
Ailwood, J. (2008). Learning or earning in the 'smart state': Changing tactics for governing early childhood. *Childhood*, 15, 535–551.
Alford, B.L., Rollins, K.B., Padrón, Y.N., & Waxman, H.C. (2016). Using systematic classroom observation to explore student engagement as a function of teachers' developmentally appropriate instructional practices (DAIP) in ethnically diverse pre-kindergarten through second-grade classrooms. *Early Childhood Education Journal*, 44, 623–635.
Apple, M.W. (2001). *Educating the "right" way: Markets, standards, god, and inequality*. New York: Routledge.
Argyris, C., & Schon, D.A. (1974). *Theories in practice: Increasing professionalism*. San Francisco: Jossey-Bass, Inc.
Barnett, W.S., Friedman-Krauss, A.H., Gomez, R., Horowitz, M., Weisefeld, G.G., Clark Brown, K., & Squires, J.H. (2016). *The state of preschool 2015*. New Brunswick, NJ: National Institute for Early Education Research.

Bassok, D., Latham, S., & Rorem, A. (2016). Is kindergarten the new first grade? *AERA Open*, 1, 1–31.

Beatty, B. (1995). *Preschool education in America: The culture of young children from colonial era to the present*. New Haven, CT: Yale University Press.

Bredekamp, S. (Ed.) (1987). *Developmentally appropriate practice in early childhood programs serving children birth through age 8*. Washington, DC: National Association for the Education of Young Children.

Bredekamp, S., & Rosengrant, T. (Eds.) (1995). *Reaching potentials: Transforming early childhood curriculum and assessment, volume 2*. Washington, DC: National Association for the Education of Young Children.

Brewer, C., Gasko, J.W., & Miller, D. (2011). Have we been here before? Lessons learned from a microhistory of the policy development of universal kindergarten. *Educational Policy*, 25, 9–35.

Brosterman, N. (1997). *Inventing kindergarten*. New York: Abrams/Times Mirror.

Brown, A.L., & Brown, K.D. (2010). Strange fruit indeed: Interrogating contemporary textbook representations of racial violence towards African Americans. *Teachers College Record*, 112, 31–67.

Brown, C.P. (2007a). Unpacking standards in early childhood education. *Teachers College Record*, 109, 635–668.

Brown, C.P. (2007b). It's more than content: Expanding the conception of early learning standards. *Early Childhood Research and Practice*, 9, 1–15.

Brown, C.P. (2008). Keep it cheap, keep it local, and keep it coming: Standards-based accountability reform in Wisconsin. *Educational Policy*, 22, 250–294.

Brown, C.P. (2009a). Pivoting a pre-kindergarten program off the child or the standard? A case study of integrating the practices of early childhood education into elementary school. *The Elementary School Journal*, 110, 202–227.

Brown, C.P. (2009b). Confronting the contradictions: A case study of early childhood teacher development in neoliberal times. *Contemporary Issues in Early Childhood*, 10, 240–259.

Brown, C.P. (2010). Children of reform: The impact of high-stakes education reform on preservice teachers. *Journal of Teacher Education*, 61, 477–491.

Brown, C.P. (2013). Reforming preschool to ready children for academic achievement: A case study of the impact of pre-k reform on the issue of school readiness. *Early Education & Development*, 24, 554–573.

Brown, C.P. (2018). Attempting to fracture the neoliberal hold on early educators' practical conceptions of teaching: A case study. *Global Studies of Childhood*, 8, 53–74.

Brown, C.P., & Englehardt, J. (2016). Conceptions of and early childhood educators' experiences in early childhood professional development programs: A qualitative metasynthesis. *Journal of Early Childhood Teacher Education*, 37, 216–244.

Brown, C., & Lan, Y. (2015). A qualitative metasynthesis comparing U.S. teachers' conceptions of school readiness prior to and after the implementation of NCLB. *Teaching and Teacher Education*, 45, 1–13.

Brown, C.P., & Lee, J.E. (2012). How to teach to the child when the stakes are high: Examples of implementing developmentally appropriate and culturally relevant practices in pre-kindergarten. *Journal of Early Childhood Teacher Education*, 33, 322–348.

Brown, C.P., & Mowry, B. (2017). "I wanted to know how they perceived jail": Studying how one early educator brought her students' worlds into her standardized teaching context. *Early Childhood Education Journal*, 45, 163–173.

Brown, C., Weber, N., & Yoon, Y. (2015). The practical difficulties for early educators who tried to address children's realities in their high-stakes teaching context. *Journal of Early Childhood Teacher Education*, 36, 3–23.

Bryant, D.M., Clifford, R.M., & Peisner, E.S. (1991). Best practices for beginners: Developmental appropriateness in kindergarten. *American Educational Research Journal*, 28, 783–803.

Bullough Jr., R.V., Hall-Kenyon, K.M., MacKay, K.L., & Marshall, E.E. (2014). Head Start and the intensification of teaching in early childhood education. *Teaching and Teacher Education*, 37, 55–63.

Burchinal, M., Kainz, K., & Yaping, C. (2011). How well do our measures of quality predict child outcomes? A meta-analysis and coordinated analysis of data from large-scale studies of early childhood settings. In M. Zaslow, I. Martinez-Beck, K. Tout, & T. Halle (Eds.), *Quality measurement in early childhood settings* (pp. 11–32). Baltimore, MD: Paul H. Brookes.

Burger, K. (2010). How does early childhood care and education affect cognitive development? An international review of the effects of early interventions for children from different social backgrounds. *Early Childhood Research Quarterly*, 25, 140–165.

Cochran-Smith, M., & Lytle, S.L. (1999). Relationships of knowledge and practice: Teacher learning in communities. *Review of Research in Education*, 24, 249–305.

Cuban, L. (1998). How schools change reforms: Redefining reform success and failure. *Teachers College Record*, 99, 453–477.

Dahlberg, G., Moss, P., & Pence, A. (1999). *Beyond quality in early childhood education and care: Postmodern perspectives*. London: Falmer Press.

De Lissovoy, N. (2014). Pedagogy of the impossible: Neoliberalism and the ideology of accountability. *Policy Futures in Education*, 11, 423–435.

Dombkowski, K. (2001). Will the real kindergarten please stand up?: Defining and redefining the twentieth-century US kindergarten. *History of Education*, 30, 527–545.

Doucet, F., & Adair, J.K. (2013). Addressing race and inequity in the classroom. *Young Children*, 68, 88–97.

Erickson, F. (2014). Scaling down: A modest proposal for practice-based policy research in teaching. *Education Policy Analysis Archives*, 22, 1–14.

Fine, M. (1988). Of kitsch and caring: The illusion of students at risk. *The School Administrator*, 45, 16–23.

Freeman, E.B., & Hatch, J.A. (1989). What schools expect young children to know and do: An analysis of kindergarten report cards. *The Elementary School Journal*, 89, 594–605.

Georgia Department of Early Care and Learning (2018). *Georgia's pre-K program 2018–2019 school year pre-K providers' operating guidelines*. Atlanta, GA: Author.

Gnezda, M.T., & Bolig, R. (1988). *A national survey of public school testing of prekindergarten and kindergarten children*. Paper prepared for the National Forum on the Future of Children and Families and the National Association of State Boards of Education.

Gomez, R.E., & Rendon, T. (2019). Early childhood policy and its impact on the field: Historical and contemporary perspectives. In C.P. Brown, M.B. McMullen, & N. File (Eds.), *The Wiley handbook of early childhood care and education* (pp. 493–514). Somerset, NJ: Wiley Blackwell.

Graue, E., Clements, M.A., Reynolds, A.J., & Niles, M.D. (2004). More than teacher directed or child initiated: Preschool curriculum type, parent involvement, and children's outcomes in the child-parent centers. *Education Policy Analysis Archives*, 12, 1–36.

Gupta, A. (2015). Pedagogy of third space: A multidimensional early childhood curriculum. *Policy Futures in Education*, 13, 260–272.

Hall, G.S. (1900). Some defects of the kindergarten in America. *Forum*, 28, 579–591.
Hart, B., & Risley, T.R. (1995). *Meaningful differences in the everyday experiences of young American children*. Baltimore, MD: Brookes Publishing.
Hatch, J.A. (2002). Accountability shovedown: Resisting the standards movement in early childhood education. *Phi Delta Kappan*, 83, 457–462.
Hatch, J.A. (2015). *Reclaiming the teaching profession: Transforming the dialogue on public education*. Lanham, MD: Rowman & Littlefield Publishers.
Heckman, J.J. (2000). Policies to foster human capital. *Research in Economics*, 54, 3–56.
Howes, C., Burchinal, M., Pianta, R., Bryant, D., Early, D., & Clifford, R. (2008). Ready to learn? Children's pre-academic achievement in pre-kindergarten programs. *Early Childhood Research Quarterly*, 23, 27–50.
Lee, K. (2017). Making the body ready for school: ADHD and early schooling in the age of accountability. *Teachers College Record*, 119, 1–38.
Lincoln, Y.S., & Cannella, G.S. (2004). Dangerous discourses: Methodological conservatism and governmental regimes of truth. *Qualitative Inquiry*, 10, 5–14.
Loh, J., & Hu, G. (2014). Subdued by the system: Neoliberalism and the beginning teacher. *Teaching and Teacher Education*, 41, 14–21.
Magnuson, K., Ruhm, C., & Waldfogel, J. (2007). Does prekindergarten improve school preparation and performance? *Economics of Education Review*, 26, 33–51.
Majone, G. (1989). *Evidence, argument, and persuasion in the policy process*. New Haven, CT: Yale University Press.
Meier, D. (2000). Educating in democracy. In D. Meier (Ed.), *Will standards save public education?* (pp. 3–34). Boston, MA: Beacon Press.
Meisels, S.J. (1989). High stakes testing in kindergarten. *Educational Leadership*, 46, 16–22.
Meisels, S.J. (1992). Doing harm by doing good: Iatrogenic effects of early childhood enrollment and promotion policies. *Early Childhood Research Quarterly*, 7, 155–174.
Moll, L.C., Amanti, C., Neff, D., & González, N. (1992). Funds of knowledge for teaching: Using a qualitative approach to connect homes and classrooms. *Theory into Practice*, 31, 132–141.
National Commission on Excellence in Education (1983). *A nation at risk: The imperative for educational reform*. Washington, DC: Author.
National Education Goals Panel (1997). *Getting a good start in school*. Washington, DC: Author.
National Governors' Association (1986). *Time for results*. Washington, DC: Author.
No Child Left Behind Act of 2001, P.L. 107–110, 20 USC. § 6319(2002).
Nxumalo, F., & Cedillo, S. (2017). Decolonizing place in early childhood studies: Thinking with Indigenous onto-epistemologies and Black feminist geographies. *Global Studies of Childhood*, 7, 99–112.
Nxumalo, F., Pacini-Ketchabaw, V., & Rowan, M.C. (2011). Lunch time at the child care centre: Neoliberal assemblages in early childhood education. *Journal of Pedagogy*, 2, 195–223.
O'Day, J.A. (2002). Complexity, accountability, and school improvement. *Harvard Educational Review*, 72, 293–329.
Pacini-Ketchabaw, V. (2014). Postcolonial and anti-racist approaches to understanding play. In L. Brooker, M. Blaise, & S. Edwards (Eds.), *SAGE handbook of play and learning in early childhood* (pp. 67–78). London: SAGE.
Pérez, M.S., Ruiz Guerrero, M.G., & Mora, E. (2016). Black feminist photovoice: Fostering critical awareness of diverse families and communities in early childhood teacher education. *Journal of Early Childhood Teacher Education*, 37, 41–60.

Pérez, M.S., & Saavedra, C.M. (2017). A call for onto-epistemological diversity in early childhood education and care: Centering global south conceptualizations of childhood/s. *Review of Research in Education*, 41, 1–29.

Reynolds, A.J., Temple, J.A., Robertson, D.L., & Mann, E.A. (2002). Age 21 cost-benefit analysis of the Title I Chicago child-parent centers. *Educational Evaluation and Policy Analysis*, 24, 267–303.

Rose, N. (1990). *Governing the soul: The shaping of the private citizen*. London: Routledge.

Sabol, T.J., & Pianta, R.C. (2012). Patterns of school readiness forecast achievement and socio-emotional development at the end of elementary school. *Child Development*, 83, 282–299.

Schweinhart, L.J., & Weikart, D.P. (1980). Young children grow up: The effects of the Perry Preschool Program on youths through age 15. *Monographs of the High/Scope Educational Research Foundation*, 7. Ypsilanti, MI: High Scope Education Research Foundation.

Scott-Little, C., Kagan, S.L., & Frelow, V.S. (2006). Conceptualization of readiness and the content of early learning standards: The intersection of policy and research? *Early Childhood Research Quarterly*, 21, 153–173.

Shepard, L.A. (1994). The challenge of assessing young children appropriately. *Phi Delta Kappan*, 76, 206–212.

Shepard, L., & Smith, M.L. (1988). Escalating academic demand in kindergarten: Counterproductive policies. *Elementary School Journal*, 89, 135–145.

Solley, B. (2007). On standardized testing: An ACEI position paper. *Childhood*, 84, 31–37.

Souto-Manning, M. (2017). Generative text sets: Tools for negotiating critically inclusive early childhood teacher education pedagogical practices. *Journal of Early Childhood Teacher Education*, 38, 79-101.

Souto-Manning, M., Cahnmann-Taylor, M., Dice, J., & Wooten, J. (2008). The power and possibilities of performative critical early childhood teacher education. *Journal of Early Childhood Teacher Education*, 29, 309–325.

Taylor, A., & Pacini-Ketchabaw, V. (2015). Learning with children, ants, and worms in the Anthropocene: Towards a common world pedagogy of multispecies vulnerability. *Pedagogy, Culture & Society*, 23, 507–529.

Tout, K., Starr, R., Soli, M., Moodie, S., Kirby, G., & Boller, K. (2010). *Compendium of quality rating systems and evaluations*. Washington, DC: Office of Planning, Research, and Evaluation, Administration for Children and Families, US Department of Health and Human Services.

Tyack, D.B. (1974). *The one best system: A history of American urban education*. Cambridge, MA: Harvard University Press.

Westinghouse Learning Corporation (1969). *The impact of Head Start: An evaluation of the effects of Head Start on children's cognition and affective development (ED036321)*. Washington, DC: Clearinghouse for Federal Scientific and Technical Information.

Yosso, T.J. (2005). Whose culture has capital? A critical race theory discussion of community cultural wealth. *Race, Ethnicity, and Education*, 8, 69–91.

Zellman, G.L., & Fiene, R. (2012). *Validation of quality rating and improvement systems for early care and education and school-age care*, Research-to-Policy, Research-to-Practice Brief OPRE 2012–2029. Washington, DC: Office of Planning, Research, and Evaluation, Administration for Children and Families, US Department of Health and Human Services.

3

STANDARDS, CORRELATIONS, AND QUESTIONS

Examining the Impact of the Accountability Regime on Early Childhood Curriculum

Jennifer J. Mueller and Nancy File

Introduction

Over the past 20 to 30 years, the landscape of early childhood education has witnessed the pervasion of prescribed learning outcomes, scope and sequence planning, and packaged curricula in teaching and learning. This has been spurred by more widespread participation of children in formal early childhood education settings, the ever-tighter connections with early childhood and its perceived role in promoting "readiness" for later schooling, along with the continued push-down of elementary practices and approaches into early childhood settings.

Within this context, early childhood curricula continue to evolve. Part of our purpose here is to examine the impacts that the standards movement, as put forth by the national disciplinary associations and the movement toward early learning standards (ELS) implemented nationwide at the state level, are having on the field – particularly in what is considered "essential" to teaching and learning in the early childhood classroom. Further, we want to examine the impact that this context has had on curricula in early childhood education, a field that is relatively new to packaged and predetermined curricula as the mechanisms for teaching and learning in classrooms.

As we know, this is occurring within a context where the value placed on accountability looms large across all levels of education. Indeed, in what we will call this accountability regime, we seem to consider this current hyper-focus on accountability as *the* means to educational improvement. If we can predetermine desired educational outcomes, we can assess those outcomes so we know if children have learned them; then we can also prescribe the behaviors (learning) in which children must engage in order to reach the "desired" outcomes. Learning is solely demonstrated via results (standardized) on the assessments, and the teachers and schools can be held accountable for the outcomes of their work via the results of the assessments. While much of the early childhood age span has been spared the degree of testing undertaken with older children, the pressure created by future accountability measures looms large. The accountability regime has taken hold in the field of early childhood as much as any other level.

Given the nearly universal connection of kindergarten to the elementary school, for the purposes of this discussion, we focus on the Pre-K context. We begin by considering the professional association standards from the four major disciplinary areas (language arts, mathematics, science, and social studies) and how they do or do not attend to or connect with the early learning context. We contemplate what they have to offer the field of early learning. We consider this alongside of the work of the National Association for the Education of Young Children (NAEYC) and the development of benchmarks for developmentally appropriate practice (DAP). Next, we briefly examine the promulgation of standards for early learning across the states, considering the impacts that the broader standards context has had. Finally, we consider a select set of packaged early childhood curricula within this standards context. What we will eventually argue is that the result has been an expansive emergence of alignment and correlation matrices underlying curriculum development in the early learning realm. This itself aligns with the desires of the accountability regime, and what we have then lost is the possibility for the emergence of children as learning, developing, and engaged beings as our guide for early learning processes.

The Sources of Standards

As the standards movement took hold in education, the professional organizations related to each of the content areas took up the charge of delineating standards for teaching and learning in their disciplines. With teaching and learning as complex endeavors, the work of these professional organizations was put forth as means to guide teachers in understanding the important components of each subject area as agreed upon by the experts in each field, knowing that each teacher could not be a disciplinary expert across all subjects. Additionally, presumably, these efforts also served to establish the expertise of each field to determine what was important for children to know and learn in each area.

Generally speaking, organizations took up this project with a focus on the K–12 grade band, with some later coming to consider teaching and learning in Pre-K. NAEYC and the states took up the cause of establishing the specialized knowledge base required for teaching and learning with young children, which we will also examine in this section.

In the following we provide a brief overview of the development of the standards for each of the content areas, considering what each offered early learning and the potential influences on curriculum development and enactment in early childhood. We then specifically discuss the DAP document and consider state-level early learning standards.

National Council of Teachers of Mathematics

The National Council of Teachers of Mathematics (NCTM) began putting forth standards for content and practice in mathematics in 1989. The original standards were defined for grades K-12. "Pre-K" was added as an area of focus in 2000. In 2014, the association published the guide called *Principles to Actions: Ensuring Mathematical Success for All*, where attention to Pre-K continued.

The NCTM documents focus attention to ten mathematical content strands: Number and Operations; Algebra; Geometry; Measurement; Data Analysis & Probability; Problem Solving; Reasoning and Proof; Communication; Connections; and Representation. They address each of these strands across grade bands, including Pre-K–second grade. The foundational standards document is extensive in scope, with a lengthy chapter devoted to each grade band. Mathematics learning is arguably one of the most researched curricular areas and the team of contributors to the standards document provides a large research base, centered largely on the work related to how young children learn within each of the ten content strands. The intent is to provide guidance for teachers to support them to enact a problem-based, conceptually focused mathematics classroom.

While the larger standards document is expansive, the *Principles to Actions* (NCTM, 2014) document is more specified and succinct, helping teachers to understand particular "Curriculum Focal Points" for each individual grade level (including Pre-K) and the ten strands within. Additionally this document provides associated "Expectations for the Content Standards" providing even more specificity and helping to align the curriculum focal points with the larger standards document. For example, a curricular focal point for Pre-K is "Number and Operations: Developing an understanding of whole numbers, including concepts of correspondence, counting, cardinality, and comparison." The content expectation is that children will "count with understanding and recognize how many within sets of objects" (p. 31).

The *Principles to Actions* authors are careful to point out that the document does not tell educators and policymakers what to do or how to implement the standards. The "what to do" is then found within the curriculum, which should be carefully chosen or developed. They document further teaching practices to guide teachers in how to approach the expectations and to support rich, conceptually based curricular and instructional decision-making.

The larger standards document, and particularly *Principles to Actions* (NCTM, 2014), are laid out in ways that invite curricular alignment. Charts and bulleted lists with quite specified activities to support the learning of the various curricular focal points are throughout. In the larger standards document, examples are included of classroom activities with rich explanations of how children might engage with the concept at hand, and in the Pre-K sections these are supported by research related to how young children develop in their mathematical thinking. NCTM has emphasized the importance of conceptual learning in context for young children, where adults support them to problem solve and grapple with mathematical thinking without the expectation of mastery, and within the context of play.

Next Generation Science Standards

The Next Generation Science Standards (NGSS) were developed out of the *Framework for K-12 Science Education* (National Research Council, 2012). These standards are notable in that they are built on a "fuller architecture than traditional standards" (p. 2, Executive Summary), which speaks to their complexity and prescriptive nature. They pull together disciplinary core ideas (four domains[1]), performance expectations (called science and engineering practices[2]), and five crosscutting concepts[3] for each standard. These are delineated for each grade level, beginning with kindergarten.

Each grade level chart presents recommended topics that fit within the disciplinary core. With each topic the performance expectations are aligned, along with the related crosscutting concepts. For instance, in kindergarten it is recommended that in the Physical Science core area children study, "Motion and Stability" through "Forces and Interactions." One of the practices to address is "plan and conduct an investigation to compare the effects of different strengths or different directions of pushes and pulls on the motion of an object." The other is "analyze data to determine if a design solution works as intended to change the speed or direction of an object with a push or a pull." "Clarification" statements are also included which provide suggested ways to teach these concepts, along with "assessment boundaries" (National Research Council, 2012, p. 5, DCI Arrangement Appendix).

In terms of curriculum development, the executive summary does put forth that standards are not curriculum, but rather are "goals that reflect what a student should know and be able to do" (NGSS, 2013, p. 2). The authors are careful to note that the intention is not to "dictate the manner or methods by which the standards are taught." The discussion includes the idea that schools and districts would have the responsibility to determine how the standards are reached. This set of standards, however, is quite complex, highly specified, and specifically engineered.

There is virtually no mention of connections to preschool learning within the NGSS documents. Interestingly, in 2014, the National Science Teachers Association published a position statement regarding young children and science learning. Drawing largely from the NAEYC document on developmentally appropriate practice (Copple & Bredekamp, 2009), it essentially put forth the idea that young children can engage in science practices and they will develop foundational science understandings at a conceptual level through discovery, exploration, experiences, and play. They also note that adults should support and guide this learning in both formal and informal settings.

National Council for the Social Studies

The social studies standards written by the National Council for the Social Studies (NCSS) have represented intensely contested terrain since their inception in the late 1990s, largely due to the complex disciplinary network that this broader area represents and to the tensions related to the inclusion of pluralism, diversity, and multiculturalism across these areas. The debates have centered on what children in schools need to know and learn, whose perspectives are included and whose are excluded, and how social and cultural groups are to be represented across these areas of study. These standards shifted from being structured as ten themes with recommended content across age/grade bands, to its current format of four process standards as delineated in *The College, Career, and Civic Life (C3) Framework for Social Studies State Standards: Guidance for Enhancing the Rigor of K-12 Civics, Economics, Geography, and History* (NCSS, 2013).

The C3 Framework (NCSS, 2013) is to be used to support the development of state social studies content standards that encourage students to engage in the overall goal of being "actively engaged in civic life." The authors note that "engagement in civic life requires knowledge and experience; children learn to be citizens by working individually and together as citizens. An essential element of social studies education, therefore, is experiential—practicing the arts and habits of civic life" (p. 6).

The research base for this work is specifically termed the "scholarly rationale" (NCSS, 2013, p. 83) and is focused on research about how students learn and develop the understandings necessary for the ultimate goal of active civic engagement. This scholarly rationale does not dictate particular content to be taught, and notes the importance of local control in developing robust social studies content but with parameters laid out of particular kinds of learning to be supported. The research presented supports a deeper understanding for policymakers and educators about the importance of the creation of authentic "problem solving spaces" (p. 84) to grapple with the significant questions of each discipline. This authentic space would include understanding and using evidence, working collaboratively to develop understanding, and developing of socio-cultural awareness. Inquiry is used for the economic, geographic, historical, and civic minded thinking in which students should engage.

This approach would seem to fit well with the call for experience and participation as a foundational component of early learning settings. However, this framework was developed for K-12 and does not include specific attention to preschool. The document (NCSS, 2013) uses grade bands to delineate learning progressions with a suggested "K-12 Pathway" showing how students' proficiencies might develop over time for the included skills and concepts. These pathways are organized developmentally and "acknowledge students' developing capacity for understanding more sophisticated ideas and completing more demanding inquiries across the grade bands of K–2, 3–5, 6–8, and 9–12" (p. 13). It is interesting to note that in the introduction, the authors specifically state that the document does not address the differing abilities, background experiences, or cultural approaches that students may bring into their school-based social studies learning.

English/Language Arts

Standards for English and the Language Arts (ELA) were first published in 1996 and later reaffirmed in 2012 by the National Council of Teachers of English and the International Reading Association (NCTE/IRA). The standards cover 12 areas and focus on reading for many purposes; strategies used to understand and analyze text; effective use of spoken, written, and visual languages; and using resources for information. The general goal is full participation in society via skills in understanding and using language in its many forms.

The standards are presented through extended discussion that lays out the nature of each, what each means, and why it is important. They are intended to set a shared vision for teachers in this area while also reflecting high standards for all children (NCTE/IRA, 1996). An important point throughout the document is the multiple languages and language norms that exist; therefore, there is more attention to diversity in these standards compared to those we examined from the other professional disciplinary associations.

The framers of the document were clear that the standards would be translated and applied within local contexts. Furthermore, they do not offer any recommendations regarding levels of achievement for children. Examples are described for various grade levels, but more generally schooling is conceptualized as elementary, middle, or high school levels. More narrowly defined grade bands were addressed in supplementary documents, which offered examples of practice consistent with the standards; one such guide addresses kindergarten through second grade (Crafton, 1996). Importantly, the lowest level addressed is kindergarten (NCTE/IRA, 1996). Preschool is mentioned only occasionally in regard to referencing what experiences children might have had, or not had, before entering kindergarten.

The standards are described as reflecting what is valued within the field. As well, it is stated that the goals and interests of learners are key to the classroom. The standards are meant to be suggestive and the authors state that "we do not mean to imply that the standards can or should be translated into isolated components of instruction" (NCTE/IRA, 1996, p. 18).

National Association for the Education of Young Children

Led by NAEYC, the field of early childhood took an early stand to define "good" early childhood approaches and practices and to protect practice from what was viewed as the "push down" of elementary approaches to teaching and assessment with young children. After initial publication in 1986, NAEYC has since updated *Developmentally Appropriate Practice in Early Childhood Programs*

Serving Children from Birth through Age 8 (Copple & Bredekamp, 2009) – hereafter DAP. The influence of this document has been far-reaching, evidenced in part by how widely the acronym DAP is known.

In its most recent edition (Copple & Bredekamp, 2009), the DAP document lays out a comprehensive framework which includes the five domains of development. The theoretical underpinnings of DAP largely reflect Piagetian developmental theory ascribing to the notion that development occurs in a largely predictable and universal manner. DAP is organized across age bands, and within each age band there are specific "examples to consider" of practices that are developmentally appropriate, and those that are "in contrast" to that.

This most recent edition is contextualized within the standards/accountability context, which is described as "powerful" (Copple & Bredekamp, 2009, p. 3), while it acknowledges the importance of the goal of high achievement for all children. The authors noted (perhaps predicted) some of the possible problems with large scale standardization and rigid adherence to standards in early childhood. They warned of "standards overload" that could be "overwhelming for teachers" and could lead to "problematic teaching practices" including an "insistence that teachers follow rigid, tightly paced schedules" with a curtailing of "rich play" (p. 4).

Copple and Bredekamp (2009) argued that standards should be the starting place for early childhood programs to be able to choose or develop curriculum that was appropriate to their local contexts. Teacher expertise and decision-making was put at the center of this process, in which the work is too complex and individual to allow advance prescription of a teacher's every move.

The larger DAP document does provide quite a bit of direction specifically related to curriculum development and implementation. Copple and Bredekamp (2009) stress the importance of planning curriculum toward the "knowledge, skills, abilities, and understandings children are to acquire," noting that these outcomes should be "developmentally and educationally significant" (p. 20). Within the domain of cognitive development for preschoolers, the document makes connections to the specific content areas (mathematics, science, language and literacy, technology, social studies, and creative arts). It is recommended throughout that curriculum development in these areas be aligned to the national professional organizations connected to these subject/curricular areas and to curriculum offered in K–3 schools. While the work of NCTM is specifically discussed in the preschool and kindergarten section, the practice recommendations for language and literacy at both age bands are largely drawn from research. No mention is made of NCSS, and the NGSS were not yet written; overall, the social studies and science learning components in both age bands are much shorter than the language/literacy and mathematics sections.

State-level Early Learning Standards

In the early 2000s, the standards movement was well under way and kindergarten was firmly connected to elementary schools in most states (Bracken & Crawford,

2009). In 2002, the George W. Bush Administration put forth its "Good Start, Grow Smart" initiative intended to strengthen early childhood education in the United States. One recommendation of this initiative was to connect early childhood more clearly to the K-12 standards movement. The recommendation was (with federal dollars to determine the work) that states develop "quality criteria for early childhood education" that were to include "pre-reading and language skills activities that align with K-12 standards." Further, this initiative allocated $45 million toward research "to identify effective pre-reading and language curricula and teaching strategies" (White House, 2002). The standards and accountability movement firmly made its way into early childhood education.

In an early examination of state-developed ELS for 3- to 5-year-olds, Scott-Little, Kagan, and Stebbins-Frelow (2006) analyzed documents from 46 states. They found remarkable variation. For instance, not all states included all of the following five dimensions of development: physical, social-emotional, language/communication, cognitive/general knowledge, and approaches to learning. From state to state, there were differences in emphases among these domains and in the number of indicators within the domain categories. Documents developed within a state department of education (as opposed to, for example, some form of human services) were more likely to reflect less emphasis on the social-emotional and approaches to learning domains. Half of the documents were presented as aligned with their states' K-12 standards documents, while the other half were not. The categories and indicators used within documents included both developmental and academic subject labels. The research team also found a similarity across states, in that all documents were slanted toward emphasizing the language/communication and cognition/general knowledge domains. Interestingly, in another early paper, Scott-Little et al. (2007) found through a survey that some state representatives reported developing their ELS documents by extending K-12 standards downwards, while others reported starting from an early childhood vantage point, considering the ELS to be foundational and not necessarily requiring a neat correspondence to K-12 standards.

A more recent review of just ten states' ELS documents revealed that differences among states continue. In this study, the research team (Scott-Little et al., n.d.) found most consensus in the literacy and mathematics areas. Again, they noted that the language/communication and cognition/general knowledge domains were invariably most highly emphasized.

In a more comprehensive and recent review, DeBruin-Parecki and Slutzky (2016) noted that the 54 documents they reviewed continued to vary from state to state. They found that as time has passed, revisions in these documents has been the norm. As a result of these revisions, the content disciplines are more apparent: 100 percent of the reviewed documents included language and literacy as well as mathematics while science was included in varied ways in 94 percent and social studies in 78 percent. According to respondents' comments about how ELS were developed and revised, there is no indication that the work of the disciplinary associations was consulted. A total of 34 percent of the respondents noted that their states utilized resources from "organizations focusing on education, children and families" with NAEYC and Zero to Three being cited as exemplars (DeBruin-Parecki & Slutzky, 2016, p. 16). The most common resource mentioned was the research base on children's development and learning.

Before leaving this topic, we must make note of the one nationwide set of standards for young children, the Head Start Early Learning Outcomes Framework (Office of Head Start, 2015). Given the variation in states' ELS, it would be stating the obvious to observe that these guidelines are yet again unique. The framework is presented as a continuum of developmental progressions in each of the areas addressed. There is an emphasis on the idea that children in Early Head Start and Head Start programs should be moving along this continuum toward the endpoint of kindergarten readiness.

Summary

This admittedly swift review of standards that impact the field of early childhood offers one easy conclusion: there is a proliferation of ideas about what children should know and be able to do during the early years. Standards have risen and been influenced by many sources: content experts, state systems staff, and researchers whose work is being utilized in forming standards. It is also true that for some standards developers, learning begins at kindergarten (although the structure of school systems has changed to widely include younger children). Children not yet in kindergarten are ignored by the majority of professional disciplinary associations. If alignment is the goal, Pre-K teachers are given no guidance from the ELA, science, and social studies associations. Yet, given that Pre-K is not experienced as universally by children as kindergarten, might it be good to avoid setting assumptions of a learning sequence begun at age four or younger? How do we consider alignment in the case of non-universal experiences? It is also true that professional associations have approached this work very differently, ranging from highly engineered, sequenced prescriptions about what should be addressed grade-by-grade to broadly described visions of what is important for children to learn and be able to do, tied to broad levels of schooling.

There is not consensus across the United States about what young children should learn and be able to do if they attend formal early childhood settings prior to kindergarten enrollment. For teachers in these settings (as well as those in the grade bands universally addressed by standards documents) attempting any sort of understanding formed *across* the current silos of standards is a dizzying prospect. Yet it is clear there are certainly expectations that young children from a variety of program auspices (and from exclusively parental and/or extended family care?) should be arriving at kindergarten with *some* battery of skills and knowledge. These expectations are part and parcel of the accountability regime.

More and more, guidance for early childhood professionals is being provided via published curricula. We turn now to how publishers have addressed the varying standards in place for early childhood programs.

Early Childhood Curriculum Packages

In this section we examine the claims offered by those who publish curriculum packages for early childhood Pre-K classrooms. We focused on curriculum for children in the year (or two) prior to kindergarten for several reasons. First, the stakes have become higher in this age group. As noted previously, children entering kindergarten are expected to arrive with a repertoire of skills and understandings and engage quickly with academics. Second, children spend the year before kindergarten in a variety of program auspices if they are in group settings, including Head Start, pre-kindergarten within a school district building, pre-kindergarten provided in partnership between the school district and a community-based agency, and child care. These settings differ in regard to teacher qualifications, policy mandates and oversight, composition of the classroom, and many other characteristics. The variations occur both within a state and from state to state. Curriculum developers must address the different auspices, as they represent markets that cannot be ignored. Finally, as noted in the previous section, the Pre-K year has been addressed very differently by different versions of standards. Thus, learning is differently conceptualized, authorized, and guided during this particular year of children's lives.

Our review of publishers' claims is informed by Hatch's (2002) arguments about the threats he perceived if standards-based instruction was pursued inappropriately in early childhood classrooms – in his words, if accountability efforts were shoved down. We will note in the discussion to follow where we witnessed these threats reflected in curriculum packages currently marketed by major publishers. We examined curricula that are recommended for Pre-K programs in the state of Georgia (Georgia Department of Early Care and Learning, 2018), as a public list is available. The Georgia Pre-K program includes a variety of settings in braided funding streams, including Head Start, public schools, and private programs. The assumption is that the recommended curriculum packages are suitable for all auspices. We selected six widely marketed packages from the list of approved curricula and examined the claims made in the initial quest for customers, the information available on websites without further request or restricted access. These packages were: Creative Curriculum (Teaching Strategies, 2018), OWL – Opening the World of Learning 2014 (Pearson, 2014), We Can Early Learning Curriculum (Voyager Sopris Learning, 2018), Frog Street Pre-K (Frog Street Press, 2017), Big Day for Pre-K (Houghton Mifflin Harcourt, 2015), and Learn Every Day (Gryphon House, 2012).

The curricula share many common features. All claim to address learning and development comprehensively and are built around units of study or thematic units. There are units common across many or even all of the packages, related to topics such as self and family, classroom, community, as well as topics related to animals and/or insects or movement and/or building. The packages share common learning modes as well, invariably including small and large group experiences and interest/learning centers. In addition, there were differences. The content of the curriculum also varied according to themes found in only one or a smaller subset of the packages, for example, deserts, jungles, and oceans. Thus, there was not a common body of knowledge promulgated across the packages.

These curricula are marketed upon the promise of successful learning for young children. The websites all carried variations of a theme related to the curriculum's "positive outcomes" for children or the curriculum as a "key to success" and/or readiness for future learning in kindergarten and above. But of course, this opening pitch would seem crucial to productively marketing this sort of product. What is reflected in the pitches, however, is the assumption that a pre-determined curriculum trumps all – a well-planned and competently-implemented curriculum is sufficient. This is regardless of other program resources, teacher knowledge and skill, and individual differences among children in how they relate to, experience, and take up the information and skills embedded in the curriculum. Also implicit within the promises made by the developers is the assumption that there is a shared and clear vision of what it means to be successful and "ready" for kindergarten.

Widely apparent in our examination of these curricula was the impact of the ELS movement. A ubiquitous claim for these curricula is that they are aligned to important standards documents. Thus, one finds the correlation documents, which typically illustrate in detail which components of the curriculum (e.g., a lesson, an activity, a page number) are aligned to the components of a set of standards. In the correlations for any of these curricula, one can find documents related to some, or even all states (and the District of Columbia), as well as the Head Start Early Learning Outcomes Framework. None of the publishers correlated their curriculum with the standards of the one disciplinary association which included Pre-K, NCTM.

As Hatch (2002) noted, early childhood programs are not immune to the influences of the accountability phenomenon. In our examination, we witnessed how the threats Hatch discussed appear in these curriculum packages, well over a decade later.

Hatch (2002) first discussed the threat of pressure on children. In one sense, these packages do not evidence pressure on children. There are no high-stakes outcomes being demanded. The packages included ideas for adapting experiences to children who needed more challenge or simpler concepts, children learning English as an additional language, or children with special needs. On the other hand, almost all of the curricula were described as attending to a scope and sequence of skill- and knowledge-building, with teaching and learning being a process built sequentially and deliberately across the year. In this sense, the idea that children in a Pre-K group are moving lock-step toward a finish line – readiness – there is pressure for those children whose learning is not so neatly mapped and completed.

As well, Hatch (2002) noted that accountability put pressures on teachers. We found that the marketing for these packages very explicitly aimed in the opposite direction – claiming to take pressure off of teachers. The specificity and inclusiveness of the materials were designed to put all a teacher needs at reach. "Everything" is provided, making the curriculum "easy" to implement. For most packages, it is possible to purchase manipulatives and children's books, making the package a true one-stop shop for the classroom and clarifying that all decisions are pre-made. Potential customers were assured, as well, that with these materials they didn't have to be concerned that they were missing anything important toward the children's success; in the words of the Creative Curriculum, they could "have confidence" that standards would be met because "guesswork" had been taken out of the equation (Teaching Strategies, 2018). In this sense, the curricula are marketed as relieving the burden on the teacher. In the case of standards overload, there seems to be some logic here. However, we wonder about pressures on teachers from another direction. What of the potential stressor of trying to fit young children to the engineered curriculum? If teaching with a published curriculum is claimed to be "easy," how do teachers come to terms with the real-life messiness and complexity of early childhood classrooms?

However, Hatch (2002) included another concern related to teachers, that the accountability culture would lead to deprofessionalization of their work. We would argue that the evidence in the preceding paragraph points in this direction. In fact, teachers have few decisions to make with these all-inclusive packages. Preparing for a unit is often presented as a list of to-do tasks and materials to gather. While some packages present general suggestions for some regular components of the daily activities, others provide scripts for all teaching moves in the classroom, from the questions to use during a read-aloud to the choices to present to children for a smooth transition to another activity. While it is true in early childhood that teachers in various program auspices come to their work with a range of professional educational experiences, the curricula are overwhelmingly written to the least prepared educator, the teacher not capable of curricular decision-making, or as in the preceding paragraph, the teacher prone to engaging in guesswork while planning curriculum in the current standards-heavy climate.

In addition to the previously noted concerns, Hatch (2002) discussed the potential of children's learning experiences being narrowed due to accountability. We noted evidence of this happening in the curriculum packages in regard to child-driven, open-ended play and exploration. Traditional elements of free play, such as child-based decision-making and spontaneity (Nell & Drew, n.d.), are curtailed in the packages in favor of play that is more directed and/or aligned with the thematic unit. For example, in Learn Every Day, it is suggested during one unit that children sort healthy and non-healthy foods in the dramatic play center. Where the dramatic play area is typically ripe for free play opportunities, in this curricular iteration, play becomes determined toward a specific learning objective. A rather common theme among the packages was that teachers could make every experience valuable to learning, in the words of Opening the World of Learning, allowing the teacher to "make every moment count." The question is, count toward what and whose ends? This stance requires a teacher always ready to step in and direct the activity as prescribed by the curriculum toward ends that are most likely not determined by the children or the teachers.

This points us to one other concern raised by Hatch (2002), which is that accountability would result in devaluing individuals. We saw this as endemic to the curriculum packages. Suggestions for individualization (defined broadly) were widespread and some packages were even translated into Spanish. On the other hand, all of the potential recipients were rather similarly-imagined individuals. Children were universalized, and language differences were not embedded within a culture. These curricula are highly engineered and yet touted as suitable for all and any children. For instance, one scripted transition in Frog Street Pre-K suggests dismissing children on the basis of whether the chore they would prefer would be making food, taking care of a pet, or mowing the lawn, ignoring the fact that children in the desert southwest or built-out apartment blocks have little personal experience with lawns, or that pets are not common to all. Defined parameters and leading questions framed the quest toward learning, while local context and meaningfulness were sacrificed for assurances that this package would take children (any and all) where they needed to go. Cultural responsiveness was assumed and not specifically addressed.

In sum, in these packages, teaching and learning were all business, even if oriented in purposeful play and/or game-like formats. There was seemingly no allowance for children to be 4-year-olds who needed time and space to wonder, wander, and converse, let alone ask their questions, try out their ideas, and express curiosity about their interests. Teachers were cast as technicians delivering a protocol, rather than as professionals capable of nuance, intuition, and professional decision-making.

An early publication focused on practice in settings below kindergarten seemed to downplay the potential impact of ELS on teachers' work. As expressed by Gronlund (2006),

> Planning curriculum with ELS in mind does not require a complete change in teaching practices. . . . Incorporating standards requires adding a layer of awareness to your planning and implementation so that you can clearly see where standards are being addressed and add ways to bring them more to the forefront. In that way you can incorporate the language of those standards. . . . This is necessary so that parents, community members, and policymakers understand that what looks like play and fun has learning and skill development within it.
>
> (p. 16)

While Gronlund envisioned little impact of standards on early childhood practice, a dozen years later, few, if any, individuals might assert that the demands exist only in connecting standards-based language to the classroom practices that have been traditionally utilized by preschool teachers. Standards within the accountability regime loom large in early childhood practice across all settings, including Head Start, state-funded pre-kindergarten, and child care. The emphasis for curriculum development is becoming predicated upon following pre-engineered paths that we think of as the "promise of standards-fulfillment." Alignment becomes the goal of curriculum development rather than support of teaching and learning. We view this development as reflecting many of the red flags raised by Hatch (2002) in relation to the impact of accountability on our youngest learners.

Conclusion

In this chapter we have offered a brief history of the entities promulgating standards, how they have and have not influenced each other, and how they have and have not connected to curricular approaches for young children. Across levels, and including early childhood, standards have become the approach to ensure that all children learn. It is clear, however, that standards are derived in very different ways, with varying intents and purposes. Furthermore, there is little overlap across standards documents; it is a field heavy with silos. Standards are developed in many different ways, expressed in many different styles, and seemingly, without a common sense of how they may be enacted in teaching and learning.

While this is problematic enough – how does a teacher make sense of it all? – in the accountability regime, standards become powerful drivers within the system. Somehow, we have come to believe that if we can create and package oversight structures (standards, curriculum, etc.), that we will have solved our educational problems. The more we can predict and the more we can control, the "more" children will learn. Based on the idea that we can change ostensibly bad outcomes to better ones, pressure is now put on teachers to be better at producing learning outcomes. All curriculum is to be evidence-based and delivered with fidelity in all sites, even in places as highly variable as the world of young children, with their uneven developmental progressions and the nuances required to move individuals with different backgrounds into something resembling a group moving along at somewhat the same learning pace, give or take.

We believe that in many ways the standards documents and DAP are rich sources of knowledge about young children's learning and their potential and about what is valued for disciplinary learning. While we see a desire to frame standards as guidelines, frameworks, even explicit values, to be applied to curriculum packages, the result has been more prescriptive in nature, with topics, activities, books, and more, all selected in the absence of meeting children and learning about who they are.

Copple and Bredekamp (2009) noted in DAP that "expert decision making lies at the heart of effective teaching" (p. 5). For the entirety of DAP's existence, teachers have been advised to make decisions based in part on the children with whom they work. Now, with a dizzying array of requirements, some standards are relatively ignored (e.g., those promulgated by the professional associations, except perhaps NCTM), and others are treated as checklists (e.g., each correlation matrix checks off where a domain/standard/indicator is addressed in the curriculum package). As we have increased the complexity of the teaching/learning process in the United States, where correlation matrices abound at all levels of education, the penchant is to turn to an "all-encompassing and aligned" package that can do the job. The curriculum packages that we examined appear as suggested recipes, equally applicable anywhere. Perhaps with such an unwieldy framework as the one we have now, this should not be a surprise.

As a result, we are threatened with losing important parts of the role of the teacher. With these curriculum packages the work is increasingly technical. There will be no room for error in learning because the children "will learn" with our matrices aligned and a teacher following the plan. The intellectual pursuits and art of teaching have been replaced with to-do lists, prepared questions, and ready-chosen topics, literature, and materials.

As a result, we've lost the child in early childhood – who, as a field, we have traditionally placed (more or less) at the center of the curriculum. Any child's questions, interests, ways of making meaning, and background are subsumed into a conveyer belt of ongoing and skill-building themes. Children have become, in a common phrase, a bucket to fill.

As a result, we've severely limited the way learning is defined. Both teacher and child are actors, expected to perform in ways determined in advance. Learning is conceived as highly predictable and universal across the course of a year's worth of thematic units. Even the lack of complete universality is taken care of with specific individualization ideas as needed. The idea is lost that learning is not entirely predictable, varied, and, to be honest, downright messy. The notions that we can engage children authentically in their immediate worlds, build from the various assets they bring to our classrooms, and that learning should be emergent and generative have been forfeited.

Some might argue that in the highly variable world of early childhood before kindergarten that teachers who have less professional preparation than others need the support of a strong curriculum. By solving the issue of minimal expectations for teacher education with a teacher-proof curriculum package, we are selling both teachers and the entire field short. It is a myth that we can build a perfect system outside of the people involved in order to reach perfect outcomes with those people.

Notes

1 The physical sciences; the life sciences; the earth and space sciences; and engineering, technology, and applications of science.
2 Asking questions, developing and using models, planning and carrying out investigations, analyzing and interpreting data, designing solutions, engaging in argument from evidence, and obtaining, evaluating, and communicating information.
3 Patterns; cause and effect; systems and system models; interdependence of science, engineering, and technology; and influence of engineering, technology, and science on society and the natural world.

References

Bracken, B.A., & Crawford, E. (2009). Basic concepts in early childhood educational standards: A 50-state review. *Early Childhood Education, 37*(5), 421–430.

Copple, C., & Bredekamp, S. (Eds.) (2009). *Developmentally appropriate practice in early childhood programs serving children from birth through age 8.* Washington, DC: National Association for the Education of Young Children.

Crafton, L.K. (1996). *Standards in practice: Grades K–2.* National Council of Teachers of English. (ERIC Document Reproduction Service No. 461 861).

DeBruin-Parecki, A., & Slutzky, C. (2016). *Exploring pre-K age 4 learning standards and their role in early childhood education: Research and policy implications* (Policy Information Report; Research Report No. RR-16–14). Princeton, NJ: Educational Testing Service. http://dx.doi.org/10.1002/ets2.12099

Frog Street Press (2017). *Frog Street Pre-K.* Retrieved from www.frogstreet.com/curriculum/pre-k/

Georgia Department of Early Care and Learning (2018). *Georgia's pre-K program 2018–2019 school year pre-K providers' operating guidelines.* Atlanta, GA: Author.

Gronlund, G. (2006). *Make ELS come alive: Connecting your practice and curriculum to state guidelines.* Upper Saddle River, NJ: Pearson.

Gryphon House (2012). *Learn every day.* Retrieved from www.learneverydayabout.com/

Hatch, J.A. (2002). Accountability shovedown: Resisting the standards movement in early childhood education. *Phi Delta Kappan, 83*(6), 457–462.

Houghton Mifflin Harcourt (2015). *Big day for pre-K.* Retrieved from www.hmhco.com/products/big-day-Pre-K/

National Council for the Social Studies (NCSS) (2013). *The college, career, and civic life (C3) framework for social studies state standards: Guidance for enhancing the rigor of K-12 civics, economics, geography, and history.* Silver Spring, MD: NCSS.

National Council of Teachers of English/International Reading Association (NCTE/IRA). (1996). *Standards for the English language arts.* Retrieved from www.ncte.org/library/NCTEFiles/Resources/Books/Sample/StandardsDoc.pdf

National Council of Teachers of Mathematics (2000). *Principles and standards for school mathematics.* Reston, VA: NCTM.

National Council of Teachers of Mathematics (2014). *Principles to actions: Ensuring mathematical success for all.* Reston, VA: NCTM.

National Research Council (2012). *A framework for K-12 science education.* Washington, DC: National Academies Press.

National Science Teachers Association Board of Directors (2014). *NSTA position statement: Early childhood science education.* Retrieved from www.nsta.org/about/positions/earlychildhood.aspx

Nell, M.L., & Drew, W.F. (n.d.). *Five essentials to meaningful play.* Retrieved from www.naeyc.org/our-work/families/five-essentials-meaningful-play

Next Generation Science Standards (2013). *The next generation science standards: Executive summary.* Retrieved from www.nextgenscience.org/sites/default/files/NGSS%20Executive%20Summary%20-%206%2017%2013%20Update.pdf

Office of Head Start (2015). *Head Start early learning outcomes framework: Ages birth to five.* Retrieved from https://eclkc.ohs.acf.hhs.gov/sites/default/files/pdf/elof-ohs-framework.pdf

Pearson (2014). *Opening the world of learning.* Retrieved from www.pearsonschool.com/index.cfm?locator=PSZpNy

Scott-Little, C., Kagan, S.L., Reid, J.L., Sumrall, T.C., & Fox, E.A. (n.d.). *Common early learning and development standards analysis for the North Carolina EAG Consortium: Summary report.* Retrieved from www.buildinitiative.org/Portals/0/Uploads/Documents/Common%20Early%20Learning%20and%20Development%20Standards%20Analysis%20for%20the%20North%20Carolina%20EAG%20Consortium%20-%20SUMMARY%20REPORT.pdf

Scott-Little, C., Kagan, S.L., & Stebbins-Frelow, V. (2006). Conceptualization of readiness and the content of ELS: The intersection of policy and research? *Early Childhood Research Quarterly, 21,* 153–173.

Scott-Little, C., Lesko, J., Martella, J., & Milburn, P. (2007). ELS: Results from a national survey to document trends in state-level policies and practices. *Early Childhood Research and Practice,* 9(1). Retrieved from www.ecrp.uiuc.edu/v9n1/little.html

Teaching Strategies (2018). *The creative curriculum for preschool.* Retrieved from www.teachingstrategies.com/solutions/teach/preschool/

Voyager Sopris Learning (2018). *We Can early learning curriculum.* Retrieved from www.voyagersopris.com/literacy/we-can/overview

White House (2002). *Good start, grow smart: The Bush administration's Early Childhood Initiative.* Retrieved from www.georgewbushwhitehouse.archives.gov/infocus/earlychildhood/earlychildhood.html

4

FROM THEORY TO CURRICULUM

Developmental Theory and Its Relationship to Curriculum and Instruction in Early Childhood Education

J. Amos Hatch

I studied early childhood education in a college of education. My terminal diploma says that I have a PhD in curriculum and instruction. The transcripts from all three of my degrees show that I had extensive coursework in child development and early childhood education, but I was also exposed to heavy doses of curriculum theory and design as well as lots of coursework in instructional theory and research. My path as an early childhood professor has taken me far away from my roots as a student of curriculum and instruction, but the notion that curriculum can be thought of as a separate and distinct discipline from instruction provides an interesting tool for considering the topic on which I have been invited to write: the application of developmental theory to early childhood curriculum.

Given the way developmental theory is usually construed in our field and my take on curriculum as the intellectual substance that should be taught in educational settings, I argue that the connections between developmental theory and curriculum are tenuous at best. To organize my case, I present a brief description of what I take to be the hegemony of developmental perspectives in theorizing and policy making in mainstream early childhood education. I then make distinctions between curriculum and instruction and point out how these distinctions are largely missing when child development theories dominate the discourses of early childhood. Describing the impact of developmental theory on early childhood instruction (as opposed to curriculum), I contrast the implications of applying precepts from Piaget to those from Vygotsky. I conclude with examples from math and science that demonstrate the advantages of distinguishing curriculum from instruction and highlight the disadvantages of the field's overreliance on Piagetian-influenced developmental theory.

Developmentally Appropriate Thinking

Developmentally appropriate practice (DAP) is a brand. It is *the* brand of the National Association for the Education of Young Children (NAEYC), and as a brand, it has been adopted (sometimes co-opted) by countless programs, policies, and products in the US and around the globe. NAEYC has been thoughtful and strategic about marketing, protecting, and updating DAP – its most valuable commodity. In the second and third of three major DAP iterations so far (Bredekamp, 1987; Bredekamp & Copple, 1997; Copple & Bredekamp, 2009), NAEYC has adjusted adroitly to the complaints of its critics. The documents have changed in form and substance, but the reliance on developmental theory as the bedrock on which the DAP brand is built remains constant; it is after all, *developmentally* appropriate practice.

In a recent article (Hatch, 2010), I describe my search through a collection of current textbooks designed for early childhood college courses. My goal was to examine what future early childhood teachers are reading about teaching and learning in these texts. As might be expected, the efficacy of developmentally appropriate practice and the central importance of knowing child development theory were taken for granted throughout these contemporary textbooks. None of the texts I examined (all published in 2006 or later) had enough time to make reference to the 2009 DAP guidelines, but it is certain that their next editions will do so. It seems just as certain that child development theory will continue to dominate future versions of the DAP brand and strongly influence the materials, programs, and policies that drive the early childhood education mainstream. It would be unthinkable to disconnect DAP from NAEYC and impossible to construct a "developmentally appropriate practice" without its defining ingredient: developmental theory. But, what does this have to do with early childhood curriculum (and instruction)?

Distinguishing the What from the How in Early Childhood Education

Plenty of evidence suggests that mainstream early childhood educators are preoccupied with how children develop, how classrooms are organized, how adults interact with children, and how children interact with their surroundings. In fact, early childhood curriculum as described in the current literature, including all three DAP handbooks, is largely focused on how classrooms ought to be organized and run. Missing until recently is a careful consideration of what should be learned in these classrooms.

Curriculum in many early childhood contexts has been taken to mean setting up stimulating environments and following the lead of the child. Early childhood curriculum has emphasized child-centered approaches and child-initiated activity. In this discourse, curriculum is said to emerge from the interests and developmental capacities of children. The role of children is to act as explorers and discoverers, while teachers are to be guides and facilitators. The processes of the classroom become the focus of early education. In these settings, the intellectual substance to be learned has been little more than an afterthought.

In a book on teaching in kindergarten (Hatch, 2005), I offer a conception of curriculum and instruction that highlights the differences between the what and how of early childhood education. In this way of thinking, curriculum is focused squarely on the subject matter content that young children ought to be taught. The content comes from subject matter disciplines, including language arts, mathematics, science, social studies, health and physical education, and the arts. In contrast, instruction is conceptualized as the ways that teachers work with students to ensure that the substance of the curriculum is learned. Curriculum is what is to be taught; instruction is how the curriculum is taught.

Contrary to what is provided in most texts about early childhood education, my book lays out a wide range of teaching strategies that teachers are encouraged to apply. The conceptualizations of curriculum and instruction are intentionally clean and neat. They are meant to help teachers and future teachers avoid confusing what they teach (curriculum) with how they teach it (instruction).

Others within the field have also moved in the direction of placing more emphasis on distinguishing between curriculum and instruction. Coming from different angles, Epstein's (2007) *The Intentional Teacher: Choosing the Best Strategies for Young Children's Learning* and *Teaching Young Children: Choices in Theory and Practice* by MacNaughton and Williams (2004) are prominent examples. Epstein published her book with NAEYC, utilizing the "intentional teaching" concept "to broaden our thinking about early curriculum content and related teaching strategies" (2007, p. viii). My view is her book is valuable because Epstein takes seriously the notion that there is genuine curriculum content to be learned in early childhood classrooms. She acknowledges that curriculum comes from knowledge generated in the academic disciplines. The book does less well at broadening early childhood teachers' conceptions of teaching strategies because of its emphasis on the primacy of "child-guided" activities. However, the book's premise that it is important to include real intellectual substance in early childhood curriculum is a big step forward.

MacNaughton and Williams (2004) are Australian authors, and the focus of their book is on enriching early childhood educators' knowledge of alternative theories and expanding their repertoires of teaching strategies. They provide an extensive taxonomy of teaching strategies that include 15 general (e.g., demonstrating, grouping, questioning) and 10 specialized (e.g., deconstructing, empowering, philosophizing) teaching techniques. For each of the specialized teaching strategies, MacNaughton and Williams provide a theoretical overview to support teachers' understandings. The theorists they draw on in these sections include some who are not often found in early childhood curriculum texts, including Derrida (deconstructing), Freire (empowering), and Lipman (philosophizing). Although they acknowledge traditional notions related to the impact of developmental forces, MacNaughton and Williams honor the cognitive capacities of young children to process genuine curriculum content, and they provide instructional tools for teachers that mark clear boundaries between the what and how of early childhood teaching. Both books support my case that early childhood curriculum need not and should not be conflated with early childhood instruction.

Like MacNaughton and Williams (2004), I used my kindergarten book to identify sets of teaching strategies so that early childhood teachers could see that their roles as instructors go beyond setting up stimulating environments and waiting for opportunities to facilitate development (Hatch, 2005). Given real curriculum content and real children who need to learn that content, the teaching strategies are presented as options designed to improve teachers' chances of helping all children be successful learners. These strategies are arranged on a continuum that range from incidental to direct teaching, and include three kinds of thematic teaching (units, projects, and integrated theme studies) and seven types of tactical teaching (grouping, modeling and demonstrating, coaching, tutoring, discussing, practicing, and individualizing). No strategies are given more attention or status than any others. Teachers are called on to use the continuum to frame instructional decisions that maximize all children's chances of learning the material in the curriculum.

Like Epstein (2007), my kindergarten book identifies curriculum content synthesized from academic disciplines (e.g., literacy, math, science, social studies, health, physical education, and the arts). Both books rely on recommendations from professional organizations in the various disciplines as content is selected for inclusion, and for both books the message is the same: real content is important in early childhood curriculum, and we have a good idea of what that content should be.

The kindergarten curriculum I describe is meant to be an example of what is possible; it is not intended to be *the* kindergarten curriculum. In my sample kindergarten curriculum, I stayed away from the using the terms "objectives" and "standards," preferring "elements" to name the distinct pieces of content to be taught. That is because I want to provide early childhood teachers with a roadmap of what ought to be learned in kindergarten. It is not a capitulation to manic attempts to create arbitrary standards, then apply ill-suited measurements to assess them – what I have called accountability shovedown (Hatch, 2002). I want to promote teaching real content because doing so makes sense for young children. I do not want the identification of elements to be appropriated by those who would say that the mastery of these "objectives" or the accomplishment of these "standards" ought to become the criteria by which young children or their teachers are judged.

Developmental Theory and Early Childhood Curriculum and Instruction

I know that curriculum can be defined in many ways and that early childhood definitions based on developmental theory have their own logic once basic premises are accepted, but I think those premises need to be challenged. Here, I am challenging the utility of developmental theory as a source for understanding the what of early childhood curriculum. Curriculum content, the substance of early childhood education, cannot logically be identified based on knowledge of child development theory; that is, figuring out what subject matter knowledge should be taught does not follow from understandings of what children are like at particular ages and stages. This helps explain why descriptions of developmentally appropriate early childhood curriculum are so often devoid of serious consideration of the intellectual content children should be expected to learn (Kessler & Swadener, 1992; Stone, 1996).

If developmental theory has little to tell early childhood professionals about the intellectual content that young children can and should be learning (i.e., the curriculum), what about its relationship to instruction? The short answer is that developmental theory can tell us a lot more about instruction than it can about curriculum. However, it gets complicated very quickly because applying constructs from different developmental theorists leads to classroom practices that look quite different from one another. As a prime example, differences between the constructivist theories of Piaget and his followers (e.g., Piaget, 1968; Piaget & Inhelder, 1969; Furth, 1970) and the socio-cultural theoretical approach of Vygotsky and his disciples (e.g., Vygotsky, 1978; Luria, 1976; Wertsch, 1985) lead to quite different instructional stances.

As I have argued elsewhere (Hatch, 2010), the field likes to lump developmental theories together and pretend that early childhood educators can comfortably meld Piagetian and Vygotskian approaches in the classroom. However, the basic assumptions of these two seminal developmental theorists with regard to the relationship between learning and development lead to conceptions of instruction that are not easily reconciled. Piaget's position is that cognitive development needs to be in place *before* learning can be meaningful and effective. One of Piaget's most quoted axioms encapsulates this key feature of his theory: "Learning is subordinated to development and not vice-versa" (Piaget, 1964, p. 17). The point is hammered home by one of Piaget's most prominent interpreters: "Learning is inconceivable without a theoretically prior interior structure" (Furth, 1970, p. 160).

Vygotsky has a different view of the relationship between learning and development. For him, learning *leads* development. Learning is conceived to be an inherently social activity, and interactions between children and more capable others are the vehicle for generating developmental progress. In his words, "learning awakens a variety of internal developmental processes that are able to operate only when the child is interacting with people in his environment" (Vygotsky, 1978, p. 90).

Yes, knowledge of developmental theories like those associated with Piaget and Vygotsky can be used to inform instruction, but educators need to be much more discerning about how they apply developmental theory in early childhood practice. It is not a surprise that those who fail to see the need for content-rich curriculum in early childhood classrooms are those who favor the application of Piagetian principles. If they agree with Piaget that "when we teach too fast, we keep the child from inventing and discovering himself" (as quoted in Duckworth, 1964, p. 3), then activities that aim to teach certain curriculum content will not have a prominent place in their classrooms. What is a surprise is that they do not see (or at least acknowledge) the inherent contradiction between their approach and the application of Vygotskian theoretical principles. Vygotsky is always cited in DAP and other mainstream early childhood texts, but the application of his ideas related to the place of learning as the engine that drives development is virtually ignored.

If Vygotsky's notion that learning leads development were taken seriously, then "appropriate" classrooms would look and operate differently than those based primarily on Piagetian principles. Teacher and student roles would be constructed in new ways, and the curriculum and instruction experienced by students would be different than are prescribed in the current early childhood literature. If learning as opposed to development were the defining element in early childhood classroom experiences, then curriculum content would have a much more prominent place. If learning via social interaction with more capable others took the place of individual exploration and discovery, then *teaching* intellectual substance as opposed to *facilitating* individual development would be much more visible. Teachers would actually be applying knowledge of Vygotskian concepts such as the zone of proximal development (Vygotsky, 1978; Bedrova & Leong, 2007; Berk & Winsler, 1995) in their work. They would focus their instruction on scaffolding skills and concepts that are just beyond the students' level of independent functioning. They would be actively engaged in interactions with children that are strategically designed to send the message to students that what they can do with the teacher's support today, they will be able to do alone tomorrow. In sum, teachers would be planning activities and implementing instructional strategies that emphasize learning over development (see Hatch, 2010).

In this chapter, I am trying to make the case that developmental theory as it is being conceptualized in contemporary discourses has little to offer in terms of defining the substantive curriculum to be learned in early childhood classrooms. A central issue is that early childhood educators have conflated notions of curriculum and instruction, assuming that the "how" of setting up and facilitating early experiences takes precedence over the "what" that might be included in a carefully designed content-rich curriculum. While developmental theories are not useful in deciding what content ought to be included in early childhood curriculum, they do have profound implications for how instruction is conceptualized and enacted. Examining the differences between Piagetian and Vygotskian notions of the relationship between learning and development, and recognizing how Piaget's ideas have trumped Vygotsky's, provides insight into why curriculum and instruction have not been considered distinct entities in our field. If Piaget (as quoted in Duckworth, 1964, p. 3) is correct in asserting that "the goal of education is not to increase the amount of knowledge, but to create opportunities for a child to invent and discover," then a concern with including specified "knowledge" in the curriculum seems misplaced. In the next section of this chapter, I use specific examples from math and science to argue that unchallenged Piagetian precepts may be limiting how early childhood educators think about curriculum and instruction and undermining opportunities for young children to learn and develop.

Math and Science Learning

In this section, I offer examples of how making clear distinctions between curriculum and instruction can improve young children's chances of learning important content in early childhood classrooms. I utilize recent research on young children's capacities to process math and science content and contrast that research with precepts from developmental theory that continue to dominate early childhood practice. Using examples of specific content, I also point out the potential inadequacies of math and science teaching based on outdated developmental axioms.

I have chosen to focus on math and science for three reasons. First, it seems clear that math and science instruction should be receiving more attention in early childhood because of the current emphasis on the STEM fields (science, technology, engineering, and mathematics) in K-12 and higher education (President's Council of Advisors on Science and Technology, 2010). Second, research on the capacities of young children to learn math and science content has demonstrated that assumptions at the base of traditional early childhood approaches have underestimated the cognitive capacities of young children (e.g., Bransford, Brown, & Cocking, 2000; Meadows, 2006). Third, based on reactions to research syntheses that showed the efficacy of actively teaching key reading skills and concepts (National Reading Panel, 2000; Neuman, Copple, & Bredekamp, 2000; Snow, Burns, & Griffin, 1998), significant progress toward systematically including literacy content in early childhood curricula has already been made.

It is worth noting at the outset of this discussion that the Piagetian orthodoxy that dominates mainstream early childhood thinking has been thoroughly critiqued by scholars from across many disciplines, including developmental psychologists. Cognitive scientists (e.g., Bransford et al., 2000; Meadows, 2006) who study how children learn have discovered that young children are capable to mental processing that was considered impossible based on Piagetian notions of cognitive development. For example, these scientists have documented that young children can think about their own thinking, metacognitively monitor their own learning, and intentionally adjust their own mental processes to adapt to different learning situations. These findings directly challenge Piagetian understandings that children are capable of metacognitive thinking only after they have reached the formal operational stage of cognitive development (about age 12).

In addition, studies in disciplines such as cultural anthropology (Lave, 1988; 1993) and cultural psychology (Rogoff, 1990) have shown how learning happens in a variety of social and cultural contexts. Findings from these studies demonstrate that children do not learn new skills and information in isolation; learning happens in social interaction with adults or more capable others. Children are not expected to be "little scientists" who explore and experiment on their own in order to discover the cultural knowledge that they need. Learning happens best when they act in the role of "apprentice thinkers" who learn directly from "more skilled partners" (Rogoff, 1990, p. 15), a conceptualization that looks more like the application of Vygotskian than Piagetian constructivist theory.

Research into young children's mathematics learning demonstrates the inadequacy of expecting children to construct complex understandings based on free play, independent exploration, and discovery. Challenging Piagetian assumptions about how children acquire logico-mathematical knowledge, Ginsburg and colleagues (2006, p. 174) summarize:

- Young children are competent in a wider range of mathematical abilities than Piaget's (1952) theory might lead one to believe;
- When given instruction, young children are ready to learn some rather complex mathematics;
- Free play is not enough to promote early mathematical thinking.

Math content is not currently emphasized in early childhood curriculum or meaningfully addressed in typical early childhood teaching. Based on a comprehensive National Research Council review of research on mathematics teaching in early childhood settings, Cross, Woods, and Schweingruber (2009, p. 275) conclude:

> Young children in early childhood classrooms do not spend much time engaged with mathematics content. The time that is spent engaged in mathematics is typically of low instructional quality and, more often than not, is conducted as part of whole class activities or embedded in center time or free play. Early childhood teachers rarely teach mathematics in small groups. They report that they are much more likely to use embedded mathematical strategies or do the calendar, which they consider to be teaching mathematics, rather than provide experiences with a primary focus on mathematics.

As a university instructor, I have been guilty of perpetuating the paucity of high quality mathematics teaching in early childhood settings. By way of example, for years I preached to students in my kindergarten methods classes that it was developmentally inappropriate to expect kindergartners to master the concept of missing addends (e.g., 2 + __ = 5). Citing an article by Kamii, Lewis, and Booker (1998) and their reference to Inhelder and Piaget (1964), I taught my students that children up to about age 7 should not be taught missing addends because they were not developmentally ready to reverse their thinking (they would likely respond by adding 2 and 5 and writing 7 in the blank). I used the Piagetian notion of reversibility (i.e., the ability to think in opposite directions simultaneously) to make a larger point about the futility and potential dangers of expecting young children to master mathematics content that they were not cognitively capable of understanding.

My approach now in the same classes is to encourage future kindergarten teachers to take students as far as the students can go in their math learning. I show preservice teachers a progression of math concepts and skills drawn from my book (Hatch, 2005) and from other sources (Clements, Sarama, & DiBiase, 2004; NCTM, 2000), and I provide a range of instructional strategies that make it possible for young children to acquire mathematics knowledge that has been thought to be beyond their capacities in the past. With regard to missing addends, young children can learn the deep structure of mathematical sentences so that they understand the fundamental algebraic axiom that both sides of an equation must be equal. When confronted with equations like 2 + __ = 5, their mental processing turns to making sure that elements on both sides of the equal sign are equivalent. Going beyond the limitations associated with children's cognitive development as described by Piaget and his interpreters means that young children can and should be learning more mathematics content in early childhood classrooms.

Similar issues apply in early childhood science curriculum and instruction. Genuine science content has even less prominence than mathematics in most early childhood curricula. Children are given opportunities to explore and discover, but systematic teaching of scientific concepts and processes is difficult to find. Again, the assumption that young children are not cognitively ready to comprehend abstract scientific principles and that they should be given opportunities to explore and construct scientific understandings on their own dominates mainstream thinking about early childhood science. But, as with mathematics, there is evidence that this kind of thinking shortchanges children's chances to form solid foundations in science. As Duschl, Schweingruber, and Shouse (2007) have noted, "Contrary to older views, young children are not concrete and simplistic thinkers. . . . Children can use a wide range of reasoning processes that form the underpinnings of scientific thinking" (pp. 2–3). And others question the appropriateness of Piaget's view of "child as little scientist." Segal (1996, p. 152) points out that the content and processes of science are too complex to understand without instruction and support, noting that to discover science principles on his or her own, the child has to be not just a little scientist but "quite a brilliant theorist."

My approach to introducing preservice teachers to early childhood science teaching has also changed over the years. In the past, I emphasized setting up opportunities in kindergarten classrooms for children to explore objects and materials related to science concepts, for example, learning centers that allowed children to experiment with physical properties like magnetism, gravity, and buoyancy. I passed along the same Piagetian logic I was taught in my own early childhood science preparation, logic exemplified in a widely used contemporary early childhood curriculum text's advice to prospective teachers:

> Science is, and should be, a natural part of a child's daily experience. It is not a separate subject to be reserved for specific experiences in the curriculum; it is present everywhere in the world around the children, and they are anxious to explore it, discover answers, and build new understandings.
> *(Eliason & Jenkins, 2008, p. 239)*

My approach to teaching about science teaching has changed. I take the same tack as I use with math and the other subject matter areas. I tell my students there is real science to be learned in kindergarten, and it is their responsibility to actively teach science content and science processes. Instead of just setting up the science table with an assortment of objects (e.g., rocks) for children to manipulate, explore, and "play" with, I recommend (and have preservice teachers practice) designing activities that teach specific scientific processes (i.e., observation, classification, hypothesizing, investigation, interpretation, and communication) along with real content in the areas of life science, physics, and earth and space science (Hatch, 2005). For example, the scientific process of classification can be systematically taught in ways that help children use their senses to get reliable information from the world, identify similar and different attributes of objects, make distinctions between objects based on those attributes, form conceptual categories based on those distinctions, and start to understand that all knowledge can be organized into a hierarchy of superordinate, coordinate, subordinate categories. So children can be taught to observe and classify rocks by their attributes while they also learn the basics of rock taxonomy (e.g., sandstone and limestone are kinds of sedimentary rock).

It is clear to anyone who has spent time observing children's "science play" or talking to young children about their conceptions of science that their scientific understandings are limited and frequently distorted. We have dismissed these gaps and misunderstandings based on our assumptions about young children's limited developmental capacities, rationalizing that the processes of exploration and discovery are more important than acquiring accurate scientific understanding (Lind, 1999). But the contention that young children are cognitively incapable of processing real scientific content and learning real scientific processes does not hold up. The key is that scientific understandings are taught in ways that respect the intellectual capacities of young children and that teachers carefully scaffold connections between what is familiar and unfamiliar to their young students (Bransford et al., 2000; National Research Council, 2001).

Conclusions

In this chapter, I argued that developmental theory has almost nothing to say about curriculum, when curriculum is understood to be the content that young children are exposed to in early childhood classrooms. Noting the hegemonic influence of developmental theories on early childhood policy and practice (as exemplified in the branding of the DAP), I made the case that the dominance of developmental theory leads the field to blur differences between curriculum and instruction. I described frequently ignored differences between precepts at the core of Piagetian and Vygotskian theories related to the relationship between learning and development and pointed out implications of those differences for early childhood instruction. I concluded by presenting examples from the curriculum areas of math and science that show the disconnect between the field's emphasis on Piagetian developmental theories and current research on the learning capacities of young children. These examples demonstrate that the field needs to take a careful look at its overdependence on developmental theory and consider the advantages of making clear distinctions between what is considered to be curriculum and what is taken to be instruction in early childhood classrooms.

References

Bedrova, E., & Leong, D.J. (2007). *Tools of the mind: The Vygotskian approach to early childhood education*. Upper Saddle River, NJ: Pearson.

Berk, L.E., & Winsler, A. (1995). *Scaffolding children's learning: Vygotsky and early childhood education*. Washington, DC: National Association for the Education of Young Children.

Bransford, J.D., Brown, A.L., & Cocking, R.R. (Eds.). (2000). *How people learn: Brain, mind, experience, and school*. Washington, DC: National Academy Press.

Bredekamp, S. (Ed.). (1987). *Developmentally appropriate practice in early childhood programs*. Washington, DC: National Association for the Education of Young Children.

Bredekamp, S., & Copple, C. (Eds.). (1997). *Developmentally appropriate practice in early childhood programs* (Rev. ed.). Washington, DC: National Association for the Education of Young Children.

Clements, D.H., Sarama, J., & DiBiase, A.M. (Eds.). (2004). *Engaging young children in mathematics: Standards for early childhood education*. Mahwah, NJ: Erlbaum.

Copple, C., & Bredekamp, S. (Eds.). (2009). *Developmentally appropriate practice in early childhood programs* (3rd ed.). Washington, DC: National Association for the Education of Young Children.

Cross, C.T., Woods, T.A., & Schweingruber, H. (Eds.). (2009). *Mathematics learning in early childhood: Paths toward excellence and equity*. Washington, DC: The National Academies Press.

Duckworth, E. (1964). Piaget rediscovered. In R.E. Ripple & V.N. Rockcastle, *Piaget rediscovered: A report of the conference on cognitive studies and curriculum development* (pp. 1–5). Ithaca, NY: Cornell University School of Education.

Duschl, R.A., Schweingruber, H.A., & Shouse, A.W. (Eds.). (2007). *Taking science to school: Learning and teaching science in grades K-8*. Washington, DC: National Academies Press.

Eliason, C., & Jenkins, L. (2008). *A practical guide to early childhood curriculum* (8th ed.). Upper Saddle River, NJ: Pearson.

Epstein, A.S. (2007). *The intentional teacher: Choosing the best strategies for young children's learning*. Washington, DC: National Association for the Education of Young Children.
Furth, H.G. (1970). *Piaget for teachers*. Englewood Cliffs, NJ: Prentice-Hall.
Ginsburg, H.P., Kaplan, R.G., Cannon, J., Cordero, M.I., Eisenband, J.G., Galanter, M., & Morgenlander, M. (2006). Helping early childhood educators to teach mathematics. In M. Zaslow & I. Martinez-Beck (Eds.), *Critical issues in early childhood professional development* (pp. 171–202). Baltimore, MD: Paul H. Brookes.
Hatch, J.A. (2002). Accountability shovedown: Resisting the standards movement in early childhood education. *Phi Delta Kappan*, 83, 457–462.
Hatch, J.A. (2005). *Teaching in the new kindergarten*. Clifton Park, NY: Thomson Delmar Learning.
Hatch, J.A. (2010). Rethinking the relationship between learning and development: Teaching for learning in early childhood classrooms. *The Educational Forum*, 74, 258–268.
Inhelder, B., & Piaget, J. (1964). *The early growth of logic in the child*. New York: Harper & Row.
Kamii, C., Lewis, B.A., & Booker, B.M. (1998). Instead of teaching missing addends. *Teaching Children Mathematics*, 4, 458–461.
Kessler, S., & Swadener, B.B. (Eds.). (1992). *Reconceptualizing the early childhood curriculum: Beginning the dialogue*. New York: Teachers College Press.
Lave, J. (1988). *Cognition in practice: Mind, mathematics, and culture in everyday life*. New York: Cambridge University Press.
Lave, J. (1993). The practice of learning. In S. Chaiklin & J. Lave (Eds.), *Understanding practice* (pp. 3–32). New York: Cambridge University Press.
Lind, K.K. (1999). *Science in early childhood: Developing and acquiring fundamental concepts and skills*. American Association for the Advancement of Science Project 2061. www.project2061.org/publications/earlychild/online/experience/lind.htm.
Luria, A.R. (1976). *Cognitive development: Its cultural and social foundations*. Cambridge, MA: Harvard University Press.
MacNaughton, G., & Williams, G. (2004). *Teaching young children: Choices in theory and practice*. Berkshire, UK: Open University Press.
Meadows, S. (2006). *The child as thinker: The development and acquisition of cognition in childhood*. New York: Routledge.
National Reading Panel (2000). *Report of the National Reading Panel: Teaching children to read*. Washington, DC: National Institute of Child Health and Human Development.
National Research Council (2001). *Eager to learn: Educating our preschoolers*. Washington, DC: National Academy Press.
NCTM (2000). *Principles and standards for school mathematics*. Reston, VA: National Council of Teachers of Mathematics.
Neuman, S.B., Copple, C., & Bredekamp, S. (2000). *Learning to read and write: Developmentally appropriate practices for young children*. Washington, DC: National Association for the Education of Young Children.
Piaget, J. (1952). *The child's conception of number*. London: Routledge & Kegan Paul.
Piaget, J. (1964). Development and learning. In R.E. Ripple & V.N. Rockcastle, *Piaget rediscovered: A report of the conference on cognitive studies and curriculum development* (pp. 7–20). Ithaca, NY: Cornell University School of Education.
Piaget, J. (1968). *Six psychological studies*. New York: Random House.
Piaget, J., & Inhelder, B. (1969). *The psychology of the child*. New York: Basic Books.
President's Council of Advisors on Science and Technology (2010). *Prepare and inspire: K-12 education in science, technology, engineering, and math (STEM) for America's future*. www.whitehouse.gov/assets/documents/PCAST_H1N1_Report.pdf

Rogoff, B. (1990). *Apprenticeship in thinking: Cognitive development in social context.* New York: Oxford University Press.

Segal, G. (1996). The modularity of theory of mind. In P. Carruthers & P. Smith (Eds.), *Theories of Theories of Mind* (pp. 141–157). Cambridge, UK: Cambridge University Press.

Snow, C.E., Burns, M.S., & Griffin, P. (1998). *Preventing reading difficulties in young children.* Washington, DC: National Academy Press.

Stone, J.E. (1996). Developmentalism: An obscure but pervasive restriction on educational improvement. *Educational Policy Analysis Archives,* 4, 1–29.

Vygotsky, L.S. (1978). *Mind in society: The development of higher mental processes.* Cambridge, MA: Harvard University Press. (Original work published in 1930).

Wertsch, J.V. (1985). *Vygotsky and the social formation of mind.* Cambridge, MA: Harvard University Press.

5

THE CURRICULUM THEORY LENS ON EARLY CHILDHOOD

Moving Thought into Action

Jennifer J. Mueller and Kristin L. Whyte

Given that this is a volume about early childhood curriculum, in order to understand our past, present(s), and potential, it is important that we consider early childhood education (ECE) within the larger contexts from which it has and is evolving. Understanding our past, and how we came to the places and spaces within which we currently exist, is a key means for the field to progress in the ways that our young children so desperately need us to do. This larger context has been examined, conceptualized, and theorized by the field of curriculum studies. Part of the purpose of this chapter is to connect the evolution of early childhood curriculum with the movements in and related to curriculum studies. Through this connection, we will realize the other purpose of the discussion, which is to help move all of us into "what could be" in early childhood curriculum — a site of strong democracy in education supporting a "commitment of the learner to a relationship to knowledge" and with the potential to "free the learner to have new thoughts and even think the 'not yet thought'" (Young, 2013, p. 107).

In the first edition of this book, this chapter ended in the space of critical theory and the impact of the "reconceptualists" on the direction of the field of early childhood curriculum. In particular, in ECE, just as in curriculum studies as a field, there was (and still is) a struggle with the dynamism of theory and practice as it applies to the reality of day-to-day classroom work. The argument at that time landed in the space of "what next?" and "how do we?" moments in consideration of curriculum in ECE. And, as noted in the literature in curriculum studies (Apple, 2018; Baker, 2015; Wheeler-Bell, 2017; Young, 2013; Zeichner, Payne, & Brayko, 2018), curriculum studies has not necessarily provided the tools (literal or epistemological) we need as educators to enact the practices it espoused, or change the practices it critiqued.

In this new version of the chapter, we again present the overview of the history that helps to place the evolution of early childhood curriculum within the context of curriculum studies. And since the time of the first chapter, as one might expect, curriculum studies has taken on the struggle to evolve in its work and to redefine its charge in the purposes of both critiquing and reshaping the educational/curricular landscape (Baker, 2015). Shifts in enactment of early childhood curriculum have also ensued (many of which are discussed in this volume), the nature of which, it can be argued, have operated to standardize, commodify, and marketize the types of knowledge and learning to which young children have access (Au, 2011).

What we will eventually argue is that the ongoing tension between theory and practice in the space where that practice occurs can and should be the site of the struggle for authentic participation, voice, and emancipation and transformation. It is here that those marginalized or kept from accessing the educational enterprise in early childhood can bring their perspectives and experiences forward as the basis for equality and social justice. It is at the nexus of theory and practice that we can enact what Apple (2018) (and others) calls a robust or thick form of democratic participation that has the potential to transform both curriculum studies, and early childhood education. Apple (2018) defines thick democracy as "understandings of democracy that provide full collective participation in search for the common good and the creation of critical citizens" (p. 4). And it will be this thick form of democratic participation that, if we can embody it, will be the genesis of change and opportunity in the field of ECE. What was not included in the last version of this chapter is this larger context of the contestation for democracy – the struggle for power, representation, voice, and value of knowledge – that can be seen in all of the shifts we have witnessed curriculum move through.

Curriculum, Curriculum Studies, and Curriculum Theory – A Brief and Selective Overview

Defining curriculum has proven to be a contested project over time with the very existence of the field of curriculum studies as evidence. We often consider curriculum to be the formal products and documents that guide what is to occur in classrooms. If we think of curriculum as the "stuff" of what happens in schools, there are many avenues to pursue in considering what that might mean. Pinar (2004) posits that curriculum actually is school, in total, as experienced by students and teachers.

Curriculum studies has evolved in two veins – one of curriculum development and the other of curriculum theorizing. If we understand curriculum to be the study of that which constitutes knowledge, questions that comprise a study of curriculum include: how we conceive of the nature of knowledge; how students (children) come to learn that knowledge; and which knowledge is of greatest value and importance (Apple, 2018). The shifting nature of the socio-cultural-historical contexts of our society and, thus, education and curriculum over more than a century demonstrates that conceptions of curriculum are always contested terrain.

Curriculum studies as a field emerged at the turn of the 20th century as the country struggled to define the aims and goals of education amidst a changing population and an ever-shifting social and cultural milieu (Kliebard, 2004). Kliebard describes the debates around the purposes and aims of education during the 20th century as defined by four predominant interest groups. The humanists rested on the idea that education and curriculum ought to focus on the "development of reasoning power" (p. 9) and a steeping in Western-based subject areas. The developmentalists operated from the "assumption that the natural order of development in the child was the most significant and scientifically defensible basis for determining what should be taught" (p. 11) in schools. Adherents to a social efficiency model focused on the elimination of waste in the curriculum through "scientific management techniques" (p. 20), precise measurement and differentiation of education according to students' perceived proclivities and ultimate "destinations." And, the social meliorists believed that education was the key to social progress, correction of social ills, and promulgation of social justice.

The Technocratic View

Overarching these debates was predominance of the scientific/rationalist/empiricist paradigm during most of the 20th century. This, according to Cornbleth (1990), shaped concepts of curriculum in all four factions. Out of this paradigm of thought emerged what Cornbleth calls the "technocratic" view of curriculum. In this view curriculum is construed as a product, separate from policy and from classroom use. Curriculum is also necessarily set apart from politics, giving it the appearance of neutrality and separation from the competing values and interests of any historical time. This view indicated that curriculum was scientifically, objectively, and rationally derived, was objectives-focused, and thus could have a knowable and attainable end result or outcome. This was derived from an assumption that the "means-end" progression is a "direct path" where the "precision and control over the otherwise disorderly nature of curriculum and teaching" is paramount, thus conveying the image "of scientific efficiency, effectiveness, and progress" (Cornbleth, 1990, p. 15).

This view of curriculum has arguably been one of the greatest influences on what we know as curriculum, and we can see the continued predominance of this approach in schools today. Indeed we can argue that there has been a robust return to this approach via the testing regime (Cochran-Smith et al., 2018), the focus on the accountability and performativity aspects of teachers' work (Kilderry, 2015), and the adherence to a theory of marketization/competition as the means to educational improvement (Zeichner, Payne, & Brayko, 2018).

In laying out what he calls seven "curriculum episodes" of the past century, Scott (2008) makes the case for the predominance of the theory of social efficiency as the blueprint for school curriculum. Major scholars of the time including Bobbit,

Charters, and Tyler in the 1920s and '30s argued for "precision, objectivity, and prediction" in curriculum development and proffered that we could determine exactly "what should be taught in schools and how educational knowledge should be structured" (Scott, 2008, p. 6). Out of this movement came the suggested importance of behavioral objectives where knowledge and skills could be broken down into their essential elements. The important skills were determined by the objective examination of experts in fields of study and curricular goals could be derived. The skills were then translated into teaching strategies and objective testing could determine if the learner had acquired the skills.

Alongside this movement, and thus also influenced by the technocratic model, was the faction of educational scholars who adhered to the doctrine of developmentalism, as noted previously. Led by G. Stanley Hall, this group operated from the belief that one could catalog what happened in the minds of children, and a systematic and accurate cataloging would conclude what should be taught in schools (Kliebard, 2004). Buoyed by the scientific, empiricist paradigm, research entailed careful, systematic "observation and recording of children's behavior at various stages of development" (p. 11). The developmentalists believed that "the curriculum riddle could be solved with ever more accurate scientific data" (p. 24).

In addition, the larger debates of the time focused on whether or not all children could learn a select body of important knowledge or content, and given a vast array of capabilities and destinations curriculum needed to be differentiated to meet the capacities of learners (which could be scientifically discovered) (Kliebard, 2004). Here Hall contributed by suggesting the idea of "probable destination" where through careful study of child development the life outcome of a child could be determined, and then a curriculum devised to support that destination. And indeed, Kliebard suggests, "predicting future destination as the basis for adapting the curriculum to different segments of the school population became a major feature of curriculum planning" (p. 13).

Bloch, in several publications (1991, 1992, 2000), illustrated the connections of current early childhood research and curriculum to the developmentalist faction. She noted (1991) that Hall's ideas began the child study movement that connected psychology, science, and child development, which also coupled science with the study of pedagogy and curriculum in early childhood education.

Bloch explained that eventually a departure from Hall's version of child study was necessitated by better science – in other words, more scientific and objective ways of researching children to formulate a pattern of "normal" child development. And while strong ties between psychology and pedagogy shaped both elementary/secondary and early childhood, early childhood ran a somewhat separate course from that of elementary and secondary education, where in these latter fields social reconstructionist theories had more influence for theorists and educators to focus on school as a means of social reform. Early childhood, on the other hand, in order "to appear to be a fairly 'hard' science," stayed heavily aligned with "psychology, psychiatry, home economics, and child and family studies programs at the university level" (Bloch, 1992, p. 13). Bloch (2000) further highlighted that since the fields of child development and developmental psychology were dominated by "quantitatively oriented psychological studies" (p. 258), thus so was the field of early childhood education.

Goffin (1996) pointed out that this scientism initially (and importantly) supported the professionalization of the field of early childhood. She noted that the faith put into the ability for "scientifically derived solutions" to solve social ills ran parallel with "an undervaluation of children as public responsibility." This required that early childhood take on an advocacy role, and the emergence of "predictable and achievable child development outcomes" supplied an "important lever for arguing the inadequacy of many existing early childhood education settings and for promoting the importance of better prepared and compensated personnel... child development knowledge provide[d] a concrete frame of reference for improving classroom practice" (p. 125).

The Dawns of Change

Moving forward in our historical overview, Kliebard (2004) highlighted the social meliorist faction of educational theory that emerged initially with the Great Depression "from the undercurrent of discontent about the American economic and social system." Curriculum via this faction became the means through which "social injustice would be redressed" (p. 154). Forwarding quickly to the mid to latter parts of the 20th century we saw a period of increased awareness and social unrest regarding inequitable distribution of opportunity across social groups – a time where sociology of education in particular began to more carefully document the actual experiences of children in schools, the impact that children and teachers had on the curriculum, and inequality of access to educational opportunities in schools (e.g., Gracey, 1972; Lubeck, 1985; Rist, 1970). And, while early critiques of the social meliorist movement stemmed from an initial behaviorist bent and over-subscription to determinism (Kessler & Swadener, 1992), the sociology of the curriculum elucidated the existing dynamism between curriculum and children and teachers, revealing that the "process of schooling [was]...complex, context-bound, interactive" (p. xxiv), drawing attention to the idea that schools could be sites and spaces for rich democratic participation.

It was in this context that work of particular curriculum theorists (Huebner, MacDonald) laid "important groundwork for *reconceptualizing* the field" (Pinar, Reynolds, Slattery, & Taubman, 1995) of curriculum theory that began in the 1960s and '70s. According to Pinar et al., the work of these theorists supported the field in questioning the basic assumptions of the mainstream. Malewski (2010) suggested that this set the stage for understanding the contextualized notion of curriculum where the consideration of curriculum via "democratic ideology, media representations, and issues of power and access" (p. 2) were revealed. As a result, the field experienced a dramatic shift in the concepts and questions on which it focused, the inquiry methods it used, and the purposes of its work. This represented a move from a focus on curriculum development and curriculum as a transcendent product, to the idea of "understanding" curriculum as a sociological, contextualized *process* laden with issues of power, authority, phenomenology, and interpretation (Pinar, 2004).

Early Childhood Participates   *equality*

Returning now to early childhood, as the reconceptualist movement was unfolding in curriculum studies, early childhood programming was in a social meliorist movement engaged in addressing the war on poverty and issues of the "deprived" child. The continued push for professionalization in the field resulted in the publication of the seminal *Developmentally Appropriate Practice in Early Childhood Programs Serving Children from Birth through Age 8* (Bredekamp, 1987) – hereafter referred to as DAP. The emergence of DAP was in response to the push down of the rationalist, behavioral objective-oriented curriculum of the elementary school (Copple & Bredekamp, 2009). During the latter part of the 20th century, as more and more public school systems took on younger and younger students as part of their purview, those in the field of early childhood spoke out against the "direct instruction academic oriented" (Bloch, 1991) view of teaching and learning that was presumed characteristic of the elementary curriculum.

While rejecting the behavioral objective and academic orientation toward curriculum, the DAP document maintained a rationalist scientism and a positivist approach, given its roots in developmental and child psychology. DAP really represented a re-emergence of the developmentalist perspective, certainly with the child as the focus, though now with better science to support its claims. The most recent iteration of the DAP document (Copple & Bredekamp, 2009) firmly states that its position is "grounded. . . in the research on child development and learning" (p. 1), with the claim being that developmental science provides "much clearer guidance for programming decisions than do other, more value laden philosophies" (Bredekamp, 1991, pp. 202–203).   *value-laden*

However, "value-laden philosophies" also emerged on the ECE scene (beginning mainly in the late 1980s and early 1990s) as a reconceptualist movement in early childhood that closely mirrored the movement in curriculum studies. Drawing heavily from critical theory (including postmodern, feminist, post-structuralist, postcolonial, and interpretivist orientations) the reconceptualists illuminated the necessity that we understand childhood, early childhood education, teachers' practice, and curriculum as inseparable from the larger politicized and value-laden contexts in which it exists. Early childhood practice is not neutral or apolitical and as Cannella and Bloch (2006) point out, the work of the reconceptualists "crossed disciplinary and geographic boundaries [and] fostered hybrid ways" (p. 6) of understanding early childhood theory and practice. The movement elucidated the relationship between knowledge and power important to our understanding of curriculum – particularly since the movement pushed the field to reconstruct ideas related to what knowledge is valued, what is important to teach in educational settings, and what children are entitled to know and learn (Kessler, 1992; Kilderry, 2015).

The reconceptualist movement in early childhood emerged partly as critique of the DAP document, and mainly via the critical theory lens, in part illustrating the DAP's predominance in the field of early childhood. Even into today, the DAP document remains the major definer of what is "good" early childhood practice (indicating that this can be defined) and how curriculum "needs" be derived out of a sophisticated understanding of child development theory and research. Mainstream early childhood curriculum remains steeped in a paradigm that ultimately suggests that there is a "best" and "right" way for development to unfold. For example, Copple and Bredekamp (2009) suggest that to minimize achievement gaps evident across social groups, one goal in early childhood classrooms should be to engage "proactive vocabulary development to bring young children whose vocabulary and oral language development is lagging. . . closer to the developmental trajectory typical of children from educated, affluent families" (p. 7). This suggests that there is an optimal trajectory of development based on one, more valued, cultural model.

The reconceptualists point out that this inherently leaves many children out. The reconceptualist critique of DAP is illustrated when Dahlberg and Moss (2005) suggest that DAP continues its adherence to developmental psychology. Via reconceptualist curriculum theory, the idea that curriculum can be "evidence based" and we can predetermine and adhere to a definitive notion of "positive outcomes" is problematic. They note that DAP provides a particular way of understanding children and thus "normalizes" them through its characterizations. The generalizations of DAP are considered universal and thus reliable, therefore governing children's development.

Dahlberg and Moss (2005) point out that:

> the quasi-scientific status of developmental norms slips from description to prescription: from a mythic norm (mythic because no one actually fits it) to statements of how people should be: whether milestones, gender types, reading ages, cognitive strategies, stages or skills. . . they become enshrined within an apparatus of collective measurement and evaluation that constructs its own world of abstract autonomous babies; of norms, deviation from which is typically only acknowledged in the form of deficit or problem.
>
> (p. 7)

The technocratic and decontextualized form of curriculum as a product that can universally guide student learning and development in a preconceived, measurable, accountable manner prevails in education. This further suggests the continued predominance of knowledge viewed in a product-oriented manner that is based in dominant culture ways of knowing and being. However, as many scholars across disciplines (and indeed the DAP document itself) note, we need only look to the larger trends of underachievement and under-attainment in schools by children of color and children from low-income families to suggest that this view of knowledge and its resultant form of curriculum have not functioned to serve all children. The reconceptualists argue that value for alternative and localized views of knowledge, multiplicity of voice, incorporation of diverse ways of making meaning, and attendance to the legitimacy of a variety of cultural ways of knowing are necessary in order for curriculum to serve all children and families.

In the 2009 revision of DAP (Copple & Bredekamp) there is evidence that the issues raised by reconceptualist scholars have been acknowledged and given credence. The document begins by noting the need to attend to "critical issues in the current context" (p. 1). These "issues" include the increase in children being served in early childhood settings whose heritage home-language is not English and in children living in poverty. In addition, Copple and Bredekamp highlight the responsibility for early childhood curriculum to attend to the problem of achievement gaps across social/cultural groups, and the cultural mismatches between home and school settings that may precipitate these gaps. And, indeed, several reconceptualist scholars are cited as part of the "research base" of DAP – though their inclusion has not changed DAP's fundamental theoretical orientations.

Our purpose for laying out the relationship between DAP and the reconceptualist movement is not to create a binary in which DAP is seen as leading teachers down an entirely wrong path. Nor is it to position the reconceptualist movement as having all the answers to early childhood's curricular woes. Rather, it is to show how DAP is reflective of technocratic views of curriculum in need of disrupting. The reconceptualists did well to point out how these linear ways of thinking about curriculum do not serve all children well. This history depicts an important moment in time for early childhood. The DAP/reconceptualist debates draw attention to the need to move forward with our thinking in a way that is more directly useful to practitioners. One way to do this is to address the tension present in this debate.

We believe, as the reconceptualists do, that the norming of development and its curricular consequences does not best serve children and the betterment of our society as a whole and that curriculum should be *of* children, their families, communities, and their numerous, culturally developed ways of knowing. But what does this mean for early childhood curriculum? How are practitioners supposed to know how to create worthwhile curricular experiences during the day-to-day action of their classrooms? This is a tension that the DAP/reconceptualist debate has left us with – the demand for robust intellectual, rather than academic (Katz & Chard, 2000), curricula that honors the complexity children bring into classrooms, while practitioners are often expected to adhere to curricula reflective of technocratic understandings. The technocratic context contributes to a lack of tools that could help practitioners imagine what this could look like for their day-to-day practice. In other words, not only is the question how should we re-envision early childhood curriculum, it is also how can we ensure that practitioners are left with authentic ways to act on these visions?

So now we are at the point where, aware of the tensions of the field, we turn our attention to issues of practicality. Pinar et al. (1995) point out that the reconceptualist movement in curriculum theory has been largely ignored in mainstream curricular products – particularly textbooks. And, we could argue that the movement in early childhood has had little effect on directives for mainstream practice in the field. We suggest in the next section that to move requires concerted focus on the practice of teachers who enact the curriculum in action and process.

"How Do We Actually Do This?" (Or, How Does Curriculum Theory Move Us into "What Next?")

Given our foray through history in this chapter, we argue that the technocratic approach to curriculum, while predominant, has not served ultimately to meet the aims and goals of the educational interests of all children. Arguably the fact that the reconceptualist movements arose gives credence to this view. Yet, curriculum theory as part of the reconceptualist movements has had seemingly little influence on practice in schools in such a way to shift the tides in our educational dilemmas. Current political contexts will do little to support teachers to move in the directions suggested by the reconceptualists, and in fact, will further entrench the technocratic model.

Farquhar and Fitzsimons (2007) posit that we have moved into a period of "intensified government involvement in educational institutions and increasing standardization of curricula" (p. 225). These authors further signify that early childhood education has been forced to conform to economic and market pressures to maintain its relevance and, indeed, its very existence. Moss (2007) points out:

> early childhood education and care includes large swathes of under-resourced "childcare" services, often competing with each other in market conditions; combined with nursery education or kindergarten provision that is subject to increasingly strong regulation through prescriptive curricula, testing and inspection systems in order to ensure they produce children who are ready for school.
>
> (p. 241)

DAP has necessarily, and some argue appropriately, responded to this context. Copple and Bredekamp (2009) note DAP's responsibility in these times of standardization and accountability measures, particularly in light of No Child Left Behind, to support preschool and kindergarten teachers to enact developmentally appropriate practice in ways that prepare teachers and children for this context. They note the DAP utilization of "accumulating evidence and innovations in practice [that] provide guidance as to the knowledge and abilities that teachers must work especially hard to foster in young children, as well as information on how teachers can do so" (p. 3). In times of uncertainty, the DAP model gives teachers support and a means to do what they can view as "good" for children. Indeed, in our current political and economic context, walking into a DAP-oriented classroom can be refreshing. However DAP remains reflective of its technocratic underpinnings that are in need of disrupting in order to realize the potentials of all children.

The call for such a disruption comes from both curriculum theory and early childhood post-modern, reconceptualist scholars. Even in this political and economic context, their arguments assume (or perhaps hope) that the movement to a more complex, contextualized, inclusive, and diverse view of curriculum will improve the state of education. However, the enactment of this must occur in the details of daily life in classrooms, in the interactional space of curriculum, teachers, and children. And, critique of critical theory influences on curriculum studies suggest that they have been long on deconstruction and short on suggestions for new direction (Cannella & Bloch, 2006). Lenz Taguchi (2007) further notes that the deconstructive approach can be challenging for educators, given that the eclectic practices necessitated by the critical, inclusive, multi-voiced approach are by their very nature relativistic and ambiguous. She suggests that because they are not "sufficiently grounded in any one (universalist or better) theory" they "lack the normative qualities expected of a robust pedagogy" (p. 285).

If reconceptualist ideas about curriculum have not been taken up in mainstream curriculum documents, Cornbleth (1990) interestingly points out that it is often the case in practice that curriculum (of any sort) is not used as intended by curriculum developers, or ignored all together by educators. Teachers and children hold pre-existing beliefs and engage in activity in classrooms before curriculum materials are applied. Thus those beliefs act on, with, and in what is intended in the curriculum and the curriculum is often adapted to those beliefs (Nuthall, 2005).

In the effort to move into "what next?" we must consider how these shifts in curriculum theory and early childhood can impact *classroom practice*. There is debate in curriculum theory currently as to whether or how its worth as a field should be defined in terms of its viability in practice (Malewski, 2010). We want to be careful not to position this line of thinking into the debate on what is often termed the "divide" between theory and practice. And we tend toward the more hybrid view purported by reconceptualist scholars that the theory/practice divide is a false dichotomy (or troublesome binary) that itself requires deconstruction, "dissolution and/or transgression" (Lenz Taguchi, 2007, p. 275).

And, here we position ourselves as early childhood teacher educators, intensely focused on the very real and on-the-ground struggles of our students – both preservice and in-service teachers. They are teaching young children in public schools where the call for fidelity to curriculum is the answer to achievement gaps and children are deemed as "behind" before they even get a start. They are teaching in childcare centers where they report that adherence to DAP in order to retain accreditation has created a tunnel vision where procedure according to DAP outstrips a focus on the actual needs of children. We espouse in their teacher education coursework a reconstructionist-oriented view of curriculum as multi-voiced, inclusive, interdisciplinary, and process-focused. Yet, in the day-to-day reality of their work with children they face the technocratic model of curriculum. While it provides them with guidance for practice, they see the daily reality that it does not necessarily or always support learning and growth for their children. In practice, the tension, for these teachers, weighs heavy. Almost every time we work together they desperately ask, "But how do we actually *do* this?" Perhaps the problem for them lies in the incongruence of trying to exert a necessarily ambiguous and tentative process into a structured, authoritative model.

Looking to Existing Curricula

We can look to research to provide some examples of localized practice, as well as theory and practice informing/becoming each other. There are examples of early childhood reconceptualist scholars working with specific groups of teachers toward more democratic, inclusive, and particular vision of curriculum and curriculum enactment with young children (e.g., Jipson, 1991; Lenz Taguchi, 2007; Lewis et al., 2006). In the variety of scenarios within this vein of research some similarities emerge. Curriculum, while it may begin from a standardized place, is posed as a site for de- and re-construction taking into account the learning needs of the children and exposing dominant discourses. Curriculum is posed as a community-based project where a variety of perspectives must be brought to bear and where outcomes emerge from the learning. In this type of curriculum, instead of having a predetermined list of discrete skills in mind, teachers are asked to pull from their deep reservoirs of pedagogical content knowledge so they can build with children in ways that encourage their intellectual development in multiple subject areas. Here the myriad of invested voices (i.e., children, families, teachers, community members, theorists, teacher educators, etc.) work in concert, continuously, to reflect the evolving learning and growth that curriculum should embody.

Certainly this kind of work was reflected in Dewey's Laboratory School at the University of Chicago where he created a model of curriculum with/in practice in an attempt to mesh and reconcile the world of the child and "the social aims, meanings, values incarnate in the matured experience of the adult" with "the educative process" as "the due interaction of these forces" (Dewey, 1902, p. 8). The Laboratory School was organized so Dewey was able to, with his teachers, engage in pedagogical tinkering such that they could, in an ongoing fashion "construct a curriculum that best facilitated that process" (Kliebard, 2004, p. 55). Kliebard reports that Dewey, along with his teachers, studied, reflected upon, and puzzled with practice so as to bring the child into the curriculum, wherever in the process that child began.

Additionally, we can see this kind of work reflected in the pedagogistas of Reggio Emilia. These consulting teachers work with the preschool teachers in an ongoing form of professional development, reflectivity, and curricular processing. This runs counter to the US model of professional teacher support where (if it exists at all) there is often a one-time smattering of information that the teacher is then expected, on his/her own, to approximate and incorporate into classroom practice. The process with the pedagogistas is an individualized relationship that is not constructed as a series of reproducible events. Rather these professionals function as "critical, caring friends offering a permanent provocation to new thinking and practice who enter a long-term commitment" to be part of the work (Dahlberg & Moss, 2005, p. 187).

The previously discussed curricula represent an ideal – something to move toward, and yet not necessarily within the reality of what many of our teachers experience. It is important to note they are not the only possibilities out there. There are other examples, such as the Project Approach (Katz & Chard, 2000) and work being done with Funds of Knowledge (Hedges, Cullen, & Jordan, 2011; Moll, Amanti, Neff, & Gonzalez, 1992) in early childhood settings that attempt to disrupt technocratic approaches to curriculum. The existence of these approaches, however, does not relieve the reality of our curricular decision making and the tensions of preparing teachers within contextualized practice. We have to come face to face with the reality, both in a critical mode and in practice, that context is a very real feature of our teachers' work that cannot simply be overridden. We need to support their efforts at subversion of the official curriculum in the name of continually and over again coming to understand what their children need as learners. And at the same time, we must find ways to reimagine curricula that both acknowledges context and pushes for change in other systems impacting said curriculum.

Seeking Democracy while Addressing Tensions

Yes, we can look to Dewey's work, Reggio Emilia, Funds of Knowledge, and the like. These are helpful tools. At the same time, tensions still exist. One being, we often look through a technocratic lens as we see the work of these innovators, creating a narrow curricular focus despite the core purposes of these types of curricula. Another, that all curriculum is seen and enacted within a capitalistic context, which, because of the conflict between transformative curriculum and capitalist tenets such as commodification, minimizes educators' capability to implement curriculum that embodies notions of a thick democracy. Acknowledging and attempting to work through these tensions also contains potential for creating ideas for more systemic curricular change (Apple, 2018).

In an effort to examine these larger issues more practically we now suggest avenues for how these tensions might be worked through. Here we identify as teacher educators working in university settings and our recommendations come from this position. We consider, who are the key actors and in what spaces could their work be carried out. We draw from Zeichner, Payne, and Brayko (2018), who offer examples of how different universities' teacher education programs have attempted to create partnerships with practitioners and community stakeholders. The purpose of these relationships has been to better prepare pre-service teachers for teaching by truly bringing various stakeholders' voices into teacher education practices. To achieve this they call for the creation of "new hybrid spaces where academic, practitioner, and community-based knowledge come together" (p. 175) with the purpose of finding innovative ways to address enduring problems with teacher education. The hope is that these spaces can become places where people coming from different, loosely-coupled systems can come together to create new practices as they work through problems such as the relationship between university coursework and how it prepares pre-service teachers for creating and/or implementing curricula.

As Zeichner and his colleagues (2018) describe how universities and the surrounding communities have taken on this work, lessons for early childhood become evident. For one example, early childhood is unique in that children, dependent on age and context, are cared for/taught in diverse settings – schools, community centers, childcare centers, homes, etc. We should see this variability as a strength, rather than something to mediate through universalizing. Teacher educators should strive to create connections with these various stakeholders, inviting them and those they serve into conversations about how they envision their idealized forms of curriculum, what helps and what discourages the enactment of these goals, and what they would like to see from their local universities. This must be done with sincerity, meaning, teacher educators must be ready to hear differing opinions and be open to dialogue and change. We encourage teacher education programs to think about how to bring these voices into their programming in a systematic way by striving to make these relationships reciprocal – considering what roles practitioners can have at the university (i.e., as instructors, supervisors, advisors, etc.), what roles teacher educators can play in the community (i.e., offering professional development, spending time at sites with children, etc.), and what roles family members and children can play (i.e., curricular advisors, guest lecturers, etc.). The overarching goal when making decisions about reimagining these systems should be tied to disrupting power imbalances and increasing participation.

The current struggle for power present in a larger societal context must be addressed. Here we align ourselves with Apple (2018) in that our aim is tied to schools, including their curricula, being envisioned as sites that disrupt systemic inequities. This often calls for a drastic rethinking of curriculum, as schools have been shown to further inequity (Anyon, 1980; Gracey, 1972; Lubeck, 1985; Rist, 1970). These ideas about thick democratic education are crucial for early childhood educators. Take, for example, current readiness discourse. Readiness is used as a rationalization for much early childhood programming. As groups of children are labeled "ready" and "not ready" for school, curricular decisions are made about what those who are deemed not ready need to do to become ready. These decisions, made in our current socio-political contexts, can limit the voice of those in most need of greater access to robust curriculum by focusing in on discrete skills through scripted curricula marketed to address readiness concerns. Baker (2015) discusses the need for empirical studies of curriculum and its relationship to capitalism and power. Readiness movements show, that to move early childhood curriculum forward, we must both commit to the empirical exploration of whose children have access to what kinds of knowledge via the curricula to which they are exposed. We believe this must be done through a critical lens and in a collaborative manner. Teacher educators, along with practitioners, community members, and families, must find ways to promote curricula, such as the ones outlined earlier in the chapter, that increase not just standardized test scores, but also the participation and overall *education* of children who have been marginalized by schools. Teacher educators can take this up in their programming, but these efforts will fall flat unless this is done in concert with the larger community.

These conversations will not be simple. Perhaps these tensions lie in what Moss (2007) characterizes as an unwillingness for the differing factions in early childhood to speak. He notes that communication across divides is constrained because the modernists tend not to see paradigm, and the postfoundationalists "see little virtue in the paradigm of modernity" (p. 233). Malewski (2010) envisions the need for "proliferation" in curriculum studies where the aim is not that "one cluster of theories overtakes another on the way toward 'one right way' approaches." Rather he pleads for us to:

> maintain a commitment to a field that celebrates the growth of its theories and stories – and to be seized by its vigor and intensity – and to assert our human inventiveness so as to personalize our theorizing regardless of how unsettling and unwieldy.
>
> *(p. 23)*

Moss (2007) and Malewski (2010) affirm that we will struggle through understanding the inevitable differing viewpoints present in these tensions, but we commit to struggling through them *with* our larger communities. In other words, we commit to thick democratic participation.

We continue to explore the processes for working with our teachers via our relationships with them in preservice preparation, then further interrogation of practice in graduate studies, along with committing to how our relationships outside our universities can be strengthened to increase participation. We also call for an increase of empirical studies of early childhood curriculum that aim to better understand the relationships between the marketization of early childhood curriculum and full participation for the common good (Apple, 2018; Baker, 2015).

During all of this, we keep an eye on the larger contexts in which we work so we can remain critical, reflective, and open to the possibilities of curriculum in motion. Curriculum theory helps us do this.

References

Anyon, J. (1980). Social class and the hidden curriculum of work. *Journal of Education*, 162(1), 67–92.

Apple, M. (2018). *The struggle for democracy in education: Lessons from social realities*. New York, NY: Routledge.

Au, W. (2011). Teaching under the new Taylorism: High-stakes testing and the standardization of the 21st century curriculum. *Journal of Curriculum Studies*, 43(1), 25–45.

Baker, D. (2015). A note on knowledge in the schooled society: Towards an end to the crisis in curriculum theory. *Journal of Curriculum Studies*, 47(6), 763–772.

Bloch, M. (1991). Critical science and the history of child development's influence on early education research. *Early Education and Development*, 2(2), 95–108.

Bloch, M. (1992). Critical perspectives on the historical relationship between child development and early childhood research. In S. Kessler & B.B. Swadener (Eds.), *Reconceptualizing the early childhood curriculum: Beginning the dialogue*, (p. 3–20). New York: Teachers College Press.

Bloch, M. (2000). Governing teachers, parents, and children through child development knowledge. *Human Development*, 43(4), 257–265.

Bredekamp, S. (1987). *Developmentally appropriate practice in early childhood programs serving children from birth through age 8*. Washington, DC: National Association for the Education of Young Children.

Bredekamp, S. (1991). Redeveloping early childhood education: A response to Kessler. *Early Childhood Research Quarterly*, 6(2), 199–209.

Bredekamp, S., & Copple, C. (1997). *Developmentally appropriate practice in early childhood programs serving children from birth through age 8*. Washington, DC: NAEYC.

Cannella, G., & Bloch, M. (2006). Social policy, education, and childhood in dangerous times: Revolutionary actions or global complicity. *International Journal of Educational Policy, Research, and Practice*, 7, 5–19.

Cochran-Smith, M., Carney, M.C., Keefe, E.S., Burton, S., Chang, W.C., Fernández, M.B., ... & Baker, M. (2018). *Reclaiming accountability in teacher education*. New York: Teachers College Press.

Copple, C., & Bredekamp, S. (2009). *Developmentally appropriate practice in early childhood programs serving children from birth through age 8*. Washington, DC: NAEYC.

Cornbleth, C. (1990). *Curriculum in context*. London: Falmer Press.

Dahlberg, G., & Moss, P. (2005). *Ethics and politics in early childhood education*. New York: Routledge Falmer.

Dewey, J. (1902). *The child and the curriculum*. Chicago, IL: University of Chicago Press.

Farquhar, S., & Fitzsimons, P. (2007). Philosophy of early childhood education. *Educational Philosophy and Theory*, 39(3), 225–228.

Goffin, S. (1996). Child development knowledge and early childhood teacher preparation: Assessing the relationship – A special collection. Early Childhood Research Quarterly, 11(2), 117–133.

Gracey, H. (1972). *Curriculum or craftsmanship: Elementary school teachers in a bureaucratic system*. Chicago, IL: University of Chicago Press.

Hedges, H., Cullen, J., & Jordan, B. (2011). Early years curriculum: Funds of knowledge as a conceptual framework for children's interests. *Journal of Curriculum Studies*, 43(2), 185–205.

Jipson, J. (1991). Developmentally appropriate practice: Culture, curriculum, connections. *Early Education and Development*, 2(2), 120–136.

Katz, L., & Chard, S.C. (2000). *Engaging children's minds: The project approach*. Stamford, CT: Ablex Publishing Corporation.

Kessler, S. (1992). The social context of early childhood curriculum. In S. Kessler & B.B. Swadener (Eds.), *Reconceptualizing the early childhood curriculum: Beginning the dialogue*, (pp. 21–42). New York: Teachers College Press.

Kessler, S., & Swadener, B.B. (1992). Reconceptualizing curriculum. In S. Kessler & B.B. Swadener (Eds.), *Reconceptualizing the early childhood curriculum: Beginning the dialogue*, (pp. xiii–xxviii). New York: Teachers College Press.

Kilderry, A. (2015). The intensification of performativity in early childhood education. *Journal of Curriculum Studies*, 47(5), 633–652.

Kliebard, H. (2004). *The struggle for the American curriculum: 1893–1958, 3rd edition*. New York: Routledge Falmer.

Lenz Taguchi, H. (2007). Deconstructing and transgressing the theory—Practice dichotomy in early childhood education. *Educational Philosophy and Theory*, 39(3), 275–290.

Lewis, T., Macfarlane, K., Nobel, K., & Stephenson, A. (2006). Crossing borders and blurring boundaries: Early childhood practice in a non-western setting. *International Journal of Early Childhood*, 38(2), 23–34.

Lubeck, S. (1985). *Sandbox society: Early education in black and white America*. London: Falmer Press.

Malewski, E. (2010). Introduction: Proliferating curriculum. In E. Malewski (Ed.), *Curriculum studies handbook: The next moment*, (pp. 1–39). New York: Routledge.

Moll, L.C., Amanti, C., Neff, D., & Gonzalez, N. (1992). Funds of knowledge for teaching: Using a qualitative approach to connect homes and classrooms. *Theory into Practice*, 31(2), 132–141.

Moss, P. (2007). Meetings across the paradigmatic divide. *Educational Philosophy and Theory*, 39(3), 229–245.

Nuthall, G. (2005). The cultural myths and realities of classroom teaching and learning: A personal journey. *Teachers College Record*, 107(5), 895–934.

Pinar, W. (2004). *What is curriculum theory?* Mahwah, NJ: Lawrence Earlbaum Associates.

Pinar, W., Reynolds, W., Slattery, P., & Taubman, P. (1995). *Understanding curriculum*. New York: Peter Lang.

Rist, R. (1970). Student social class and teacher expectations: The self-fulfilling prophesy in teacher education. *Harvard Educational Review*, 40(3), 411–451.

Scott, D. (2008). *Critical essays on major curriculum theorists*. London: Routledge.

Wheeler-Bell, Q. (2017). Standing in need of justification: Michael Apple, R.S. Peters and Jürgen Habermas. *Journal of Curriculum Studies*, 49(4), 561–578.

Young, M. (2013). Overcoming the crisis in curriculum theory: A knowledge-based approach. *Journal of Curriculum Studies*, 45(2), 101–118.

Zeichner, K., Payne, K., & Brayko, K. (2018). Democratizing teacher education. In K. Zeichner (Ed.), *The struggle for the soul of teacher education* (pp. 171–196). New York, NY: Routledge.

6

ENGAGING WITH CRITICAL THEORIES AND THE EARLY CHILDHOOD CURRICULUM

Mindy Blaise and Sharon Ryan

Introduction

The early childhood curriculum is a complex field of interrelationships amongst teachers and children, content and pedagogy, what takes place in early learning sites, and larger social contexts. Given its complexity, theory is at the heart of the early childhood curriculum. As Pinar, Reynolds, Slattery, and Taubman (1996) argue, contemporary views of curriculum are about understanding the sociocultural and political dimensions of knowledge production, not the technical development and implementation of a course of study.

The field's earliest efforts at curriculum were rooted in philosophies concerning the relations between the young child and larger bodies of knowledge (Williams, 1992). In our attempts to be recognized and accepted as a profession, most of the 20th century has involved using theories of child development and learning to advocate what content and pedagogy should constitute appropriate programs for young children. However, a number of scholars for well over two decades (e.g., Bloch, Swadener, & Cannella, 2014; Grieshaber & Cannella, 2001; Kessler & Swadener, 1992) have pushed back against psychological theory as the source of curriculum for young children. Many of these scholars have turned to critical theories drawn from philosophy, sociology, and cultural studies to examine the politics of the curriculum, particularly the assumed benign impacts of developmentally appropriate practice (e.g., Hatch, et al., 2002; Lubeck, 1998). For these critical theorists, the curriculum becomes a site where children and staff question relations of power and work together to transform society in local and contextualized ways (MacNaughton, 2005).

This chapter is an introduction to critical theories and their application to early childhood curriculum. We begin with a review of the work that has been conducted using critical theories to investigate and question taken-for-granted early childhood practices. In doing so we highlight what makes a theory critical and show how some theoretical orientations have been applied to the early childhood curriculum. The focus then shifts from a review to an examination of some of the most recent efforts to trouble and remake early childhood curriculum. We suggest that more diverse forms of critical theorizing in their efforts to dismantle the logic of dualisms inherent in Western thought (e.g., male/female, adult/child, theory/practice, global north/global south) help toward understanding how curriculum has the potential to be transformative. This chapter concludes by reasserting the importance of critical theory for contemporary early childhood practice.

Review of Critical Theorizing and Early Childhood Curriculum

Critical theory is a set of theoretical traditions that has its roots in the 19th-century philosophies of Marx, the 20th-century work of members of the Frankfurt school, and the writings of Habermas. These modern critical traditions (Popkewitz, 1999) have since been challenged by postmodern theorists whether they are post-structural, postcolonial, or some blending of frameworks such as Black feminist thought, feminist post-structural, posthuman, or queer theories. At the heart of any critical theorizing, however, is an effort to understand how power works in society through structures like schooling to perpetuate inequities. Using various conceptual tools to consider how power operates in education in relation to knowledge and authority, critical theories question taken-for-granted assumptions (or ideology) the field holds to be true about teaching, learning, childhood, and curriculum. In uncovering whose values and knowledge perpetuate particular truths about early childhood education, the assumption is that it then becomes possible to create more inclusive and just forms of curriculum.

Most of the critical work in early childhood education has been conducted using postmodern theories that draw primarily from global north viewpoints (Pérez & Saavedra, 2017). Postmodern simply means past modern, and postmodern theories "challenge the modernist focus on the macro and universal to the exclusion of the micro; they embrace ambiguity and uncertainty, and refuse modernist discourses that classify, control, and measure against what is considered the 'norm'" (Grieshaber & Ryan, 2006, p. 534). To understand how postmodern theories do these kinds of things, we begin this review with a description of post-structural theory and the influential work of Michel Foucault as his concepts of power, knowledge, and subjectivity have been applied in a large number of studies of early childhood curriculum. As postmodernists are concerned with those who are marginalized by curriculum making, we then turn to other postmodern work that draws on post-structural concepts and combines them with other theories to focus on issues of gender, (hetero)sexuality, "race," and ethnicity.

Post-structuralism

Foucault's views of power, knowledge, and subjectivity have been drawn on by a range of critical scholars in early childhood education. For Foucault (1980), power is a process operating in our social world, rather than something possessed by individuals. Power operates within all relationships and is expressed through discourse. Therefore, Foucault (1980) argues for understanding power as something that circulates and at the same time operates to produce particular kinds of subjects. For Foucault and critical theorists who use his work, "individuals are the vehicles of power, not its points of application" (p. 98). From this perspective, it becomes important to understand how the strategies and techniques of power work, not simply who has or does not have power. Emphasis is placed on locating *how* power is producing different kinds of subjectivities and knowledge.

For Foucault (1980), knowledge and power are tied in relationship to one another and expressed in and through language. Power relations exist within fields of knowledge, which produce and exercise particular forms of power relations. As meaning is created through language, then it is neither fixed nor essential. Therefore there are no certain truths, only those we speak into action using particular knowledge to support our assertions. Language and discourse are the keys to how we create meaning as socially constructed individuals or subjects. Subjectivity is a term used to capture the complexities of how the self is not a separate and isolated entity, but instead how we recognize ourselves and are always entangled and intersect with others (Mansfield, 2000). As a social and political site of struggle, language becomes the site where knowledge and subjectivities are formed, reformed, and transformed.

Human beings interact in a range of discourse communities, each of which creates a politics of truth and determines what can be said and done by different subjects in that community. For example, in the discourse of schooling, teachers potentially have more power because of their qualifications and positioning as experts compared to children and families when it comes to asserting what knowledge should constitute the curriculum. However, at the same time, teachers' actions are shaped by political discourses that limit what they can do. Currently, there are many efforts to standardize teaching in early childhood classrooms in an effort to systematize quality across birth through third grade. As a consequence, teachers are less likely to be autonomous curriculum makers and more likely to have to comply to a range of standards and curriculum requirements. At the same time, because power circulates in relation to knowledge there are also spaces within the discourse of schooling where children and parents and teachers may be able to exercise more agency and power than policies. Language in relation to knowledge, therefore, is the space where social meanings, such as what it means to be a child, girl, second language learner, etc., are open to challenges, redefinitions, and reinterpretations depending on the discourses circulating in early childhood classrooms and who speaks them into action.

Educators using post-structuralism in their daily work engage in a critical questioning of their practice by asking themselves what discourses are at work here, whose knowledge is shaping the curriculum, who benefits and who loses if I use this knowledge, and what other knowledges and practices might I bring into play to create a more equitable curriculum for students? One educator who has written about this kind of critical questioning is Giugni, a teacher researcher whose work is documented by MacNaughton (2005). After engaging with Foucault's ideas, Giugni began to explore what power and control were in her setting. She began this by revisiting past observations she had kept for 13 years. While rereading them she found that she described children's behavior as "socially unacceptable" and then planned for them to be "dealt with" (p. 52). She also noticed how a colleague and university supervisor affirmed her claims about this child's behavior and her practices. By rereading these observations with a post-structural eye, Giugni was able to see how these truth claims worked to normalize middle-class behaviors as socially acceptable. In doing so, Giugni recognized how developmentally appropriate practices were constructing some children as socially acceptable and others as unacceptable. By critically questioning her past practices, Giugni was able to see how she was narrowly constructing teaching, learning, and childhood as either "good" or "bad." She wrote that post-structural concepts of power and knowledge enabled her to "be creative and flexible in how meanings are constructed rather than constrained by the fixed and static meanings some psychological ways of thinking would have her believe" (p. 53).

Early childhood settings are saturated with power relations and knowledge production is continuously being (re)constructed. A large portion of post-structural research is interested in how early childhood curriculum regulates children's subjectivities. The following section reviews studies that have been inspired by post-structuralism for critically theorizing and troubling gender, (hetero)sexuality, "race," and ethnicity.

Troubling Gender

A feminist post-structuralist perspective that employs Foucault's concepts while foregrounding gender shifts away from understanding gender as biologically fixed, coherent, and stable, towards situating gender as a social, relational, and unstable construction that is always located within power relations. Additionally, children are assumed to be active agents in their gender identity work. As social actors, young children are not simply "learning" or "soaking up" the social meanings, values, and expectations of how to be a girl or a boy exclusively from their parents, teachers, peers, or the media. Rather, children themselves are producing and regulating gender by constantly "doing" and "redoing" femininities and masculinities that are available to them.

Since Davies' feminist post-structuralist gender research (1989/2003) with preschool children, a large body of research has been generated that draws on Foucault's conceptualizations of subjectivity to examine how children perform gender (see Blaise, 2014 for a comprehensive review). Davies' research is significant because it demonstrated how post-structuralist understandings of knowledge, power, and subjectivity could be used to trouble common-sense understandings of gender with young children. After reading feminist stories to preschool children and then discussing with them what they thought, Davies (1989) found that children did not simply accept the notion that boys and girls can do or be anything (i.e., boys wearing dresses or girls choosing not to marry a prince). Instead, children's resistance to these feminist storylines meant the field needed to rethink their beliefs about how children take up gender as well as the kind of curriculum that was considered to be the most effective for challenging gender bias and stereotypes. Davies also observed children in these classrooms taking up gender in multiple ways, debunking the notion that gender is fixed and stable. Instead, her findings showed the fluidity of gender by disclosing the strategies children used for transgressing gender norms or the male/ female binary despite the risk of being seen as not doing their gender "right."

Scholars in other than Western contexts are building on these feminist post-structuralist insights about gender by acknowledging the complex ways that gender discourses are always intimately shaped by the specific histories and cultures of their contexts (see Adriany & Warin, 2012; Chou, 2011; Davies & Kasama, 2004). For instance, D'Souza Juma's (2017) participatory action research with 12 early childhood teachers in Karachi, Pakistan, shows how religious patriarchy constructs understandings of gender and gender equity in an Islamic Republic. While critically engaging with both the religious discourses of gender in Pakistan and feminist post-structuralist understandings of the social construction of gender, these teachers raised questions about gender and power in their cultural context. They deliberated on the egalitarian principles that are the foundation of Islam, including "God's intent of ensuring equity for women and men regardless of their biological sex" (p. 140) and how essentialized notions of femininity and masculinity were always present in the early childhood classroom and broader society. Together, they discovered how religious discourses created boundaries of what was and was not possible in this cultural context, as children, parents, other staff, and even themselves upheld essentialized understandings of gender that got in the way of working towards gender equity. Although these teachers found feminist post-structuralism a useful framework for locating competing gender discourses, shifting their understandings about gender, and highlighting what pedagogies might be possible, it was impossible to "apply" these ideas fully within this context. This is an important reminder about the limitations of trying to apply Western theories in non-Western contexts and the necessity for theoretical diversity.

Troubling (Hetero)Sexuality

Scholars have been building on this important gender research by using insights from queer theory to continue troubling subjectivity, but now addressing (hetero) sexuality (i.e., Blaise, 2005, 2009, 2010; Blaise & Taylor, 2012; Robinson, 2005;

Semann & DeJean, 2010). Drawing on the work of Foucault (1978) and Butler (1993, 1990/1999), these scholars critique heteronormativity, or the expectation that everyone in society is heterosexual. Scholars using queer theory are committed to rethinking the relationship between sex, gender, and sexuality, proposing a new appreciation of gender as performance, and suggesting that (hetero)sexuality is an effect of gender. Queer theory acts to uncover how heterosexual ways of being are normalized.

A large portion of the queer research in early childhood that troubles gender and (hetero)sexuality involves empirical studies of children's play. This research shows that children are knowledgeable about heterosexual gender norms and how they use these discourses to regulate the gendered social order in their classroom. Blaise's (2005) qualitative case study of gender combines feminist post-structuralism and queer theory to provide an in-depth look at how power is a dimension of gender and (hetero)sexuality and how these discourses play out in the kindergarten classroom. Case studies of Madison, Penny, and Alan explore the risks that children take to transgress heterosexual gender norms, as well as the investment they have in "playing it straight."

Building on these findings, Larremore (2016) uses feminist post-structuralism and queer theory to rethink gendered narratives and childhood sexuality in her early childhood classroom. Using autoethnographic methods she documents and shares her pedagogical journey of creating a critically conscious classroom that challenges categorical thinking about gender. Like Davies (1989/2003) and Blaise (2010), Larremore uses picture books to engage children in large group discussions about gender and (hetero)sexuality. Rather than simply describing her practices, Larremore presents multiple narratives showing how she moved beyond her comfort zone of being the safe and "good" early childhood teacher. These narratives illuminate the competing teacher voices (good, disruptive, sexualized, mother) that Larremore negotiated while responding to children's perspectives, views, and questions about gender, gender differences, and (hetero)sexuality. This research shows how one teacher troubled her own gendered teaching practices by opening up new ways to listen, observe, and make sense of children's gendered play and talk.

Troubling "Race" and Ethnicity

Postcolonialism and critical race theory are used in tandem by scholars and teachers interested in locating the politics of children's and adults' racialized identities (MacNaughton & Davis, 2009). Postcolonialism connects the colonial past with the present (Ghandi, 1998) and provides conceptual tools, to understand the workings of colonialism. Colonial discourse is based on the processes of "othering" or the discriminatory practices that position particular cultures as primitive, less than, or "other." For example, Gupta (2006) and Viruru (2001) show how the British colonial past is ever present in the curriculum in early childhood classrooms in India and how Western values should not be used to judge what another culture considers to be quality early education. In conversations with children using persona dolls, MacNaughton (2005) shows how young children's present understandings of cultural diversity include past traces of colonialism. For example, most of the children in this study were able to sort the dolls according to color, a small group equated "white" with "Australian," and several Anglo and Asian Australian children found white desirable and good.

Engaging deeply with postcolonial and critical race theory, Srinivasan (2014) conducted a qualitative participatory action research study about the cultural identity practices of children, teachers, and families in a childcare center located in postcolonial Australia. Through the careful crafting of multiple cultural narratives from children, teachers, parents, and herself, Srinivasan shows the complex ways in which whiteness, power, and nationhood weave their way throughout the hidden and formal curriculum. For example, she shows how young children's "othering" is done as they classify who is "Australian" and "not Australian" by skin color. In this setting, "brownness" is rejected and equated with being "not Australian" and "whiteness" is desired and linked with being "Australian" by children. Srinivasan's research builds on MacNaughton's (2005) work with young children and persona dolls by also showing how adults' silence, discomfort, and reluctance to engage with children's othering practices maintained "white" power of the past and present. These findings are disturbing and show how the ideology of racism is at work everywhere in postcolonial Australia.

Also working with postcolonial and critical race theory, Davis (2007) shows how the discourses of "whiteness" work to privilege white people and marginalize non-whites. By interrogating how she was using images and activities in the curriculum that were intended to highlight Indigenous peoples and their ways of knowing, she wonders if these strategies were beginning to "other" Indigenous culture. It is significant how Davis's critical reflections shift from questioning curriculum practices, to a more inward look at how she was ignoring certain issues, such as prejudice and discrimination, because they made her, a white Australian female teacher, too uncomfortable. Critical race theory, with its focus on the everyday realities of racism and how racism continues to privilege whites and disadvantage non-whites (Ladson-Billings, 1998) facilitated this shift and also forced Davis to question if her beliefs, assumptions, and intentions to include Indigenous knowledges in the curriculum were actually widening, rather than closing the gap between white Australians and Indigenous peoples.

Situating their work firmly in critical postcolonialism, Pacini-Ketchabaw and Taylor (2015) draw widely from a range of critical theories (i.e., new materialism, critical race theory, Indigenous ontology, and posthumanism) to shift the focus from the child and her identity construction within an exclusive sociocultural and human world, towards resituating her relations with other living beings and things in their local "common world" environments (Common Worlds Research Collective, 2018). This perspective recognizes the significance of place, space, and relations for disrupting colonizing practices. Critical postcolonial inquiries take a situated approach. This means that place matters; materially, discursively, historically, and pedagogically.

For example, Nxumalo (2015) focuses on everyday encounters that she, children, and educators have with forest trails, tree stumps, and tree hollows while walking through the mountain forest that "lies on unceeded Musqueam, Squamish, Stó:lō, and Tseil-Waututh First Nations Territories" (p. 22) in British Columbia, Canada. Nxumalo's situating practices begins by first locating the place where these mountain forest walks occur. This troubles the notion that British Columbia's landscapes are wild, empty, and untouched. Constantly unpacking settler colonialism happens by the telling of non-innocent stories of both past colonial logging practices and the human-made walking trail. Stories of extractions and displacement of plants, animals, and people are told that present Indigenous relationships within this occupied territory that have been erased. These stories have the potential to raise teachers' attention towards the present non-innocent histories in the forest trails, tree stumps, and tree hollows that they encounter. It is possible that these storied walks allow educators and children to see the forest not as a pretty backdrop to their learning, but as a play of complex and lively encounters of which they are mutually a part.

Examinations of the early childhood curriculum drawing on post-structural, feminist, queer, postcolonial, critical race, and critical postcolonial theories illustrate how child-centered curricula practices are often normative and limiting of children's and teachers' subjectivities (Ryan & Grieshaber, 2004). Some of these common practices include conducting child observations, reading stories to children, going on walks, and using culturally diverse materials and resources with children. Critical perspectives provide a set of conceptual tools that are useful for troubling these taken-for-granted curriculum practices by revealing the sociocultural and political dimensions of teaching and learning. They allow us to consider how common curriculum practices often reproduce inequities even when teachers claim to be engaging in social justice work. However, while there has been an expansion of research using postmodern theories (see reviews by Grieshaber & Ryan, 2006; Ryan & Grieshaber, 2004; Taylor, 2018), little of this work goes beyond critique and not enough is about how practitioners are using these theoretical tools in their everyday work.

Moving from Critique toward Reconstruction and Transformation

There is an emerging body of research and practice that is concerned with developing a different logic *with* teachers, and therefore stimulating new capacities for transforming curriculum practices. This new scholarship, often referred to under the umbrella term of posthumanism, is inspired by the work of French philosophers Deleuze and Guattari (1983, 1987). They offered what is often referred to as an ontology of immanence that privileges emergence, potentiality, and connectivity. These concepts have been taken up by early childhood scholars (Kuby & Rowsell, 2017; Lenz Taguchi, 2010; Olsson, 2009; Sellers, 2010; Pacini-Ketchabaw et al., 2017) for re-orienting how we think about learning, teaching, and curriculum. This work is important because like postmodern theories it tries to challenge Western logic but at the same time these newer forms of theorizing go beyond examinations of language and discourse to consider the relations between the material world and humans, and the human and non-human. Much of this work has been done with and by teachers and as a consequence illustrates how teachers might use critical theory in their everyday work.

Troubling Western Logic

Much of Western logic is based on binary thinking. Binaries or paired concepts are usually founded on opposites (adult/child, male/female, developmentally appropriate/developmentally inappropriate, etc.) with one side of the binary always positioned as more important than the other. In this logic ideas are unable to exist without each other and there is a fixed and final result. For instance, if you are not a developmentally appropriate educator then you must be developmentally inappropriate.

Deleuze claimed that Western logic, with its aim on a fixed and final result, stops us from thinking and acting on the "in-betweens" of different ideas and their relations (Deleuze & Parnet, 1987), and he argues for a new logic that works against naturalized modes of difference and fixed notions of truth. As post-structuralists, Deleuze and Guattari's (1983, 1987) work is responding to the impossibility of founding knowledge either on experience or on systematic structures, such as language. Deleuze and Guattari did not see the impossibility of organizing life around closed structures as problematic. Instead, they saw this as an opportunity to experiment with, invent, and create different ways of knowing (Colebrook, 2002). Instead of focusing on representation and identification, which are related to knowing and determining what children can or cannot do, their work points towards how learning processes are produced and function, and what social effects they have. Deleuze and Guatarri's intellectual project is an invitation to think differently about childhood and curriculum, and several early childhood scholars have taken up this challenge by using their philosophy to engage with difference.

A growing number of early childhood researchers and teachers are beginning to put some of Deleuze and Guattari's philosophical concepts to use at the micro level of preschools (Olsson, 2009; Pacini-Ketchabaw, 2010; Pacini-Ketchabaw et al., 2017; Sellers, 2010) and early childhood teacher education (Lenz Taguchi, 2010; Palmer, 2010). In doing so, these scholars are building on the important work regarding knowledge, power, and subjectivity enacted by postmodern theorists by now using slightly different tactics that are intended to unsettle old ways of thinking and encourage new pedagogical encounters with difference. That is, they are challenging binary thinking by attempting to make use of difference, rather than trying to reduce it to simplistic either/or thinking. One of the ways they are doing this is by thinking with Deleuzian/Guattarian concepts, such as "lines of flight," "rhythms," "intensities," and "becomings" to embrace the idea of curriculum as a creative, experimental, and generative practice, open to multiple possibilities.

Although Olsson (2009) uses several Deleuzian/Guattarian concepts with Swedish early childhood teachers to challenge binary thinking, "the rhythm of the heart" project shows how a group of teachers experiment with lines of flight. As a Deleuzian/Guattarian concept, lines of flight are moments when something new or different happens and as a result produce new meanings and knowledge. Since lines of flight are unpredictable and cannot be planned for, experimentation is required, and this challenges teachers' desires to represent and recognize children's interests and learning. Olsson describes how teachers engaged with lines of flight, encouraging curriculum practices that work with the unknown and are concerned with the new.

In this project, 4- and 5-year-old children had been talking a lot about the heart and its rhythm. Because of these interests the teachers gave the children stethoscopes, paper, and pens, and asked them to illustrate how they understood the rhythm of the heart. The teachers observed and documented how the children engaged with this activity, their learning processes, and tried to understand how the children were using their illustrations to represent the rhythm of the heart beating. The teachers then discussed with each other different ways they might continue working with children's illustrations. While this type of planning using children's interests is how many teachers operate, the teachers working with Olsson went further with the children. Next, the teachers presented their pedagogical documentation to the children, but shared only part of their observations. The children reacted with disappointment because only part of their learning was recorded and represented, rather than everything they said or illustrated. The children were so upset that they did not want to investigate this idea any further.

A few days later, the teachers approached the group with all of their documentation, rather than just the parts they originally thought were relevant. This strategy works against a cause-and-effect logic because the teachers were no longer trying to extract a part of children's individual learning or interests to inform their curriculum practices. This strategy seemed to be successful as the children decided they did want to look for and illustrate more sounds outside. As the children begin exploring sounds and illustrating them, the teachers' pedagogies shifted from trying to recognize and represent what individual children were learning, to instead focusing on how new understandings about sounds were being produced. The teachers noticed how one girl changed strategies for illustrating heartbeats by using her friend's technique and then invented a new way to show a heart beating. This discovery then led the teachers to begin noticing what was happening "in-between" children, ideas, and materials. It is this moment when teachers were no longer trying to control what children would learn next, but instead allowing collective experimentation between children to occur that let learning and ideas take off and in turn create lines of flight.

Lenz Taguchi (2010) finds inspiration from Deleuze and Guattari's (1987, 1994) rhizomatic logic and Barad's (2007) material feminism, which considers the intra-active relationship between all living organisms and the material environment. She works with preservice and in-service early childhood teachers as they move towards what she calls an "intra-active pedagogy" (p. 9), which understands learning and knowing as occurring in the inter-connections that take place "in-between" different forms of matter. Lenz Taguchi is interested in what is happening relationally in the field and what might become, but she also includes the non-human. This kind of pedagogy requires teachers to shift their understanding of learning from a linear to a rhizomatic process that is multi-dimensional.

An example of how an intra-active pedagogy works is illustrated in a preservice teacher's project with 2- and 3-year-old children in Sweden (Lenz Taguchi, 2010). Using pedagogical documentation, the teacher shared how a group of boys were playing with wooden sticks, which quickly turned into gun play. After overhearing one of the boys shout that his gun was "alive," the teacher inquired further about the gun, including if it had a name, where it lived, etc. Soon, the boys became interested in the sticks beyond playing guns by turning the sticks into friends and decorating them in various ways. When shooting became impossible with the sticks, children began having different relationships with this material. The learning became more inclusive because the whole group was now interested in the sticks, and the discussions about the sticks evolved to include topics such as nature and science. An intra-activity pedagogy is employed by shifting the focus from the interpersonal interactions between the teacher and the boys and how this supports learning, to the multiple intra-active processes taking place in-between children and the materials and children's meaning making. A clear set of directions for meeting learning outcomes is not followed, but instead the teacher focuses on the in-betweens and the turning points where no one really knows what will happen. When the children start discussing nature and science, the teacher does not follow their interests and create a curriculum around the life cycle of nature. Instead, her focus is on what is emerging in the multiple inter-activities taking place. As a rhizomatic process, learning has no predetermined directions, but instead can begin anywhere and go anyplace. This requires teachers to be comfortable with not knowing where the learning will go or what will be produced. It is also important to recognize that the teacher did not have a pre-set agenda when she questioned the boys' play. Rather, she took a chance when she responded to the stick being "alive" and this turned the play and learning around because it activated the boys' interests in an unpredictable way. The teacher's actions set off multiple intra-activities, in which all are considered significant. Lenz Taguchi argues that this intra-active pedagogy transgresses binary divides such as discourse/matter and theory/practice, and lines of flight have been made possible.

A third example of Deleuzian/Guattarian inspired scholarship is found in the ways in which Pacini-Ketchabaw et al. (2017) engaged with the concept of experimentation to radically transform life in the early childhood classroom. Experimentation is an open-ended practice that does not have an end goal, nor does it try to interpret what something means. Instead, it is concerned with "how" something functions. Experimentation requires teachers to "try out" new methods, techniques, or practices. It is about exploring what is new and emerging, rather than something that has already happened or been experienced. In this project, teachers worked with experimentation to show what is possible when focusing on child-material encounters and relations. This was not a project that sought to understand how common materials found in preschool, such as paper, paint, charcoal, or blocks, effect children or vice-versa. Instead, teachers worked with experimentation to show what is possible when unpredictable child-material encounters become the focus of inquiry. In short, teachers learned how to pay attention differently. Their experimentation with child-material encounters and relations forced them to shift from knowing what a material is (i.e., paper, paint, charcoal), to what or how it "does" (i.e., moving, emerging, assembling, fostering). Experimentation was about paying attention to the incomprehensible, rhythms of repetition, and to the play between bodies. Embracing experimentation transformed life in the preschool because curiosities, processes, and problems became the focus, not products and solutions.

Together, these studies inspire educators to reconsider the relations between teaching and materials in early childhood classrooms, to question our gaze on individual children and our efforts to use knowledge to impose curriculum events on them, and they suggest that we might think of curriculum making as momentary, less able to be planned, or viewed as theory into action.

The Importance of Critical Theories to the Early Childhood Curriculum

Critical theory is a range of theories that expose the biased and problematic aspects of everyday curriculum practices. The studies reviewed here show that practices as benign as periods for play, providing children with materials to act on the world and observation and documentation are imbued with hidden meanings that have the potential to limit both teachers' and children's agency. Yet, as it has also been illustrated in this review, critical theoretical constructs are complicated, somewhat elusive, and for some may seem irrelevant in an era of accountability and increasing standards-based reform. However, it is precisely because we live and work at this moment in the field's history that we believe we have no choice but to use critical theories.

The field has long had a commitment to improving the lives of young children and for at least 40 years now we have made various efforts to address inequity and injustice. The fact remains however, that while the students we teach become increasingly diverse, we have yet to find ways to level the playing field so every child succeeds. Complicating this issue further is the reality that how children learn and the information and tools available to them with sophisticated technologies means that it is not possible for educators to apply generic theories of learning and development. Therefore even as policymakers attempt to standardize curriculum and impose research proven practices, if educators are not aware of whose knowledge is being given authority in the curriculum, and how knowledge enacts a politics that marginalizes some students, then it will not be possible to be inclusive of every child's learning.

Early childhood teachers also need critical theory if they are to be able to understand how power is playing out in everyday classroom life. Studies of children's play using critical theory have shown children are active agents in the curriculum, regulating each others' subjectivities and yet also using spaces to subvert adult discourses. Teachers also are often unaware of their own positioning in various discourses and how their own subjectivity values particular ways of knowing and being thereby constraining their pedagogical actions. In short, educators need critical theory to see how children are exercising power and what they might do pedagogically to engage with children in ways that build on the learning moment, and also challenge children's presumptions about race, class, sexuality, gender, etc.

Teaching young children in the 21st century requires that we do things differently. In assuming that our developmentally-based curricula are inclusive of all learners, we have been unjust to some students and families. Early childhood educators need critical theory because it enables them to examine the political nature of the curriculum, and in so doing challenges normative views of young children and outdated views of childhood. However, it is one thing to be able to use critical theory to uncover bias, it is another to act on bias to change it. Like the teacher researchers described in this chapter, we believe it is time for all of us to start engaging with some of the newer forms of critical theory, documenting and sharing our efforts, helping each other to engage with these concepts in ways that do not just trouble but reinvent what it means to teach young children in these new times.

References

Adriany, V., & Warin, J. (2012). Gender power relations within the school's space and time: An ethnography study in an Indonesia Kindergarten. In Paper Presented at the Space, Place, and Social Justice in Education Conference, July 13, 2012. Manchester: Manchester Metropolitan University.

Barad, K. (2007). *Meeting the universe halfway: Quantum physics and the entanglement of matter and meaning.* Durham, NC, & London: Duke University Press.

Blaise, M. (2005). *Playing it straight! Uncovering gender discourses in the early childhood classroom.* New York: Routledge.

Blaise, M. (2009). 'What a girl wants, what a girl needs': Responding to sex, gender, and sexuality in the early childhood classroom. *Journal of Research in Childhood Education*, 23(4): 450–460.

Blaise, M. (2010). Kiss and tell: Gendered narratives and childhood sexuality. *Special Sexualities Issue: Australasian Journal of Early Childhood*, 35(1), 1–9.

Blaise, M. (2014). Gender discourses and play. In L. Brooker, M. Blaise, & S. Edwards (Eds.), *The SAGE Handbook of Play and Learning in Early Childhood* (pp. 115-127). London: SAGE UK.

Blaise, M., & Taylor, A. (2012). Using queer theory to rethink gender equity in early childhood education. *Young Children*, 67(1), 88–96.

Bloch, M., Swadener, B.B., & Cannella, G.S. (Eds.). (2014). *Reconceptualizing early childhood care and education: Critical questions, new imaginaries and social activism*. New York: Peter Lang.

Butler, J. (1993). *Bodies that matter: On the discursive limits of "sex."* New York: Routledge.

Butler, J. (1990/1999). *Gender trouble: Feminism and the subversion of identity, 2nd Ed.* New York: Routledge.

Chou, Y.H. (2011). *A study of gendering culture of new Taiwanese children in their kindergarten classroom*. PhD Dissertation, Kent State University, Kent, OH.

Colebrook, C. (2002). *Gilles Deleuze*. New York: Routledge.

Common Worlds Research Collective (2018). www.commonworlds.net, accessed June 1, 2018.

Davies, B. (1989/2003). *Frogs and snails and feminist tales: Preschool children and gender*. NSW, Australia: Allen and Unwin.

Davies, B., & Kasama, H. (2004). *Gender in Japanese preschools: Frog and snails and feminist tales in Japan*. Cresskill, NJ: Hampton Press, Inc.

Davis, K. (2007). Locating the 'Other': Stories from practice and theory. *Children's Issues*, 11(1), 21–24.

Deleuze, G., & Guattari, F. (1983). *Anti-Oedipus: Capitalism and schizophrenia* (R. Hurley, M. Seem, & H.R. Lane, Trans.). London, UK: Continuum.

Deleuze, G., & Guattari, F. (1987). *A thousand plateaus: Capitalism and schizophrenia* (B. Massumi, Trans. and foreword). London, UK: Continuum.

Deleuze, G., & Guattari, F. (1994). *What is philosophy?* (G. Burchell & H. Tomlinson, Trans.). London, UK: Verso.

Deleuze, G., & Parnet, C. (1987). *Dialogues* (H. Tomlinson & B. Habberjam, Trans.). London, UK: Athlone Press.

D'Souza Juma, A. (2017). Engaging with feminist poststructuralism to inform gender equity practice in early childhood classrooms in Pakistan. In K. Smith, K. Alexander, S. Campbell (Eds.), *Feminism(s) in early childhood: Perspectives on children and young people, volume 4*. Singapore: Springer.

Foucault, M. (1978). *The history of sexuality: An introduction (Vol. 1)*. (R. Hurley, Trans.). New York: Pantheon Books.

Foucault, M. (1980). *Power/knowledge: Selected interviews & other writings, 1972–1977*. (C. Gordon, Ed., C. Gordon, L. Marshall, John Mepham, & K. Soper, Trans.). New York: Pantheon Books.

Ghandi, L. (1998). *Postcolonial theory: A critical introduction*. New York: Columbia University Press.

Grieshaber, S., & Cannella, G.S. (Eds.). (2001). *Embracing identities in early childhood education: Diversity and possibilities*. New York: Teachers College Press.

Grieshaber, S., & Ryan, S.K. (2006). Beyond certainties: Postmodern approaches and research about the education of young children. In B. Spodek & O. Saracho (Eds.), *Handbook of research on the education of young children* (pp. 533–553). Mahwah, NJ: Lawrence Erlbaum Associates.

Gupta, A. (2006). *Early childhood education, postcolonial theory, and teaching practices in India: Balancing Vygotsky and the Veda*. New York: Palgrave Macmillan.

Hatch, A., Bowman, B., Jor'dan, J., Lopez Morgan, C., Hart, C., Diaz Soto, L.S., . . . & Hyson, M. (2002). Developmentally appropriate practice: Continuing the dialogue. *Contemporary Issues in Early Childhood*, 3(3), 439–457.

Kessler, S., & Swadener, B.B. (Eds.). (1992). *Reconceptualizing the early childhood curriculum: Beginning the dialogue*. New York: Teachers College Press.

Kuby, C.R., & Rowsell, J. (2017). Early literacy and the posthuman: Pedagogies and methodologies. *The Journal of Early Childhood Literacy*, 17(3), 285–296.

Ladson-Billings, G. (1998). Just what is critical race theory and what's it doing in a nice field like education? *International Journal of Qualitative Studies in Education*, 11(1), 7–24.

Larremore, A. (2016). *Disrupting gendered pedagogies in the early childhood classroom*. New York: Peter Lang.

Lenz Taguchi, H. (2010). *Going beyond the theory/practice divide in early childhood education: Introducing an intra-active pedagogy*. New York: Routledge.

Lubeck, S. (1998). Is DAP for Everyone? A Response. *Childhood Education*, 74(5), 299–301. doi:10.1080/00094056.1998.10521954

MacNaughton, G. (2005). *Doing Foucault in early childhood studies: Applying post-structural ideas*. New York: Routledge.

MacNaughton, G., & Davis, K. (Eds.). (2009). *'Race' and early childhood education: An international approach to identity, politics, and pedagogy*. New York: Palgrave Macmillan.

Mansfield, N. (2000). *Subjectivity: Theories of the self from Freud to Haraway*. NSW, Australia: Allen & Unwin.

Nxumalo, F. (2015). Forest stories: Restorying encounters with 'natural' places in early childhood education. In V. Pacini-Ketchabaw & A. Taylor (Eds.), *Unsettling the colonial places and spaces of early childhood education* (pp. 21–42). New York/London: Routledge.

Olsson, L.M. (2009). *Movement and experimentation in young children's learning: Deleuze and Guattari*. New York: Routledge.

Pacini-Ketchabaw, V. (Ed.). (2010). *Flows, rhythms, & intensities of early childhood curriculum*. New York: Peter Lang.

Pacini-Ketchabaw, V., Kind, S., & Kocher, L.M. (2017). *Encounters with materials in early childhood education*. London/New York: Routledge.

Pacini-Ketchabaw, V., & Taylor, A. (2015). *Unsettling the colonial places and spaces of early childhood*. New York/London: Routledge.

Palmer, A. (2010). Let's dance! Theorising alternative mathematical practices in early childhood teacher education. *Contemporary Issues in Early Childhood Education*, 11(2), 130–143.

Pérez, M.S., & Saavedra, C.M. (2017). A call for onto-epistemological diversity in early childhood education and care: Centering global south conceptualizations of childhood/s. *Review of Research in Education*, 41(1), 1–29.

Pinar, W.F., Reynolds, W.M., Slattery, P., & Taubman, P.M. (1996). Understanding curriculum: An introduction. In W.F. Pinar, W.M. Reynolds, P. Slattery, P.M. Taubman (Eds.), *Understanding curriculum* (pp. 1–66). New York: Peter Lang.

Popkewitz, T.S. (1999). Critical traditions, modernisms, and the "posts." In T. Popkewitz & L. Fendler (Eds.), *Critical theories in education: Changing terrains of knowledge and politics* (pp. 1–16). New York: Routledge.

Robinson, K.H. (2005). Queerying gender: Heteronormativity in early childhood education. *Australian Journal of Early Childhood*, 30(2), 19–28.

Ryan, S., & Grieshaber, S. (2004). It's more than child development: Critical theories, research, and teaching young children. *Young Children*, 5(6), 44–52.

Sellers, M. (2010). *Young children becoming curriculum: Deleuze, Te Whāriki and curricular understandings*. London: Routledge.

Semann, A., & DeJean, W. (Eds.). (2010). *The sexuality issue: Australasian Journal of Early Childhood*, 35(1). Canberra: Early Childhood Australia, Inc.

Srinivasan, P. (2014). *Early childhood in postcolonial Australia: Children's contested identities*. New York: Palgrave Macmillan.

Taylor, A. (2018). Engaging with the conceptual tools and challenges of poststructural theory. In M. Fleer & B. van Oers (Eds.), *International handbook of early childhood education*, (pp. 91–115). Springer Netherlands.

Viruru, R. (2001). *Early childhood education: Postcolonial perspectives from India*. New Delhi, India: SAGE.

Williams, L.R. (1992). Determining the curriculum. In C. Seefeldt (Ed.), *The early childhood curriculum: A review of current research (2nd ed.)*, (pp. 1–15). New York: Teachers College Press.

7

INFANT-TODDLER CURRICULUM

Reconsider, Refresh, and Reinforce

Diane M. Horm, Kyong-Ah Kwon, and Deborah E. Laurin

Introduction

In the 2012 edition of this book, the chapter on infant-toddler curriculum was titled "Infant-Toddler Curriculum: Review, Reflection, and Revolution" (Horm, Goble, & Branscomb, 2012). In that chapter we *reviewed* key features, strengths and limitations, and similarities and differences of three widely used curricula with infants and toddlers in group care – Resources for Infant Educarers (RIE), the Program for Infant-Toddler Care (PITC), and *Creative Curriculum for Infants & Toddlers*. We used our 2012 *review* and *reflection* as a platform to discuss factors necessary for a *revolution* to transform and improve infant-toddler care.

The 2018 title of "Reconsider, Refresh, and Reinforce" foreshadows the intent of this revised chapter. We will *reconsider* not only these three curricula but also the meaning of curriculum when considered in the context of infant-toddler care. We *refresh* and update information by citing current initiatives that have implications for infant-toddler care as well as noting recent additions or modification to the three reviewed curricula. We also *reinforce* the continued need to recognize the uniqueness of the infant-toddler period as we seek needed quality improvements. We acknowledge the three curricula – RIE, PITC, and *Creative Curriculum for Infants & Toddlers* – are just three of multiple approaches available today. We maintain our focus on these three because they continue to be widely used in the US.

As noted in the 2012 chapter, an examination of infant-toddler curriculum is important for a variety of reasons. Many of the reasons remain the same, but have grown in prominence since 2012. A large number of infants and toddlers continue to experience nonparental care. For example, approximately half of all US infants and toddlers (under the age of 3) have a regular child care arrangement, with enrollment in center-based care increasing with age (National Survey of

Early Care and Education [NSECE], 2015). A growing body of research documents that high-quality infant-toddler care can have significant short- and long-term effects on children's development (Vandell et al., 2010; Yazejian et al., 2017). This deepening research base, in concert with the persisting reports of the low to moderate quality of much of the available care (La Paro, Williamson, & Hatfield, 2014; Phillips & Lowenstein, 2011; Vogel et al., 2011), continues to serve as a clarion call to improve the quality of infant-toddler group care, especially for young children growing up in poverty who have been shown to gain the most from high-quality care (La Paro et al., 2014). Additionally, policy makers continue to demonstrate increasing interest in investments in early childhood education, including enhancing the availability, accessibility, and quality of programs for infants, toddlers, and their families (Administration for Children and Families [ACF], 2014). With the goal to improve quality, increasingly federal and state policies have required programs to demonstrate use of an empirically-based curriculum. Examples of mandates requiring this include Early Head Start at the federal level, and state-level Quality Rating and Improvement Systems (Chazan-Cohen et al., 2017). These multiple factors have placed infant-toddler programs in the spotlight with attention to their availability, accessibility, quality, and curriculum.

The curriculum is an important feature of quality because it provides "an organized framework" guiding content (what children are to learn), processes (classroom practices), and context (the environment – both social and physical) (Bredekamp & Rosegrant, 1992, p. 10). The 2012 chapter summarizes the theoretical bases, key components, contributions, strengths, and cautions associated with RIE, PITC, and *Creative Curriculum for Infants & Toddlers*. That information is still relevant and will not be repeated here. Instead, we will *refresh* it by updating recent developments or innovations for each approach and focus on a common weakness identified in 2012 – the lack of research on these curricula, especially related to documenting implementation processes and child outcomes. Last, we will *revisit* and *reinforce* the recommendations we provided in 2012 based on this updated information.

Review of Recent Research (2012–Present) on Infant-Toddler Curriculum

In 2012, we argued that the zeitgeist – or dominant ideas of a time period – impacts the focus and nature of infant-toddler curricula. Since 2012, important topics influencing early childhood education, including curricula, consist of heightened attention to the importance of caregiver-child interactions, concerns about school readiness and a resulting focus on academic content, and examination of the workforce.

Given the unique developmental characteristics of infants and toddlers, practitioners and policy makers need to place a specific focus on developing and supporting relationships between young children and their teachers (Horm, Norris, Perry,

Chazan-Cohen, & Halle, 2016). This reasoning, and the research base to support it, is documented in recently published research summaries. One example is NAEYC's 2015 Research in Review on *Teacher Interactions with Infants and Toddlers* (Norris & Horm, 2015). A key conclusion of this literature review is that sensitive-responsive interactions between caregivers and infants-toddlers are associated with positive child outcomes including social skills, receptive language, expressive language, early literacy capabilities and engagement, and school readiness.

Recognizing that relationship-based care practices are a priority for strengthening the quality of infant-toddler group care (Schmit & Matthews, 2013), ACF commissioned a brief to describe relationship-based care practices and summarize the research support. This brief, titled *Including Relationship-Based Care Practices in Infant-Toddler Care: Implications for Practice and Policy* (Sosinsky et al., 2016), highlights two specific practices: primary caregiving and continuity of care. A few recent empirical studies provide some evidence of associations of continuity of care with the quality of teacher-child interactions and child outcomes (Horm et al., 2018; Ruprecht, Elicker, & Choi, 2016). In addition, caregiving routines, including those unique to infant-toddler care such as diapering, have recently received research attention that documents their potential power to provide unique opportunities for meaningful teacher-child interactions. For example, Laurin, Guss, and Horm (2018) found teacher sensitivity during diapering was associated with child engagement and offered a platform for facilitation of child learning and development.

School readiness has been a driving force in US education since the National Education Goals Panel (NEGP, 1991) articulated that "by the year 2000, all children in America will start school ready to learn" (p. 1). Initially the consequences of this goal focused attention on Pre-K and preschool, resulting in expansion of programs and debates about their content and effectiveness. However, recent research has documented that development during the first three years of life is foundational for later school readiness and success. This research is summarized in an ACF-commissioned brief titled *Developmental Foundations of School Readiness for Infants and Toddlers: A Research to Practice Report* (Horm et al., 2016). Based on current research, this brief reconceptualizes school readiness by considering the developmental characteristics and needs of infants and toddlers and offers the following conclusions:

- infancy/toddlerhood is the time when foundations of school readiness begin in the context of relationships – adults who interact with infants and toddlers must be aware of the opportunities that exist to appropriately support early developing abilities;
- supporting the foundations of school readiness during the infant-toddler period requires attention to all developmental domains;
- the unique developmental characteristics of infants and toddlers require age-appropriate strategies for supporting the foundations of school readiness.

These recommendations highlight that the foundations for school readiness develop early and require responsive relationships with adults who know and understand holistic infant-toddler development and how to appropriately support it.

These conclusions underscore the critical importance of the specialized knowledge and skills required to appropriately facilitate infant-toddler development and lead to questions about the supports available to infant-toddler caregivers. Questions concerning the implications of research for the professionals who work with young children were amplified in the landmark report *Transforming the Workforce for Children Birth Through Age 8: A Unifying Foundation* (The Institute of Medicine [IOM] and National Research Council [NRC], 2015). The report notes that although much is known about what professionals who provide care and education for young children need to know and be able to do, this information is not demonstrated in today's programs. Specifically, our research-based knowledge

> is not fully reflected in the current capacities and practices of the workforce, the settings in which they work, the policies and infrastructure that set qualifications and provide professional learning, and the government and other funders who support and oversee these systems.
>
> *(IOM & NRC, 2015, p. 1)*

While this report offers recommendations for strengthening the workforce based on the science of child development and early learning, it does not provide much specific information for infant-toddler programs. While the recommendations are likely consistent with supports needed to strengthen the infant-toddler workforce, special attention to this group is needed due to recent reports documenting that the infant-toddler workforce has less formal education than those who work with preschoolers (NSECE Project Team, 2013). Research shows that higher education programs tend to focus more on preschool- and primary-level content in early childhood programs than on best practices for supporting infants and toddlers (Early & Winton, 2001). The recent 2017 ACF report (Chazan-Cohen et al., 2017) noting the importance of infant-toddler caregivers' knowledge of development and assessment, combined with the lack of coverage of these topics in higher education, raises questions about whether caregivers have the observation and assessment skills and developmental knowledge to deliver appropriate infant-toddler curriculum.

Perhaps the most compelling disruption in the zeitgeist is Chazan-Cohen et al.'s (2017) publication overtly discussing the meaning and definition of the word "curriculum" when applied to infant-toddler programs. They address questions raised by policy makers and practitioners responding to the mandate to document the use of "empirically-based curricula for infants and toddlers." As mentioned previously, this is increasingly a requirement of state and federal systems striving to improve the quality of infant-toddler care. While well-intentioned, the term *curriculum* used in this context could be misconstrued to imply content and methods that are inappropriate for infants and toddlers. Combined with the expanding focus on school readiness, concerns abound about push-down of content and methods more appropriate for older children into infant-toddler classrooms. To address these concerns, Chazan-Cohen and colleagues clarify that the "what" of infant-toddler curriculum includes environments and planned experiences/activities that are developmentally appropriate and tailored to individual children; and the "how" is delivery in the context of relationships that are supportive and characterized by responsive interactions. The authors note the "why" of curriculum involves selecting an approach that aligns with the caregivers' or program's understanding of early development. The selected approach serves as a resource for implementing practices that support infants and toddlers in reaching appropriate goals. Thus, compared to curriculum for older children, curriculum for infants-toddlers should be more individualized; more spontaneous; embedded in caregiving routines (Laurin et al., 2018), play opportunities, and on-going individual teacher-child interactions; and less scripted and group-oriented. As noted by Chazan-Cohen et al. (2017), when defining curriculum for older children a distinction is made between the teaching process (the how) and the content (the what); but in the infant-toddler period, "it is impossible to remove the responsive interactions and relationships, the *how*, from the *what*" (p. 4). With these distinctions and characterizations in mind, we will now turn to the three commonly-used curricula and *refresh* our knowledge and understanding of these approaches.

Updates for Three Major Infant-Toddler Curricula

Recent innovations and research focused on the three curricula are summarized in the following sections. Although a brief overview of each curriculum is offered in the following sections, the reader is referred to the 2012 chapter for additional details.

Resources for Infant Educarers (RIE)

Overview

Frequently grouped together because of similarities in ideas and practices, RIE and the Pikler approach are both founded on the principles of respectful interactions with infants (Hammond, 2016). Both the RIE philosophy and Pikler approach emphasize caregiving during routines as part of the curriculum (Petrie & Owen, 2005). Both approaches focus on relationships where learning is embedded in the everyday concrete experiences of the care routines of dressing, diapering, mealtimes, and nap preparation. RIE and Pikler also share a unique emphasis on freedom of movement highlighting motor development in an environment where a child's exploration, independence, and learning are supported. Crucially, both approaches share the belief that the child "has a curriculum" where caregiving practices are based on the child's interests and explorations (Lally, 2000, p. 6). Despite these similarities, the two differ in their histories and emphases (Hammond, 2016) as noted in the following.

Not a methodology with rigidly defined ideas, the term "Pikler approach" was intentionally chosen by Anna Tardos, former director of the Pikler Institute and daughter of Dr. Pikler. Dr. Emmi Pikler (1902–1984), a pediatrician, pioneered the approach in her private practice in Budapest and later extended it to children in institutionalized settings. Pikler's approach emphasized physical and emotional safety, the well-being of every child in the residential nursery, and especially the competence of the developing child (Chahin & Tardos, 2017). This approach contrasted sharply with hospitalism, a devastating practice for institutionalized children that resulted in failure to thrive due to lack of stimulation from caregivers and the environment. An important feature of the Pikler approach is an on-site interdisciplinary team at the Pikler House in Budapest comprised of caregivers, pediatricians, Pikler pedagogues, psychologists, and occupational therapists to support caregiver practices and child development through classroom observations and team meetings.

Gerber was introduced to Dr. Pikler's unique pediatric practices when Pikler treated her daughter's illness. Gerber was so impressed with Pikler's demonstration of respect toward the child that she eventually joined Dr. Pikler at the Pikler/Loczy Institute in Budapest to train the nursing staff (Hammond, 2016). After moving to the US Gerber introduced her philosophy of care known as *educaring* that extended Pikler's ideas to family and child care center contexts in California (Gerber, 1998). She referred to RIE as a philosophy and worked predominantly with parents in the US to support attachment with their infants (Hammond, 2016). Both Pikler and RIE offer weekly Parent-Infant Guidance Classes to parents and caregivers to observe their infants or toddlers as they play and move freely, learn to be with other children, and seek out their parent or caregiver as needed (Hammond, 2016).

New Developments

In 2011, the Hungarian government adopted a foster care model and as a result, closed all infant homes. Pikler's legacy is preserved, and her work is continued at the Emmi Pikler Daycare Center, Pikler Loczy Association Hungary, and Loczy Foundation for Children, operating in the same building in Budapest as the former infant's home (Chahin & Tardos, 2017). Pikler and RIE ideas continue to be championed by parents and professionals worldwide (Chahin & Tardos, 2017; Hammond, 2016).

Both offer specialized training. Pikler pedagogues must complete basic courses in child free play, gross motor development, and Pikler culture and care. They then have two separate three-day observations at the Emmi Pikler Day Care in Budapest followed by thematic courses in Social Learning and Piklerian Observation. Case study presentations and a final thesis cap the Pikler pedagogical training. In 2016, the first two Pikler pedagogues in the US received certification to teach courses in the Pikler approach. RIE training is offered in a two-pronged approach. RIE training begins with a basic theory course followed by a RIE practicum, then internship upon recommendation of the RIE trainers. Certified RIE associates are eligible to join the RIE alliance and teach certified RIE courses.

Recent Research

While a dearth of research on RIE and its effectiveness remains since the 2012 edition of this book, some intervention research has emerged. For example, McCall and colleagues (2010) conducted a pre-post intervention study with children in Latin and Central American orphanages where caregivers were trained to increase sensitivity, warmth, and responsiveness during the care routines of feeding, bathing, and diapering consistent with the principles of the WestEd Program for Infant Toddler Care (Lally, Mangione, & Young-Holt, 1992) and the Pikler approach (Tardos, 2007). After intervention, caregivers displayed more warm, sensitive, and responsive interactions with children, and children improved an average of 13.5 developmental quotient (DQ) points after four or more months' exposure to the pilot intervention. Furthermore, 82 percent of the children had DQs less than 70 before the intervention; this was reduced to 28 percent after intervention (McCall et al., 2010).

Much of Pikler's research and documentation is archived at the Pikler Institute and, to date, remains unavailable in English. Zeanah (2010), whose body of work focused heavily on institutionalized settings and the impact of early trauma on infant and toddler development, has urged that formal evaluations of Pikler's "fascinating approach and its role in contemporary infant mental health" (p. 16) be conducted. While institutionalized care is largely relegated to the past, the pervasive impact of early trauma on development is increasingly recognized, making Zeanah's call for action urgent. For example, the National Association of Childcare Resource & Referral Agencies (NACCRRA, 2010) reported that approximately 110,000 to 154,000 of the 11 million children under age 5 in US nonparental care face social and emotional challenges requiring mental health interventions.

Program for Infant/Toddler Care (PITC)

Overview

The PITC is a relationship-based curriculum and an early childhood professional development model developed in 1986 by WestEd in partnership with the California Department of Education to improve the quality of care and support the learning of infants and toddlers (Lally & Mangione, 2017; Weinstock et al., 2012). Based on developmental theories, neuroscience, and research on child development and best practices (e.g., Shonkoff & Phillips, 2000), the PITC aims to promote essential program practices that address six topics: continuity of care, cultural sensitivity, inclusion, individualized care, primary care, and small groups (PITC, 2018). To address these practices, the PITC training is typically organized in four modules that cover social-emotional growth and socialization; group care; learning and development; and culture, family, and providers (PITC, 2018). The training is offered in various types and formats and can be customized to meet the needs of infant-toddler teachers, trainers of infant-toddler teachers, program directors, and home visitors (Weinstock et al., 2012).

New Developments

Since its development, the PITC has continued to expand and has provided training to more than 6,000 infant-toddler teachers (Weinstock et al., 2012) and over 2,200 PITC certified trainers across 49 states and a few other countries including Canada, New Zealand, and Hong Kong. In recent years, resources have been updated with new research and evidence-based programs and new materials (e.g., best practices for planning curriculum for young children; family partnership and culture). The complete set of the training resources, including DVDs, guides, and manuals, are available in both English and Spanish.

The PITC also developed an instrument designed to specifically assess key components of high quality relationship-based care (Mangione, Kriener-Althen, & Marcella, 2016). This tool, the PITC-Program Assessment Rating System (PITC-PARS), measures components from caregiving interactions to the physical environment to program policies and administrative structures, which are well aligned with the PITC's philosophy and contents (Mangione et al., 2016). This tool uses multiple methods and data sources such as direct observation, interviews, and document reviews, and is a reliable and valid measure (Mangione et al., 2016). The PITC-PARS forms and trainings and the related information is available in English, Spanish, and Chinese to expand to more culturally diverse contexts.

Teachers trained in the PITC are expected to provide relationship-based care and improve the quality of their interaction, which, in turn, will foster positive outcomes including children's school readiness (Weinstock et al., 2012). The PITC's program expansion, development of various types of training, and the associated assessment are aligned with this intent and are considered strengths of the program. However, it is unclear how the PITC's overall emphasis on relationship-based care is directly transferred to children's learning and school readiness.

Recent Research

Although the PITC is a widely adopted curriculum, its effectiveness had not been studied through rigorous evaluation research. To address this issue, Berkeley Policy Associates, the University of Texas, and Survey Research Management conducted evaluation research on the effectiveness of the PITC on program quality and child development (Weinstock et al., 2012). This effort is noteworthy because it is the first rigorous impact evaluation of the PITC and is one of few studies with a true experimental design focusing on an approach to and curriculum for infant-toddler child care and its impact on child development.

After collecting baseline program-level data (e.g., program characteristics), a sample of 936 children from 92 child care centers and from 159 licensed family child care homes in California and Arizona were randomly assigned to an intervention or control group. Random assignment was conducted at study locations using the child care program as the unit within three program categories: child care center, English-speaking family child care home, and Spanish-speaking family child care home. The intervention was delivered in a combination of 64 hours of direct caregiver training and 40 hours of on-site coaching or other tailored technical assistance. The control groups did not receive the PITC training but could participate in other available trainings as usual. Child care quality, as well as children's behavior, language, and cognitive development were assessed in two follow-up waves.

The findings showed the PITC did not produce a significant effect on children's behavior, cognitive, or language development, measured about six months after the program ended. It also did not have a significant effect on global program quality or on teacher-child interaction quality, measured by the Infant/Toddler Environment Rating Scale-Revised (Harms, Cryer, & Clifford, 2006) and the PITC-PARS (Mangione et al., 2016). There are several limitations of this research including a high attrition rate (e.g., 251 programs in baseline reduced to 172 programs by second follow-up), and a fidelity issue (e.g., low levels of teacher participation). In particular, as an intent-to-treat study, the effect of the training was assessed for all children, including children who withdrew from child care enrollment before full PITC implementation. Although a common challenge for a long-term intervention study, the widely varying exposure of children to PITC may have obscured or minimized the treatment impact. Given these limitations, further research is needed to investigate the effectiveness of the PITC curriculum.

Creative Curriculum

Overview

Teaching Strategies first published *The Creative Curriculum for Infants & Toddlers* in 1997 (with the second edition in 2006, and third edition in 2015) in response to repeated requests from the field for guidance in working with infants and toddlers (Dombro, Colker, & Dodge, 1999). Dodge, Rudick, and Berke (2006) note that *Creative Curriculum* focuses on the importance of meeting basic needs, fostering social-emotional development, developing secure attachments, and supporting cognitive and brain development. A central concept is the importance of building responsive relationships among teachers, children, families, and the community within the context of daily routines and typical classroom activities such as morning welcome/greeting, eating/mealtimes, book reading, and pretend play (Dodge & Bickart, 2000). Teachers are considered "the foundation of the curriculum" (Dodge & Bickart, 2000, p. 34). Routines are another core feature and are recognized as opportunities to build positive relationships and promote learning. The companion assessment, *Creative Curriculum's* GOLD assessment system, was first offered in an online format in 2010 for use with children birth through kindergarten. The assessment and curriculum are based on 38 specific objectives organized into nine areas including social-emotional, physical, cognitive, oral language, literacy, math, science and technology, social studies, and the arts. The 38 objectives are based on widely held expectations, drawn from the literature, and state early learning standards (Teaching Strategies, 2010) as well as the Head Start Early Learning Outcomes Framework (ACF, 2015). *Creative Curriculum* has a variety of materials for professional development specifically designed for staff, both new and seasoned, working with infants and toddlers.

New Developments

The most recent edition (third), offered in English, Spanish, and bilingual versions, has added "expanded daily support, guidance, and inspiration to teachers and caregivers" (Teaching Strategies, 2018a). This expanded support includes *The Foundation*, three volumes that summarize research and theory on the *what* and *why* of responsive caregiving, and *Daily Resources*, that offer the *how* to foster children's learning and development. The rather extensive supports include: *Intentional Teaching Cards* (provide playful activities with background justifications, materials, teaching sequences linked to assessment system's checkpoints, tips for including all children, and guides to observing); *Might Minutes* (brief activities, by main and related objectives, that support learning in the content areas and general development during routines); *Highlights Hello* (books for young children designed to foster language and literacy skills). They also consist of *Book Conversation Cards* (specific guidance for caregivers' conversations during read-alouds tailored for young infants, mobile infants, toddlers, twos, and families); and *LearningGames* (research-validated activities for both home and classroom use). A *Resource Organizer*, a binder to assemble daily resources, is available. *The Guide* provides an overview of all these components and "explains how everything works together to help teachers provide consistent, responsive care to children" (Teaching Strategies, 2018a).

Reflecting the focus on promoting school readiness and child outcomes, *Creative Curriculum* offers a web-based resource (Teaching Strategies, 2018b) that shows alignment with states' early learning standards and guidelines (ELGs) and the Head Start Early Learning Outcomes Framework (ACF, 2015). This includes the alignment of *Creative Curriculum* objectives with state's ELGs for infants and toddlers for the 45 states having infant-toddler ELGs (Chazan-Cohen et al., 2017). The Head Start Early Learning Outcomes Framework also includes specific learning goals for infants and toddlers across the major developmental domains and *Creative Curriculum*'s document shows explicit alignment with these goals (Chazan-Cohen et al., 2017).

Teaching Strategies continues to offer a variety of professional development resources. New resources specific to working with infants and toddlers include fidelity tools for both teachers and administrators consisting of implementation checklists to monitor use of *Creative Curriculum*'s components including daily routines in the five core areas of physical environment, structure, teacher-child interactions, families, and assessment; and implementation of the GOLD assessment system. Teaching Strategies has also developed a companion publication that outlines the essential elements of the coaching process including preparation, observation, feedback, and planning next steps tailored to *Creative Curriculum*'s objectives and indicators.

Recent Research

Teaching Strategies has a section of their website devoted to research (Teaching Strategies, 2018c). However, the studies summarized focus on outcomes of the curriculum when used with preschool-age children or on the psychometric properties of the GOLD assessment system. Additionally, the reviewed study examining the effects of training and ongoing coaching on implementation of the *Creative Curriculum* also was conducted in preschool settings. When turning to the broader literature, no studies investigating the characteristics, implementation, or outcomes of the *Creative Curriculum for Infants and Toddlers* were found in the published literature. Thus, research is needed on this infant-toddler curriculum.

Final Thoughts and Recommendations for Moving Forward

Despite an urgent need, little systematic and rigorous research has been conducted to examine the components and outcomes of infant-toddler care and education programs (Zaslow, Tout, Halle, Whittaker, & Lavelle, 2010). Most of the extant research that identifies effective curriculum and strategies focuses on preschoolers (Fukkink & Lont, 2007; Preschool Curriculum Evaluation Research Consortium, 2008). Rigorous evaluation research on infant-toddler curriculum has only begun to emerge (e.g., PITC evaluation research) but does not provide clear evidence that supports its effect on child care quality or children's outcomes. RIE and the *Creative Curriculum* have not conducted systematic evaluation research to date. As noted by Chazan-Cohen et al. (2017),

> The curricula currently being used in infant/toddler settings are evidence-derived, that is, based on what is known from research about the development of young children. However, the curricula are generally not *evidence-based:* their effectiveness in improving child outcomes has not been evaluated.
>
> (p. 10)

In short, the current research base is too limited to adequately address the issue of effective infant-toddler curriculum and makes it difficult to adopt evidence-based approaches. There is much to be learned about the relative strengths of the existing infant-toddler curricula and what constitutes effective curriculum and strategies to promote positive and appropriate developmental outcomes for infants and toddlers.

Based on our review of three infant-toddler curricula, we offer several recommendations that may help improve the current status. First, to ensure intended effects and outcomes, it is important that the key elements of the curriculum are implemented with sufficient fidelity, consistency, intensity, and frequency (Wolery, 2011). The current evaluation research has often not sufficiently addressed this issue (e.g., dosage issues such as widely varying exposure of children to the program in the PITC evaluation research). *Creative Curriculum*'s recent addition of fidelity tools is a step in the right direction and communicates to practitioners that it is important to implement the curriculum as designed and intended. More systematic and rigorous research that considers curriculum fidelity is needed to produce empirical evidence on the effects of infant-toddler curricula. That said, does the spontaneous, less-scripted nature of appropriate infant-toddler care align with current notions of fidelity and our ability to assess it? This question has not been sufficiently debated in the infant-toddler literature to date.

Second, the three curricula reviewed in this chapter provide various types and levels of trainings and resources. Given the limited resources and access to targeted professional development typically available for infant-toddler teachers (Norris & Horm, 2016; Zwahr, Davis, Aviles, Buss, & Stine, 2007), these resources are of great importance. However, there are limitations, such as high cost, time constraints for participation, the need for more ongoing coaching and professional development supports, as well as dated information (e.g., the majority of PITC training videos were developed between 1988 and 1992 with some second editions developed in mid-2000). Although various types of trainings are offered for the aforementioned curricula, less attention has been paid to systematic ongoing coaching and PD supports across these curricular approaches. In the pilot study of the impact of the *Creative Curriculum* for Preschool, teachers who received ongoing coaching support for two years significantly improved their classroom quality (Teaching Strategies, 2018c). Although focused on preschool classrooms, the findings suggest the importance of ongoing coaching and mentoring consistent with previous research (Bryant et al., 2009; Kreader, Ferguson, & Lawrence, 2005). Looking to the larger literature, some successful professional development models include features such as individualized plans for participants and on-site intensive mentoring emphasizing reflective practice and self-evaluation (National Child Care Information Center, n.d.; Zwahr et al., 2007). As noted earlier, responsivity, based on ongoing observation and deep understanding of development and individual characteristics, is a basic principle of infant-toddler programming. Given its complexity, it is most likely not attained through short-term professional development efforts, but through ongoing coaching, mentoring, and reflective supervision.

These comprehensive professional development supports are needed, especially in infant-toddler group care, where it has been reported that caregivers typically have less formal education than their peers working with preschoolers (NSECE Project Team, 2013). Additionally, although a bit dated, it has been reported that specialized teacher preparation programs that include content on children age 4 and younger are scarce (e.g., 29 percent of US colleges or universities) (Early & Winton, 2001), and less than half offer at least one infant-toddler focused course (Maxwell, Lim, & Early, 2006). Therefore, it is important to develop and strengthen various levels and types of teacher preparation, training, and ongoing support to meet different needs and learning styles of participants, and address effective strategies and models that facilitate infant-toddler development and learning. The scant existing research suggests tailored supports for the infant-toddler workforce are needed for both pre- and in-service professional development.

Third, the current infant-toddler curriculum models need to be re-examined and reconsidered in light of both current research and the zeitgeist. Recent pressures to promote school readiness in the early years have been controversial. The central issue is the appropriateness of focusing on academic content over valuing infants' present, holistic development (Chazan-Cohen et al., 2017). However, school readiness and developmentally appropriate programming are not necessarily mutually exclusive. High quality infant-toddler care supporting children's current developmental strengths and needs will foster the development of the whole child in the present. This ensures the child develops the foundations of school readiness (Horm et al., 2016) and is able to meet learning challenges in the future (Sosinsky et al., 2016).

In addition, as advocated in the *Creative Curriculum*, content knowledge can be appropriately integrated into play-based care without introducing formal academic instruction or inappropriate expectations. We believe that key elements such as relationship-based and responsive care in RIE and the PITC will provide an important social-emotional foundation for children's later learning, but these curricula may be too global to produce more targeted outcomes such as age-appropriate language development. Similar to the emerging findings with preschool-age children (Nguyen, Jenkins, & Whitaker, 2018), more intentional cognitive scaffolding and language modeling may need to be provided to support optimal development. This is an important question for future research.

Fourth, the review of the three curricula clearly demonstrates their recent expansion and applications to diverse populations and contexts as well as enhanced focus on inclusion and culturally responsive practice. For example, PITC's resources are available in other languages and the training modules specifically address inclusion and culturally responsive practices. In addition, all three curricula offer various types and formats of training, but they mostly focus on participants working in center-based settings. More research is needed to address appropriate curriculum and training for caregivers in other care settings including family child care and relative care, which are the most commonly used types of care for younger children and children from low-income families (Kreader et al., 2005).

Last, policy makers and other stakeholders need to recognize that infant-toddler care and education is a specialized profession and provide more funding and support, through licensing regulations, teaching certificate requirements, mandatory ongoing professional development, and other initiatives such as Quality Rating and Improvement Systems (Zwahr et al., 2007). An example is Oklahoma's Early Childhood Program, a public-private partnership created to expand and enhance infant-toddler services statewide. In 2006, the State Board of Education created a pilot infant-toddler program (State Pilot Program; later re-named Oklahoma Early Childhood Program) that raised standards of structural quality (e.g., group size, ratio, teacher education) for centers serving children under age 4 while providing the necessary fiscal infrastructure. The program also includes ongoing training and on-site technical assistance. Project funds were used to expand or create new infant-toddler classrooms meeting higher standards or to enhance the quality of existing classrooms (e.g., hiring a bachelor's-degreed teacher, improving family support caseload ratios, or improving facilities through construction projects). Oklahoma was recognized as one of only four states implementing this type of innovative infant-toddler policy initiatives (Cohen, Gebhard, Kirwan, & Lawrence, 2009). More typically, the focus is on preschool programs, and while the lack of specialized support for infant-toddler caregivers may be recognized, to date it is rare in the US for it to be overtly addressed. It is also important to build evaluation into such initiatives in order to make data-driven decisions to strengthen the workforce (Kreader et al., 2005). Relative to the Oklahoma Early Childhood Program, program evaluations indicated the project was successful in improving the availability and quality of infant-toddler group care with some evidence for positive child outcomes in language development (Horm et al., 2009).

Our 2018 *reconsideration* of the three curricula and the status of infant-toddler programming in general, leads us to end this chapter by *reinforcing* our previous 2012 call for a *revolution*. While progress has been made, the progress does not include the volume of robust research needed to inform efforts to improve infant-toddler curricula. While research has begun to emerge in the past six years, we are far from the strong body of existing findings needed to confidently design curricula and guide the development of associated supports. In the meantime, we are still too tied to common-sense approaches and activities that happen to align with theories and standards, but all too often are grounded on tradition or enjoyment, rather than demonstrated developmental and educational effectiveness. Our observations suggest others err in the direction of pushing down narrowly-focused academic content based upon misconceptions of school readiness and how learning occurs during the infant-toddler period. We hope that in 2025, when the next edition of this book will perhaps be published, that we can frame our work using three different Rs – *Research, Research-based*, and *Renaissance*.

References

Administration for Children and Families (2014). *101: Early Head Start-child care partnerships*. Washington, DC: Author. Retrieved from https://www.acf.hhs.gov/sites/default/les/ecd/ehs_ccp_101_ nal_hhsacf_logo_2014.pdf

Administration for Children and Families (2015). *Head Start Early Learning Outcomes Framework: Ages birth to five*. Washington, DC: Author. Retrieved from https://eclkc.ohs.acf.hhs.gov/sites/default/files/pdf/elof-ohs-framework.pdf

Bredekamp, S., & Rosegrant, T. (Eds.). (1992). *Reaching potentials: Appropriate curriculum and assessment for young children (Vol. 1)*. Washington, DC: NAEYC.

Bryant, D., Wesley, P., Burchinal, P., Sideris, J., Taylor, K., Fenson, C., . . . Iruka, I. (2009). *The QUINCE-PFI study: An evaluation of a promising model for caregiver training*. Chapel Hill, NC: University of North Carolina, Frank Porter Graham Child Development Center.

Chahin, E., & Tardos, A. (2017). *In loving hands*. Bloomington, IN: Xlibris.

Chazan-Cohen, R.C., Zaslow, M., Raikes, H.H., Elicker, J., Paulsell, D., Dean, A., & Kriener-Althen, K. (2017). *Working toward a definition of infant/toddler curricula: Intentionally furthering the development of individual children within responsive relationships*. Office of Planning, Research and Evaluation, Administration for Children and Families; U.S. Department of Health and Human Services.

Cohen, J., Gebhard, B., Kirwan, A., & Lawrence, B.J. (2009). *Inspiring innovation: Creative state financing structures for infant-toddler services*. Washington, DC: ZERO TO THREE and Ounce of Prevention Fund.

Dodge, D., & Bickart, T. (2000, November 5–7). *How curriculum frameworks respond to developmental stages: Birth through age 8*. Paper presented at the Lilian Katz Symposium, University of Illinois, Urbana-Champaign, IL.

Dodge, D., Rudick, S., & Berke, K.L. (2006). *The Creative Curriculum for infants, toddlers, and twos*. Washington, DC: Teaching Strategies.

Dombro, A.L., Colker, L.J., & Dodge, D. (1999). *Creative Curriculum for infants & toddlers revised edition*. Washington, DC: Teaching Strategies.

Early, D.M., & Winton, P.J. (2001). Preparing the workforce: Early childhood teacher preparation at 2- and 4-year institutions of higher education. *Early Childhood Research Quarterly*, 16, 285–306.

Fukkink, R.G., & Lont, A. (2007). Does training matter? A meta–analysis and review of caregiver training studies. *Early Childhood Research Quarterly*, 22, 294–311.

Gerber, M. (1998). *Dear parent: Caring for infants with respect*. Los Angeles, CA: Resources for Infant Educarers.

Hammond, R. (2016). Resources for infant educarers. In D. Couchenour & J. Kent Chrisman (Eds.), *The SAGE encyclopedia of contemporary early childhood education*. (p. 1184). Thousand Oaks, CA: SAGE Publications, Inc.

Harms, T., Cryer, D., & Clifford, R.M. (2006). *Infant/toddler environment rating scale-revised*. New York: Teachers College Press.

Horm, D., File, N., Bryant, D., Burchinal, M., Raikes, H., Forestieri, N., & Cobo-Lewis, A. (2018). Associations between continuity of care in infant-toddler classrooms and child outcomes. *Early Childhood Research Quarterly*, 42, 105–118.

Horm, D., Goble, C., Boatright, M., Decker, C., Noble, N., & Norris, D. (2009). Oklahoma's Pilot Early Childhood Program Birth through Three Years: Description, evaluation, and policy implications. *National Head Start Association Dialog: A Research to Practice Journal for the Early Intervention Field*, 12(4), 360–373.

Horm, D.M., Goble, C.B., & Branscomb, K.R. (2012). Infant toddler curriculum: Review, reflection, and revolution. In N. File, J.J. Mueller, & D.B. Wisneski (Eds.), *Curriculum in early childhood education: Re-examined, rediscovered, renewed.* New York: Routledge.

Horm, D., Norris, D., Perry, D., Chazan-Cohen, R., & Halle, T. (2016). *Developmental foundations of school readiness for infants and toddlers, a research to practice report.* OPRE Report # 2016-07, Washington, DC: Office of Planning, Research and Evaluation, Administration for Children and Families, U.S. Department of Health and Human Services.

Institute of Medicine (IOM) & National Research Council (NRC) (2015). *Transforming the workforce for children birth through age 8: A unifying foundation.* Washington, DC: The National Academies Press.

Kreader, J.L., Ferguson, D., & Lawrence, S. (2005). Impact of training and education for caregivers of infants and toddlers. Research-to-Policy Connections No. 3. Child Care and Early Education Research Connections. https://doi.org/10.7916/D84T6T4J

La Paro, K., Williamson, A., & Hatfield, B. (2014). Assessing quality in toddler classrooms using the CLASS-Toddler and the ITERS-R. *Early Education and Development,* 25, 875–893.

Lally, J.R. (2000). Infants have their own curriculum: A responsive approach to curriculum planning for infants and toddlers. *Head Start Bulletin,* 67, 6–18. Retrieved from https://eclkc.ohs.acf.hhs.gov/hslc/tta-system/pd/docs/finalcurriculm.pdf

Lally, J.R., & Mangione, P. (2017). Caring relationships: The heart of early brain development. *Young Children,* 72(2), 17.

Lally, J.R., Mangione, P.L., & Young-Holt, C.L. (Eds.). (1992). *Infant/toddler caregiving: A guide to language development and communication.* Sacramento: California Department of Education.

Laurin, D.E., Guss, S., & Horm, D. (2018, June). *Child well-being and involvement during diapering routines.* Poster session presented at The National Research Conference on Early Childhood Education. Arlington, Virginia.

Mangione, P.L., Kriener-Althen, K., & Marcella, J. (2016). Measuring the multifaceted nature of infant and toddler care quality. *Early Education and Development,* 27, 149–169.

Maxwell, K.L., Lim, C.-I., & Early, D.M. (2006). *Early childhood teacher preparation programs in the United States: National report.* Chapel Hill, NC: The University of North Carolina, FPG Child Development Institute.

McCall, R., Groark, C.J., Fish, L.E., Harkins, D., Serrano, G., & Gordon, K. (2010). A socioemotional intervention in a Latin American orphanage. *Infant Mental Health Journal,* 31, 521–542.

National Association of Childcare Resource & Referral Agencies (2010). *Child care in America: 2016 state fact sheets.* Retrieved from http://usa.childcareaware.org/advocacy-public-policy/resources/research/statefactsheets2016/

National Child Care Information Center (n.d.). *South Carolina and the WestEd Program for Infant Toddler Caregivers.* Retrieved from http://nccic.acf.hhs.gov/itcc/word-Docs/SC_PITC.doc

National Education Goals Panel (NEGP) (1991). *The Goal 1 Technical Planning Subgroup report on school readiness.* Washington, DC: Author.

National Survey of Early Care and Education (NSECE) Project Team (2013). *Number and characteristics of Early Care and Education (ECE) teachers and caregivers: Initial findings from the National Survey of Early Care and Education (NSECE).* OPRE Report #2013-38, Washington, DC: Office of Planning, Research and Evaluation, Administration for Children and Families, U.S. Department of Health and Human Services.

National Survey of Early Care and Education (NSECE) (2015). *Tables on Households' ECE Usage and Cost to Parents.* Submitted to OPRE, US DHHS. Chicago, IL: NORC.

Nguyen, T., Jenkins, J.M., & Whitaker, A.A. (2018). Are content-specific curricula differentally effective in Head Start or State Prekindergarten classrooms? *AERA Open*, 4, 1–17. https://doi.org/10.1177/2332858418784283

Norris, D.J., & Horm, D.M. (2015). Research in review: Teacher interactions with infants and toddlers. *Young Children*, 70(5), 84–91.

Norris, D.J., & Horm, D.M. (2016). Introduction to the special issue on group care for infants, toddlers, and twos. *Early Education and Development*, 27, 145–148. doi:10.1080/10409289.2016.1090768

Petrie, S., & Owen, S. (2005). *Authentic relationships in group care for infants and toddlers: Resources for Infant Educarers (RIE) principles into practice*. Philadelphia, PA: Kingsley.

Phillips, D.A., & Lowenstein, A.E. (2011). Early care, education, and child development. *Annual Review of Psychology*, 62, 483–500.

Preschool Curriculum Evaluation Research Consortium (2008). *Effects of preschool curriculum programs on school readiness (NCER 2008–2009)*. National Center of Education Research, Institute of Education Sciences, U.S. Department of Education. Washington, DC: U.S. Government Printing Office.

Program for Infant/Toddler Care (2018). *PITC The Program for Infant/Toddler Care*. Retrieved from https://www.pitc.org/pub/pitc_docs/home.csp#

Ruprecht, K., Elicker, J., & Choi, J.Y. (2016). Continuity of care, caregiver-child interactions, and toddler social competence and problem behaviors. *Early Education & Development*, 27, 221–239.

Schmit, H., & Matthews, H. (2013). *Better for babies: A study of state infant and toddler child care policies*. Center for Law and Social Policy. Retrieved from http://www.clasp.org/resources-and-publications/publication-1/BetterforBabies2.pdf.

Shonkoff, J., & Phillips, D. (Eds.). (2000). *From neurons to neighborhoods: The science of early childhood development*. Washington, DC: National Academy Press.

Sosinsky, L., Ruprecht, K., Horm, D., Kriener-Althen, K., Vogel, C., & Halle, T. (2016). *Including Relationship-Based Care Practices in Infant-Toddler Care: Implications for Practice and Policy*. OPRE Research-to-Practice Brief, OPRE Report #: 2016–46, Washington, DC: Office of Planning, Research and Evaluation, Administration for Children and Families, U.S. Department of Health and Human Services.

Tardos, A. (2007). *Bringing up and providing care for infants and toddlers in an institution*. Budapest, Hungary: Pikler-Loczy.

Teaching Strategies (2010). *Research foundation: Teaching Strategies GOLD Assessment System*. Retrieved from https://teachingstrategies.com/wp-content/uploads/2017/03/Research-Foundation-GOLD-2010.pdf

Teaching Strategies (2018a). *The Creative Curriculum for infants, toddlers & twos: Product overview*. Retrieved from https://shop.teachingstrategies.com/page/76108-Creative-Curriculum-Infants-Toddlers-Twos.cfm#product_overview

Teaching Strategies (2018b). *The Creative Curriculum for infants, toddlers & twos: Alignment*. Retrieved from https://shop.teachingstrategies.com/page/76108-Creative-Curriculum-Infants-Toddlers-Twos.cfm#alignments

Teaching Strategies (2018c). *Our approach: Research*. Retrieved from https://teachingstrategies.com/our-approach/research/

Vandell, D.L., Belsky, J., Burchinal, M., Steinberg, L., Vandergrift, N., & NICHD ECCRN (2010). Do effects of early child care extend to age 15 years? Results from the NICHD Study of Early Child Care and Youth Development, *Child Development*, 81, 737–756.

Vogel, C.A., Boller, K., Xue, Y., Blair, R., Aikens, N., Burwick, A., . . . & Stein, J. (2011). *Learning as we go: A first snapshot of Early Head Start programs, staff, families, and children.* OPRE Report #2011–17, Washington, DC. Office of Planning, Research, and Evaluation, Administration for Children and Families, U.S. Department of Health and Human Services.

Weinstock, P., Bos, J., Tseng, F., Rosenthal, E., Ortiz, L., Dowsett, C., . . . & Bently, A. (2012). *Evaluation of Program for Infant/Toddler Care (PITC): An on-site training of caregivers (NCEE 2012–4003).* Washington, DC: National Center for Education Evaluation and Regional Assistance, Institute of Education Sciences, U.S. Department of Education.

Wolery, M. (2011). Intervention research: The importance of fidelity measurement. *Topics in Early Childhood Special Education*, 31, 155–157.

Yazejian, N., Bryant, D., Hans, S., Horm, D., St. Clair, L., File, N., & Burchinal, M. (2017). Child and parenting outcomes after one year of Educare. *Child Development*, 88, 1671–1688.

Zaslow, M., Tout, K., Halle, T., Whittaker, J.V., & Lavelle, B. (2010). *Towards the identification of features of effective professional development for early childhood educators.* Washington, DC: U.S. Department of Education, Office of Planning, Evaluation and Policy Development.

Zeanah, C. (2010). *The Pikler Institute and the Pikler-Loczy method.* The Signal World Association for Infant Mental Health. Retrieved from http://www.waimh.org/files/Signal/Signal3-4_2010.pdf

Zwahr, M.D., Davis, C.F., Aviles, J., Buss, K.H., & Stine, H. (2007). Professional development programs for infants/toddler caregivers: Setting the stage for lifelong learning. *Dimensions of Early Childhood*, 35, 12–21.

8

UNPACKING THE TENSIONS IN OPEN-ENDED PRESCHOOL CURRICULUM

Teacher Agency, Standardization, and English Learners in Creative Curriculum and High/Scope

Sara Michael-Luna, Lucinda G. Heimer, and Leslee Grey

Introduction

An enduring goal of public education in the United States has been to enable students to acquire the knowledge and skills necessary for living in a democratic society (Apple, 2018; Dewey, 1916; Tyack, 1974). Today, given the importance placed on maintaining economic competitiveness and quality of life, academic rigor of early childhood education has become a high priority (Fuller, 2007). Although offering equitable educational opportunities is not a new concept in U.S. education, extending this vision to include high-quality, academic-focused early childhood education to all learners marks a contemporary turn in educational expectations. Researchers have established that preschool acquisition of skills in oral language and literacy, math, science, social-emotional development, and social interactions leads to academic success in the later grades (Choi, Elicker, Christ, & Dobbs-Oates, 2014; Denham, Bassett, Zinsser, & Wyatt, 2014; Graf, Hernandez, & Bingham, 2016; Verdine, Irwin, Golinkoff, & Hirsh-Pasek, 2014). The implication that preschool readiness should be primarily academic in nature (Brown, Mowry, & Feger, 2015) is driving early childhood curriculum to align more closely with expectations previously reserved for later grades, such as the Common Core State Standards (National Governors Association Center for Best Practices & Council of Chief State School Officers, 2010) or Next Generation Standards (NGSS Lead States, 2013).

Created to provide access to 4-year-old kindergarten for all children, early childhood programs such as Head Start and Universal Pre-Kindergarten (UPK) have been modifying their curriculum choices due to the academic push of standardization, accountability, and acquisition of skills (Au & Ferrare, 2015; Spencer, 2014). In a 2017 OPRE study, the majority (75.2 percent) of Head Start programs cited Creative Curriculum as their primary curriculum, with 10.8 percent relying on High/Scope (Moiduddin, Kopack Klein, Tarullo, West, & Aikens, 2017, p. 24). Additionally, New York City's Universal Pre-Kindergarten Program, which serves over 71,337 4-year-olds, has aligned its curriculum (Interdisciplinary Units of Study) and the New York Foundations for the Common Core (Pre-Kindergarten Common Core State Standards) to the Creative Curriculum Framework (NYC DOE, 2018; Teaching Strategies, 2015). Therefore, when considering access and education for all young children it makes sense to explore the implementation of curricula used in Head Start and UPK (Resnick, 2011; Schumacher, Hamm, & Ewen, 2007): Creative Curriculum and High/Scope.

In a previous study on Creative Curriculum and High/Scope (Michael-Luna & Heimer, 2012), we questioned using a universal approach to teaching and were troubled by the lack of urgency of policy makers, administrators, researchers, and teachers to shift curricular approaches to meet the needs of all children and families, specifically English learners. In light of new editions of Creative Curriculum (Dodge, Heroman, Colker, & Bickart, 2010) and High/Scope (Epstein, 2014), we revisit the themes and findings of our previous work (Michael-Luna & Heimer, 2012). First, we consider the ways in which curriculum has been taken up and embodied as policy. Second, we ground Creative Curriculum and High/Scope historically and give a brief description of each curriculum package, highlighting how the curricula draw on developmentalist (Erikson, 1959; Maslow, 1943; Piaget, 1952) and constructivist (Vygotsky, 1978) learning theories. Finally, we present three opportunities for teachers and administrators using Creative Curriculum and High/Scope to consider: (1) the complexity of teacher agency in the implementation of open-ended curricula, (2) the impact of standards and assessments on curriculum enactment, and (3) the dangers of inappropriate application of superficial knowledge of socio-cultural and contextual influences on English learners and their families. Throughout the chapter, we carefully consider the roles that developmental universalism and socio-cultural context play in both curricula, to reflect the underlying values and norms informing the curriculum (Apple, 2018).

Early Childhood Curriculum as Policy

The need for more extensive early care and education rose as more women entered the workforce in the 1970s (Fuller, 2007). Creative Curriculum and High/Scope became prevalent during what was considered a "high water-mark" for public responsibility of the education and care of young children (Beatty, 1995). The widespread use of these packages reflects the research on accepted learning theories and "best practices" in early childhood education. However, we recognize that curricular goals and practices are always historically situated and embedded in cultural, political, and ideological assumptions (Apple, 2017), which can work to universalize practices into formal policy. For example, critical scholars have framed publicly funded preschool as a form of social control over low-income families, who were viewed as culturally deficient (Nieto, 2009; Dahlberg et al., 1999; Polakow, 2007).

Developmentally appropriate practices undergird both Creative Curriculum and High/Scope in much the same way that academic standards undergird K-12 education – as a form of power (Apple, 2012). In both contexts, power is employed through a positivist perspective that hegemonically holds developmental milestones as benchmarks, suggesting all "normal" children, regardless of home background (or cultural and linguistic origins), must perform particular tasks by a certain age. The prominence of constructivism, coupled with the endorsement of DAP by organizations such as the National Association for the Education of Young Children (NAEYC), have led these seemingly independent curricular choices to become more powerful.

Historical Development and Description

Both High/Scope and Creative Curriculum developed models of child-centered, experiential learning for children 3 to 5 years of age. The frameworks for High/Scope and Creative Curriculum resulted from two 1960s preschool intervention studies, the Perry Street Preschool and the Abecedarian Study, which focused on "at risk" children as defined by income requirements. Conceptualized in a post-Sputnik era of increased attention to scientific and mathematical models, early iterations of both programs followed the suggestions of child development psychologists such as Piaget, Bloom, and Erikson, while more recent iterations, after glasnost made Vygotsky's works available to Western readers, mirrored a larger philosophical shift toward Vygotskian learning theory (Copple & Bredekamp, 2009; Dodge, Heroman, Colker, & Bickart, 2010; Epstein, 2007; Holt, 2010). While Piagetian theory posited that child development adheres to universal stages and that children learn through active self-discovery when they are biologically ready, Vygotskian thinking suggested that learning is socially and culturally situated. For Vygotsky, the teacher sets the foundation for child learning, with subsequent knowledge gained dialectically through experimenting with the environment and the child co-constructing new experiences with peers and teachers (Vygotsky, 1978). Reflecting the larger shift in the field of early childhood development, both curricula shifted their theoretical framework from a view of child development as sequential with universal milestones to a view of development as contextual and wholistic.

High/Scope

As a part of President Johnson's War on Poverty, researchers turned an eye on how to "break the cycle of poverty" through education. One of the best-known efforts from this era, the Perry Preschool (1962–1967), was developed in Ypsilanti, Michigan, by David Weikart and his colleagues. The Perry Preschool selected 123

African American children living in poverty and at high risk of not completing school to participate in a structured preschool experience. Researchers interested in studying return-on-investment followed the core group of children receiving the "treatment" of preschool throughout their lives, conducting a longitudinal cost-benefit analysis for the preschool experience. The outcomes were based on interviews and demographic surveys completed at the ages of 15 (Erikson, 1977), 27 (Barnett, 1985; 1996), 40 (Belfield, Nores, Barnett, & Schweinhart, 2006), and 50 (Heckman, Reynolds, & Henning, 2018). Comparing the preschool group to the non-preschool group, researchers found significant differences. For example, there were decreases in the likelihood of involvement in crime (from 35 percent to 7 percent), and the high school graduation rate jumped from 54 percent to 71 percent. Based on this work, there was a $7.16 return calculated for every dollar spent on preschool (Garcia, Heckman, Leaf, & Prados, 2017; Barnett, 1996; Kirp, 2007; Heckman, Moon, Pinto, Savelyev, & Yavitz, 2010). The participants' success in the early years, compared to the control group, who did not receive a preschool experience, laid the groundwork for the federal government's funding of Head Start and resulted in the development of High/Scope Curriculum in 1970.

The High/Scope Preschool Curriculum uses direct, hands-on experiences with people, objects, events, and ideas. The curriculum (Epstein, 2014) addresses four areas:

- a set of teaching practices for adult-child interaction, arranging the classroom and materials, and planning the daily routine;
- curriculum content areas for 3- to 5-year-olds (including Language, Literacy and Communication, Social-Emotional, Physical Development and Health, Mathematics, Science and Technology, Social Studies and Creative Arts);
- assessment tools to measure teaching behaviors and child progress;
- a training model to help caregivers implement the curriculum effectively.

By creating an environment where children and teachers can actively co-construct knowledge during purposeful play, High/Scope suggests that learning is a four part process: (1) adult-child interaction which should encourage child problem solving; (2) prepared environment that presents areas and resources for child exploration and discovery of knowledge; (3) planned daily routine that includes the Plan-Do-Review cycle of learning and also takes into consideration small and large group interactions; and (4) assessment of individual children's learning needs through teacher observation.

The interaction and communication between teachers and children and teachers and parents is emphasized in High/Scope.

Creative Curriculum

Teaching Strategies, LLC, under the leadership of Diana Trister Dodge and colleagues, developed Creative Curriculum in the late 1970s (the first edition of the Creative Curriculum was 1978) based on the child-adult interactive learning experiences that were developed as the curriculum for the Abecedarian Studies (1972–2009), a decade later than the Perry Preschool. Based in Chapel Hill, North Carolina, the Abecedarian Early Childhood Intervention Project was a full-day, year-round program serving low-income children up to age 8. Initially, 101 African American children deemed "at risk" due to low birthweight were selected to engage in experiential learning activities (Sparling, Ramey, & Ramey, 2007). The effect of their early learning experience was tracked over their lifetime and the following outcomes were reported: higher IQ; improved reading and math; and fewer special education placements (Campbell, Ramey, Pungello, Sparling, & Miller-Johnson, 2002; Englund, White, Reynolds, Schweinhart, & Campbell, 2015).

Described as an "architect's blueprint" (Dodge, Heroman, Colker, & Bickart, 2010, p. xix), the fifth edition of Creative Curriculum has been expanded into five volumes, covering *The Foundation* (Volume 1) (Dodge, Heroman, Colker, & Bickart, 2010); *Interest Areas* (Volume 2) (Dodge, Colker, & Heroman, 2010); *Literacy* (Volume 3) (Heroman & Jones, 2010); *Mathematics* (Volume 4) (Copley, Jones, & Dighe, 2010); and *Objectives for Development & Learning* (Volume 5) (Heroman, Burts, Berke, & Bickart, 2010). Creative Curriculum was developed as a way to help preschool teachers organize their classrooms into well-defined "Areas of Interest" (such as blocks, dramatic play, toys and games, art, library, discovery, sand and water, music and movement, cooking, computers, and outdoors) that integrate content area knowledge (Dodge, Colker, & Heroman, 2010). In order to structure the classroom in a way that young children will find predictable and familiar, Creative Curriculum offers a daily routine, within which the teacher's role is that of observer, teacher, and assessor. Creative Curriculum guides teachers to use assessments that directly contribute to supporting individual learning as well as for program evaluation.

Implications and Opportunities

Teacher Agency in Open-ended Curricula

In this section, we unpack three implications and opportunities for teachers and administrators using Creative Curriculum and High/Scope to consider: (1) teacher agency in open-ended curricula, (2) standards and assessments, and (3) English learners and their families.

Teacher agency, control, and flexibility are core principles of High/Scope and Creative Curriculum that appeal to many educators. Creative Curriculum encourages teachers to create their own content and lessons to support individual learner skills and social competence, and teachers are advised to create a daily routine with their students.

While Creative Curriculum does not mandate specific content, lesson plans, or "scripts" for teacher-student interactions, the authors of the package stipulate that "effectiveness. . .can be achieved best if the resources are implemented as intended" (Dodge, Heroman, Colker, & Bickart, 2010, p. xix). When offered scripted curricula, which allow little teacher input, many teachers choose not to deviate from the prescribed instruction. Providing fewer opportunities for teachers to develop more comprehensive plans and to grow professionally, "scripted and narrowed curriculum moves teaching away from professionalization by not allowing teachers to rely on their professional judgment to make curricular decisions for student learning" (Milner, 2013, p. ii). Pressure from administration and policy to offer a tighter interpretation can strip teachers of professional agency in curriculum implementation.

High/Scope encourages teachers to use the active participatory learning model (Epstein, 2014, p. 11) to build integrated curriculum that is meaningful to children in the local context within the daily routine. High/Scope provides guidelines for each content area (math, science & technology, social studies, arts, and language-literacy) as well as physical, social, emotional development. Lacking daily lesson plans, High/Scope claims to create an opportunity for teachers to work in teams (Epstein, 2014, pp. 81–92). By supporting young learners' knowledge construction, open-ended curricula also supports teachers in exploring their role and agency in curriculum implementation (Apple, 2018; Michael-Luna & Grey, 2018). Teachers can positively influence the content and pedagogy in ways that create respect for individual child development and engage in creating locally meaningful lesson plans and instruction.

However, recent research found this process to be much more complex than previously suggested (Michael-Luna & Heimer, 2012). Michael-Luna & Grey (2018) found that four participating preschool teachers described their initial attempts to implement the school district's Universal Pre-Kindergarten (UPK) policy directive of child *autonomy* as particularly challenging within the bounds of open-ended curricula. The teachers initially attributed these challenges to the quality of the local district supplied open-ended curriculum, which used the Creative Curriculum framework. Analysis uncovered that implementing open-ended curricula in local practice was rife with complexities. For example, the teachers expressed frustration with the lack of guidance on how to include social-emotional development during content area lessons. Furthermore, teachers suggested that the local school district's interpretation of the open-ended curriculum was too closely tied to the K-12 content area standards, leaving no room for social and emotional development. Both High/Scope and Creative Curriculum offer opportunities for teacher agency; however, there is risk for loss of agency when the curriculum is more closely tied to standards at the local levels.

Impact of Current Education Policy on Creative Curriculum and High/Scope Enactment: Standards and Assessment

With increased attention on the early years, national organizations (NAEYC, NIEER, NAECS) as well as state departments of early education (e.g., WI, MS, MA, NY, etc.) have created early childhood education standards (Brown, 2007). The move to aligning early childhood curricular objectives with K-12 standards may facilitate planning and assessment in pre-kindergarten. However, this trend to forefront efficiency through alignment of standards across developmental domains also signals an academic push down of the K-12 assessment systems to early childhood with little acknowledgment of key growth areas for young children and consideration of diverse lived experiences. Both Creative Curriculum and High/Scope reflect alignment pressure, as their planning and assessment tools shift focus to state and national early learning standards. The need to translate young children's growth and development in a way that is accepted and understood based on early elementary school criteria provides a rationale for binding curriculum to standards. However, the movement toward creating or adapting early childhood curriculum with the sole purpose of meeting universal standards limits the potential of the early childhood classroom.

To illustrate the shift toward standardization in early education, we explore the connection between curriculum and assessment tools, specifically, Creative Curriculum and Teaching Strategies GOLD®. This assessment system offers ongoing observational tools for teachers of children birth through kindergarten and is accessible both online and in print. In Creative Curriculum *Objectives for Development and Learning*, Heroman et al. (2010) provide learning objectives for social-emotional, physical, language, and cognitive development as well as literacy, mathematics, science and technology, social studies, the arts, and English language acquisition. Each learning or developmental objective is outlined and connected to research. For example, the objective "Regulates own emotions and behaviors" is further connected in the text to a definition of emotional regulation, environmental context, and teacher role, with additional research citations related to differentiation for unique family and cultural needs. Next, Heroman et al. (2010) provide rubrics based on an age continuum for the sub-skills, such as "manages feelings": A 2-year-old should be able to "use adult support to calm self" while an 8-year-old "controls strong emotions in an appropriate manner most of the time" (p. 7). Not all local classroom contexts using Creative Curriculum use the online Teaching Strategies GOLD® assessments and there are those who use Teaching Strategies GOLD® who are not implementing Creative Curriculum. However, the rubrics in Volume 5, Teaching Strategies GOLD®, DAP's five Domains and the Next Generation and Common Core State Standards are clearly linked and share the same language. Creative Curriculum offers research and support to acknowledge variation in growth and achievement, but the danger lies in the translation to rubrics and standards in a way that streamlines growth by failing to recognize the diversity of influences on growth. While tools line up seamlessly, quantifying emotional growth to fit standards and rubrics limits interpretation and explanation of the child's true capabilities.

Similarly, in terms of assessment, High/Scope offers online links for alignment by state between the Child Observation Record (COR) and the early learning standards from each state. In most states, the early learning standards are a separate set of standards focused on the domains of learning for young children in pre-K. For example, in Wisconsin the COR assessment offers an alignment grid to provide easy reference for the Wisconsin Model Early Learning Standards (WMELS) and the COR key indicators (Teaching Strategies, 2018). COR Advantage is organized using eight areas of growth and development with 34 items for measurement. The planning and assessment for both Creative Curriculum and High/Scope are aligned seamlessly with the early learning standards of the state, whether state created or the adapted Common Core State Standards (e.g., New York). Therefore, while adding efficiency to assessment writing, such alignment runs the risk of also absorbing complex aspects of all domains of early growth in early childhood into discrete standards of measurement in the spirit of seamlessly connecting to an existing K-12 system.

As mentioned earlier, High/Scope and Creative Curriculum were created in tandem with two compensatory preschool intervention programs as a way to "level the sandbox" (Kirp, 2007). Although Creative Curriculum and High/Scope began as "open" curriculum there is pressure to address the achievement gap (as defined by performance on standardized tests). One misguided strategy to reduce the achievement gap is through increased academic rigor (Brown, Mowry, & Feger, 2015). Creative Curriculum gives depth to the content knowledge (such as the *Literacy* volume's section on phonemic awareness and comprehension) as well as pedagogic approaches. For example, the *Literacy* volume's section on storytelling includes step-by-step guides, sample classroom interactions, and ways to expand the activity with a class. Additionally, the *Literacy* volume connects storytelling to literacy skills such as oral language, vocabulary, phonological awareness, understanding of books, knowledge of print, and comprehension (p. 618). Each of the skills identified can be directly linked to both the NAEYC language and literacy standards (NAEYC, 1998) as well as the Common Core State Standards or New Generation English Language Arts Standards.

In aligning ECE curriculum with K-12 standards, we are concerned that social, emotional, and physical development have taken a back seat to some forms of cognitive and language development. Too often, a 4-year-old pre-K classroom looks like first grade with children reciting the alphabet and working on phonemic (letter-sound) coordination worksheets (Miller & Almon, 2009). In High/Scope and Creative Curriculum, this shift in classroom culture is further exacerbated by the links between the curriculum and either national or state standards. The rationale for binding curriculum to standards is based on the perceived need to more easily translate learning and achievement across developmental domains (early and elementary education). However, standardized practices exclude populations of children learning across racially, linguistically, the and culturally diverse contexts as it assumes a universal norm for development. This is particularly problematic in early education where the home community has increased influence. Although streamlining communication across educational contexts seems more efficient, Lipman (1998) notes that "accountability language, practices, social relations and ways of valuing and thinking constitute a discourse of social discipline and subjugation that is highly racialized... legitimate and produce the regulation and control of youth of color" (p. 171). Considering that one-size-fits-all measures continue to exclude the very populations these two programs intended to serve, universalized national and state standards are questionable, if not alarming.

Early childhood education practitioners, policy makers, and researchers have struggled over what curricula in early childhood should look like, weighing lifelong educative benefits against short-term content-specific goals such as generating vocabulary. Both Creative Curriculum and High/Scope have made moves to represent racially, linguistically, and culturally diverse ways of teaching and learning. One way of addressing these discrepancies is through shifting approaches from an achievement gap based on standard notions of achievement to an education debt to better understand the deeper issues connected to curricula. Using the notion of "debt" moves the conversation beyond the performance gap on standardized tests to include the compounding "historical, economic, socio-political and moral components" of inequities over time (Ladson-Billings, 2006). Rather than focus solely on students' failures to "measure up" to universal academic standards, the conversation must address the efficacy of curricula to be implemented across diverse contexts. Given this, we caution against simply connecting Creative Curriculum and High/Scope with state standards through assessment packages and rigor and instead acknowledge the work of teachers, families, and children to represent relevant and meaningful growth across developmental, racial, linguistic, and cultural domains.

English Learners: Teacher Knowledge and Support in Curricula

High/Scope and Creative Curriculum leave a gap between the open curriculum and implementing the best pedagogic practice for English learners and bilingual students. Twenty-three percent of preschool-aged children in the United States are English learners (Friedman-Krauss, Barnett, Weisenfeld, Kasmin, DiCrecchio, & Horowitz, 2018), supporting teacher knowledge of English learners (or dual-language learners) is essential (Souto-Manning & Yoon, 2018). Due to the varying professional development opportunities and teacher education requirements, this important task often falls on curriculum packages. In a previous study (Michael-Luna & Heimer, 2012), we considered how both High/Scope and Creative Curriculum indirectly, and perhaps inadvertently, drew from a deficit perspective on language learning and development. Cultural deficiencies are implied when teachers, administrators, and policy makers attribute the school-based failure of a student, or group of students, as defined through race, culture, language, or socio-economic level, to the student's family or home experience (Valencia, 1997). For example, speaking Spanish at home would be considered an obstruction to the English language and literacy learning goal(s) of the curriculum or standards. Deficit thinking positions monolingual language development as the norm, suggesting that bilingual development in young children is cognitively harmful or that young bilinguals do not develop as quickly as monolinguals. Language acquisition research has long offered evidence that contradicts these perspectives (Bialystok, 2001). While authors of both curricula have decreased comparisons of English learners to students with disabilities and increased research-based knowledge about second language acquisition, some gaps still need to be addressed.

In an earlier edition, Creative Curriculum likened the variations in bilingual development to the variations in children who have disabilities: "Just as children with the same disability may have very different strengths and needs, children learning English as a second language vary greatly" (Dodge, Colker, & Heroman, 2002, p. 38). Dodge et al. (2010) removed this comparison and expanded their text on English- and dual-language learners, citing such key findings on English learners: "Children who develop a sound foundation in their first language are more efficient in learning a second language," and "children transfer concepts and skills that they learn in their first language to their second language" (p. 45). The authors also directly confront "myths about learning a second language," (pp. 44–45) as well as "levels of English language acquisition" (p. 45). Creative Curriculum offers specific English language acquisition learning objectives (Heroman, Burts, Berke, & Bickart, 2010, pp. 163–171), which are coupled with teaching strategies. For example, "Objective 38: Demonstrates progress in speaking English," suggests a continuum (beginning to advancing) as well as guided practices such as "give English-language-learners a chance to respond in English in group situations when they can answer in chorus with all the children," or "be alert to children beginning to use English very softly, perhaps rehearsing what they want to say" (p. 171). Creative Curriculum (Heroman, Burts, Berke, & Bickart, 2010) also includes a home-language survey (p. xx), which scaffolds teacher-thinking on children's home language environment (or who speaks what to whom at home). Creative Curriculum's modified text mitigates the comparison between disability and bilingualism and increases teacher knowledge on second language acquisition.

High/Scope (Epstein, 2014) defines English learners as "fac[ing] the challenge of communicating in two or more tongues simultaneously" (Epstein, 2014, p. 133). By using the word "challenge" High/Scope draws on a deficit model. However, High/Scope has increased the knowledge presented about the stages of English language development (Tabors, 2008), and links language development to culture (Epstein, 2014, p. 146) in order to make specific suggestions for classroom strategies such as, "When possible, pair non-English-speaking children with bilingual peers to help them make the bridge" and encouraging English learners to share home-language songs and books (p. 146). Explicit information about English learners is only found at the end of the chapter on language and literacy development. Rather than integrating strategies and knowledge about English learners into the body of the curriculum Epstein (2014) adds on, such as in the final Key Developmental Indicators for language, literacy, and communication, "30. English language learning: (If applicable) Children use English and their home language(s) (including sign language)" (p. 134).

Additionally, the High/Scope (Kruse, 2006) volume on multicultural programs contained many missed opportunities. Five out of six vignettes presented described young learners who were children of immigrants, but no mention was made of home-language or English language acquisition. For example, one vignette describes a 4-year-old Vietnamese boy as being "shy," but the vignette makes no mention of his home language or the role that English language development might play in his "shyness." Kruse (2006) does make research-based recommendations, not tied to vignettes, such as using body language for communication (p. 20), or offering strategies for "working with parents who do not speak the languages used in the classroom" (p. 52). The curriculum reads as if the primary goal is English language acquisition rather than bilingualism or biliteracy.

Both Creative Curriculum (Dodge et al., 2010) and High/Scope (Epstein, 2014) have improved their support of English learners, including Spanish editions of their curriculum. Both curricula also make an effort to include knowledge on English language learning and young children in their descriptive text; however, the knowledge and support provided is inadequate. Neither curriculum addresses multilingual children who come to preschool speaking two languages and learn a third (or additional) language, nor do they address the benefits of being bilingual or multilingual. The gap between curriculum, teacher knowledge, and pedagogy around English learners is still wide for both Creative Curriculum and High/Scope.

Conclusion

In this chapter, we critically review High/Scope and Creative Curriculum for gaps between policy and embodied implementation in classrooms, specifically, the role of teacher agency within the bounds of open-ended curricula, the emphasis on standards and assessments in early childhood classrooms, and the gap in knowledge on English learners and dual language classrooms. These three areas of concern mirror the larger shifts we are seeing in early education. We began by outlining the complicated nature of "open" curriculum in terms of teacher agency. We described how the tension between curricula, teacher knowledge, and local emphasis on K-12 content area standards create a tension for teachers when implementing the curricula. Next, we explored the ways in which standards, such as the Common Core, are being connected directly to the Creative Curriculum and High/Scope assessments. This illustrates the push down of standardization rather than honoring the strengths of holistic pedagogy and family-centered programs found in early education programs resulting in content areas isolated into silos. Additionally, this has created a lack of support for and recognition of culturally and linguistically diverse learning. Separating knowledge acquisition (meeting standards) from appropriate pedagogy for young children is problematic (Dewey, 1916; Copple & Bredekamp, 2009; Helm & Katz, 2000; Wisneski & Reifel, 2012). In other words, what might be child-centered, culturally relevant packages may be implemented in ways that don't honor the complexity of practice because of the regime of accountability.

We urge teachers, teacher educators, and policy makers to reject the "push down" of standardized curriculum and assessment and instead propose a "push up" of early education approaches that honor diverse home influences. Finally, we revisited and highlighted the continued trend of excluding populations of children, and specifically English learners, as a weakness of packages with an open approach. When implemented, curricula with an open-ended approach, such as High/Scope and Creative Curriculum, may serve to perpetuate dominant culture. For example, offering curricula in English and Spanish versions alone with minimal knowledge on dual language programming or pedagogy does not address the local needs of classrooms serving dual language learners. To remedy this, curriculum must be a source of knowledge for teachers, and thus must be held to a higher standard regarding the understanding and support of significant and at risk portions of the population, such as English learners.

In conclusion, these critiques are not meant to paralyze early educators, policy makers, or advocates. Rather, we believe early childhood educators should be aware of the gaps in open-ended curricula in order to reflectively work on contextually situated solutions that support children and families. Early childhood educators have the opportunity to move beyond a standardized childhood and honor creative, equitable approaches to education and learning. Previous reform efforts in early childhood education have failed to provide sufficient and adequate opportunities for all students to learn, resulting in unequal outcomes for marginalized groups of students, particularly those from low socio-economic backgrounds and English learners who receive what Lipman refers to as an "impoverished curriculum" (1998). Without significant changes in the provision of resources for teaching and learning that honor the complexities of practice, the inequities of the past are likely to continue.

References

Apple, M.W. (2012). *Education and power*. New York: Routledge.
Apple, M.W. (2017). *Cultural and economic reproduction in education: Essays on class, ideology and the state*. New York: Routledge.
Apple, M.W. (2018). *The struggle for democracy in education*. New York: Routledge.
Au, W., & Ferrare, J.J. (Eds.). (2015). *Mapping corporate education reform: Power and policy networks in the neoliberal state*. New York: Routledge.
Barnett, W.S. (1985). Benefit-cost analysis of the Perry Preschool Program and its policy implications. *Educational Evaluation and Policy Analysis*, 7(4), 333–342.

Barnett, W.S. (1996). *Lives in the balance: Age-27 benefit-cost analysis of High/Scope Perry Preschool program*. Ypsilanti, MI: High/Scope Educational Research Foundation.

Beatty, B. (1995). *Preschool education in America: The culture of young children from the colonial era to the present*. London: Yale University Press.

Belfield, C.R., Nores, M., Barnett, W.S., & Schweinhart, L. J. (2006). The High/Scope Perry Preschool program: Cost-benefit analysis using data from the age-40 follow-up. *The Journal of Human Resources*, 41(1), 162–190.

Bialystok, E. (2001). *Bilingualism in development: Language, literacy and cognition*. New York: Cambridge University Press.

Brown, C., Mowry, B., & Feger, B. (2015). Helping others understand academic rigor in teachers' developmentally appropriate practices. *Young Children*, 70(4), 62–69.

Brown, C.P. (2007). It's more than content: Expanding the conception of early learning standards. *Early Childhood Research & Practice*, 9(1). Retrieved April 9, 2019 from http://ecrp.uiuc.edu/v9n1/brown.html

Campbell, F.A., Ramey, C.T., Pungello, E., Sparling, J., & Miller-Johnson, S. (2002). Early childhood education: Young adult outcomes from the Abecedarian Project. *Applied Developmental Science*, 6(1), 42–57.

Choi, J. Y., Elicker, J., Christ, S. L., & Dobbs-Oates, J. (2014). Predicting growth trajectories in early academic learning: Evidence from growth curve modeling with Head Start children. *Early Childhood Research Quarterly*, 36(3): 244–258.

Copley, J., Jones, C., & Dighe, J. (2010). *Creative curriculum for preschool: Volume four mathematics* (5th ed.). Bethesda, MD: Teaching Strategies.

Copple, C., & Bredekamp, S. (2009). *Developmentally appropriate practice in early childhood programs serving children birth through age 8* (3rd ed.). Washington, DC: National Association for the Education of Young Children.

Dahlberg, G., Moss, P., & Pence, A.R. (1999). *Beyond quality in early childhood education and care: Postmodern perspectives*. London: Falmer Press.

Denham, S.A., Bassett, H.H., Zinsser, K., & Wyatt, T.M. (2014). How preschoolers' social–emotional learning predicts their early school success: Developing theory promoting competency based assessments. *Infant and Child Development*, 23(4): 426–454.

Dewey, J. (1916). *Democracy and education*. New York: Macmillan.

Dodge, D., Colker, L., & Heroman, C. (2002). *Creative curriculum for preschool*. (4th ed.) Washington, DC: Teaching Strategies.

Dodge, D., Colker, L., & Heroman, C. (2010). *Creative curriculum for preschool, Volume two: Interest areas*. (5th ed.). Bethesda, MD: Teaching Strategies.

Dodge, D., Heroman, C., Colker, L., & Bickart, T.S. (2010). *Creative curriculum for preschool, Volume one: The foundation*. (5th ed.). Bethesda, MD: Teaching Strategies.

Englund, M.M., White, B., Reynolds, A.J., Schweinhart, L.J., & Campbell, F.A. (2015). Health outcomes of the Abecedarian, Child-Parent Center, and High/Scope Perry preschool programs. In Arthur I. Reynolds, A.T. Rolnick, and J.A. Temple (Eds.), *Health and education in early childhood: Predictors, interventions, and policies* (pp. 257–292). Cambridge University Press.

Epstein, A.S. (2007). *Essentials of active learning in preschool: Getting to know the High/Scope Curriculum*. Ypsilanti, MI: High/Scope Educational Research Foundation.

Epstein, A.S. (2014). *Essentials of active learning in preschool: Getting to know the High/Scope Curriculum*. Ypsilanti, MI: High/Scope Educational Research Foundation.

Erikson, E.H. (1959). *Identity and the life cycle*. New York: International Universities Press.

Erikson, K. (1977). *Everything in its path*. New York, NY: Simon and Schuster.

Friedman-Krauss, A., Barnett, S.W., Weisenfeld, G.G., Kasmin, R., DiCrecchio, N., & Horowitz, M. (2018). *The state of preschool 2017*. New Brunswick, NJ: National Institute for Early Education Research.

Fuller, B. (2007). *Standardized childhood: The political and cultural struggle over early education*. Redwood City, CA: Stanford University Press.

Garcia, J.L., Heckman, J.J., Leaf, D.E., & Prados, M.J. (2017). Quantifying the life-cycle benefits of a prototypical early childhood program. (Working Paper No. 22993). National Bureau of Economic Research. Retrieved on May 24, 2018 from https://heckmanequation.org/resource/lifecycle-benefits-influential-early-childhood-program/

Graf, E., Hernandez, M.W., & Bingham, R.S. (2016). *Preschool predictors of academic achievement in five kindergarten readiness domains: Oral language & literacy, math, science, social-emotional development & approaches to learning*. Chicago, IL: NORC at University of Chicago. Retrieved on May 24, 2018 from http://krfoundation.org/krf/site-content/uploads/2017/05/Kindergarten-Readiness-Predictors-Final-Report-120916.pdf

Heckman, J., Moon, S., Pinto, R., Savelyev, P.A., & Yavitz, A. (2010). The rate of the return to the High/Scope Perry Preschool program. *Journal of Public Economics*, 94(1–2): 114–128.

Heckman, J., Reynolds, M.J., & Henning, S. (2018). *High/Scope Perry Preschool study*. Retrieved on May 27, 2018, from http://www.norc.org/Research/Projects/Pages/highscope-perry-preschool-study.aspx

Helm, J.H., & Katz, L.G. (2000). *Young investigators: The project approach in the early years*. New York: Teachers College Press.

Heroman, C., Burts, D., Berke, K., Bickart, T. (2010). *Creative curriculum for preschool: Volume five objectives for development & learning*. (5th ed.). Bethesda, MD: Teaching Strategies.

Heroman, C., & Jones, C. (2010). *Creative curriculum for preschool, Volume three: Literacy*. (5th ed.). Bethesda, MD: Teaching Strategies.

Holt, N. (2010). *Bringing the High/Scope approach to your early years practice*. New York: Routledge.

Kirp, D. (2007). *The sandbox investment: The preschool movement and kids-first politics*. Cambridge, MA: Harvard University Press.

Kruse, T. (2006). *Building a High/Scope program: Multicultural programs*. Ypsilanti, MI: High/Scope Press.

Ladson-Billings, G. (2006). From the achievement gap to the education debt: Understanding achievement in U.S. schools. *Educational Researcher*, 35(7): 3–12.

Lipman, P. (1998). *Race, class, and power in school restructuring*. Albany: State University of New York Press.

Maslow, A.H. (1943). A theory of human motivation. *Psychological Review*, 50(4), 370–396.

Michael-Luna, S., & Grey, L.J. (2018). Navigating the policy directive of child autonomy in universal pre-kindergarten practice. *Contemporary Issues in Early Childhood*, online publication date: May 8, 2018, 1–12.

Michael-Luna, S., & Heimer, L.G. (2012). Creative Curriculum and High/Scope curriculum. In N. File, J. Mueller, and D. Basler Wisneski (Eds.), *Curriculum in early childhood education: Re-examined, rediscovered, renewed* (pp. 120–132). New York: Routledge.

Miller, E., & Almon, J. (2009). *Crisis in the kindergarten: Why children need to play in school*. College Park, MD: Alliance for Childhood.

Milner, H.R. (2013). *Policy reforms and de-professionalization of teaching*. Boulder, CO: National Education Policy Center. Retrieved from http://nepc.colorado.edu/publication/policy-reforms-deprofessionalization

Moiduddin, E., Kopack Klein, A., Tarullo, L., West, J., & Aikens, N. (2017). *A portrait of Head Start programs: Findings from FACES 2009*. OPRE Report 2017-72.

Washington, DC: Office of Planning, Research and Evaluation, Administration for Children and Families, U.S. Department of Health and Human Services.

National Association for the Education of Young Children (NAEYC) (1998). Learning to read and write: Developmentally appropriate practices for young children: A joint position statement of the International Reading Association and the National Association for the Education of Young Children. *Young Children, 53*(4), 30–46.

National Governors Association Center for Best Practices & Council of Chief State School Officers (2010). *Common Core State Standards*. Washington, DC: Authors.

New York City Department of Education (2018). *Pre-K for all: Policies and resources*. Retrieved on May 24, 2018 from: http://schools.nyc.gov/Academics/EarlyChildhood/educators/UPK.htm

NGSS Lead States (2013). *Next generation science standards: For states, by states*. Washington, DC: The National Academies Press.

Nieto, S. (2009). *Language, culture, and teaching: Critical perspectives*. New York: Routledge.

Piaget, J. (1952). *The origins of intelligence in children*. New York: International Universities Press.

Polakow, V. (2007). *Who cares for our children? The childcare crisis in the other America*. New York: Teachers College Press.

Resnick, M. (2011). Pre-K programs are a long-term investment worth making. *American School Board Journal, 198*(5), 6–7.

Schumacher, R., Hamm, K., & Ewen, D., (2007). Making pre-kindergarten work for low-income working families. *Center for Law and Social Policy Child and Early Education Policy* (5). Retrieved on May 24, 2018 from https://www.clasp.org/publications/report/brief/making-pre-kindergarten-work-low-income-working-families

Souto-Manning, M., & Yoon, H.S. (2018). *Rethinking early literacies: Reading and rewriting worlds*. New York: Routledge.

Sparling, J., Ramey, C.T., & Ramey, S.L. (2007). The Abecedarian experience. In M.E. Young (Ed.), *Early child development—From measurement to action: A priority for growth and equity* (pp. 81–99). Washington, DC: The World Bank.

Spencer, T. (2014). Preschool for all? Examining the current policy context in light of Genishi's research. *Contemporary Issues in Early Childhood, 15*(2), 176–184.

Tabors, P.O. (2008). *One child, two languages: A guide for preschool educators of children learning English as a second language*. Baltimore, MD: Brookes.

Teaching Strategies, LLC (2015). *Teaching strategies*. Retrieved on May 24, 2018 from https://teachingstrategies.com/contact/

Teaching Strategies, LLC (2018). *Teaching strategy alignment*. Retrieved on May 24, 2018 from https://highscope.org/alignments

Tyack, D. (1974). *The one best system*. Cambridge, MA: Harvard University Press.

Valencia, R. (1997). *The evolution of deficit thinking: Educational thought and practice*. Bristal, PA: Falmer Press, Taylor & Francis Inc.

Verdine, B., Irwin, C., Golinkoff, R., & Hirsh-Pasek, K. (2014). Contributions of executive function and spatial skills to preschool mathematics achievement. *Journal of Experimental Child Psychology, 126*(3): 37–51.

Vygotsky, L.S. (1978). *Mind in society: The development of higher psychological processes*. Cambridge, MA: Harvard University Press.

Wisneski, D.B., & Reifel, S. (2012). The place of play in early childhood curriculum. In N. File, J. Mueller, and D. Basler Wisneski (Eds.), *Curriculum in early childhood education: Re-examined, rediscovered, renewed* (pp. 175–187). New York: Routledge.

9
RE-EXAMINING PLAY IN THE EARLY CHILDHOOD CURRICULUM

John A. Sutterby and Deepti Kharod

Introduction

Play is a serious topic in the field of early education. The leading professional organization related to early childhood, the National Association for the Education of Young Children (NAEYC) has a specific strand for issues related to play. The Play Special Interest Group is one of the largest in the NAEYC conference. Play has long been considered as a way for children to learn and has been a part of early curriculum for centuries. Vygotsky (1978), for example, writes,

> Play creates a zone of proximal development of the child. In play a child always behaves beyond his average age, above his daily behavior; in play it is as though he were a head taller than himself. As in the focus of a magnifying glass, play contains all developmental tendencies in a condensed form and is itself a major source of development.
>
> (p. 102)

Play has also been discussed in popular literature as a driver of innovation and creativity (Johnson, 2017), as an antidote to anxiety and self-obsession (Lukianoff & Haidt, 2018), and as a critical concern in the move to universal pre-kindergarten education (Bouffard, 2017).

Unfortunately, there has been a decline in play in educational settings, as well as in home settings, due to a number of factors. This decline in play is having consequences that are being revealed through research (Brown & Patte, 2013). This chapter will go into more detail as to these challenges to play.

According to mainstream educational organizations like NAEYC and Association for Childhood Education International (ACEI), play is considered the best way of providing curriculum for children and is significant in popular culture. However, debate continues on about many aspects of play, including how it leads to learning, how best to implement it, what it actually looks like in the classroom, and whether play and schooling are actually compatible with each other.

This chapter will discuss how play is changing in academic and non-academic contexts. As part of the landscape of children's play, we will discuss the importance of play as part of the curriculum as well as the educator as part of the landscape and the changing materials for play. In addition, this chapter will discuss how play as part of the curriculum has moved into other settings such as children's museums.

Play and Learning

An important frame for the debate about the significance of play is the relationship play has with learning. Historically, major theoretical frameworks have been formed around how play and cognition interact and how this influences what happens in the early childhood classroom. Jean Piaget's theory of developmental constructivism describes play as reflecting a child's current developmental level. This theory has been a foundation of a more hands-off view of children's play, as the experience of the play itself was the foundation for learning. The cognitive stages that children engage in are reflected as children move from sensori-motor activities to symbolic activities to activities that reflect social rules. Educators from this perspective want the curriculum to reflect what the child expresses as a level of development (Fowler, 2017; Reifel & Sutterby, 2009).

Vygotsky (1978) saw play as important for learning as well; indeed, he also suggested (as included in the quotation at the start of this chapter) that play alone can lead to cognitive development. Interpreters of Vygotsky's theories also suggest there is a role for the adult in scaffolding play. Socio-dramatic play is the type of play that Vygotsky was referring to in the previous quote on how children act their ability when engaged in play (Bodrova & Leong, 2015). Nowadays, researchers are making connections between Vygotsky's theoretical models and more recent understandings about how the brain develops and functions (Vandervert, 2017).

Play's critical role in learning is also being recognized as advances in technology have allowed for an examination of the neurological connection between play and the brain. The positive emotional effect of play as well as the therapeutic nature of the activity help reduce stress in the child and allow for greater creativity (Rushton, 2011). Play is an evolved activity that helps the player to develop rapid responses to stimuli. Engaging in play with others requires the player to make predictions and adaptations based on the input from the other player. These interactions improve as the playing brain deeply engages in experiences with others (Vandervert, 2017).

Executive function is another important process that children develop through their play interactions. Executive function is the ability to focus attention, work with long term memory, plan and regulate behaviors, and practice cognitive flexibility. Socio-dramatic play enhances executive functioning as children have to keep reality and pretend separate and also engage in symbolic representations (Bjorkland & Beers, 2016).

Challenges to Play

There have been attempts recently to examine the context around how play is related to early childhood curriculum and how the goals of current early childhood curriculum may not fit with free play. Play-based programs have traditionally been built on the theoretical framework of developmental psychology, which encouraged hands-off approaches to children's play. On the other hand, social policy has focused on a school readiness discourse that is at odds with a hands-off approach. The social policy discourse seeks to control curriculum content and limit variability in educational programs (Wood & Hedges, 2016).

The landscape for children's play is made up of the physical space, the people who occupy this space, adults and children, and also societal attitudes and values about play. This landscape for children's play continues to evolve and change. In examining current literature, the use of play in early childhood can be seen as going in two different directions. In many academic contexts, play has been reduced in favor of more teacher-directed activities, while on the other hand, play is being embraced in contexts outside of traditional schools.

In examining the landscape of play, we investigate first the challenges to play. Wisneski and Reifel (2012) opened their discussion of play in early childhood by discussing this issue. Barriers to play include a growing emphasis on academics, standardized tests, lack of time, and school administration. The tension between play and the curriculum is not a new one. Early advocates of Froebelian kindergartens debated how much free play versus teacher-directed play was appropriate. So strong was the disagreement that a committee of the International Kindergarten Union was unable to find common ground after a ten-year-long process (Kuschner, 2012). The tension between play and schooling has led some to believe that there are irreconcilable differences between play and school. This has led to a change in discourse around play and academics that suggests that the word play should be left out and replaced with terms such as inquiry or serious play.

Accountability and Play

A shift in early childhood education away from early childhood care to more formal educational settings has shifted the discourse of what sorts of activities are appropriate for young children (Gibbons, 2013). Gibbons suggests that the increased emphasis on assessment is having the effect of pushing down curricula into the lower grades as the act of measurement itself encourages educators to engage in activities related to the measurements. The act of measuring encourages homogenization of the curriculum as all children are expected to have a certain set of experiences leading to similar outcomes.

The changing discourse has meant that activities which were once called play time are now referred to as learning time, and play centers have become learning centers or, even more restrictive, desks. Progress reports that were given out to previous generations have become report cards full of academic expectations (Graue, 2011). Play and accountability are often in conflict because it is difficult to measure play. Play does not result in a physical product. It is difficult for teachers to make sure that children are acquiring particular skills. A more scripted curriculum does allow for that type of measurement.

Accountability standards for learning outcomes set up by states have also limited the flexibility teachers have in selecting content and methods of teaching (Trawick-Smith, 2012). The "push down curriculum" has also been part of the conversation for why play is facing a changing landscape in the early childhood classroom. The push down curriculum involves having young children completing tasks which were once thought appropriate for older children (Barblett, Knaus, & Barratt-Pugh, 2016).

Jarrett (2016) explains that how learning looks in the classroom has changed due to accountability. The play materials are removed from the classroom and recess has been eliminated in order to increase test scores: "kindergarten became like first grade" (p. 4). Patte (2012) describes the influence of accountability as a snowball gaining speed and size as it rolls down the hill towards early childhood classrooms. In working with student teachers, Patte found that many cooperating teachers were reluctant to give up control in the classroom and that a reliance on scripted curricula hampered the implementation of playful activities in the classroom.

Teacher Attitudes

Another factor in the decline of play as part of the curriculum are the abilities and attitudes of early childhood educators. Elements of educators' ability to implement a successful play curriculum include the training and knowledge they have about play and their confidence in playful practice. Educators who want to implement playful practice need to have confidence to explain the purpose of play to administrators and parents. This confidence comes from educators' feelings that they have the theoretical and practical knowledge to implement a play curriculum. In many cases educators feel underprepared to implement a play curriculum due to lack of emphasis in their own educational programs (Howard, 2010).

Dockett (2011) found that teachers in her study saw play as learning for young children and an important part of the curriculum. However, they also mentioned using play time as an opportunity for teachers to engage in administrative tasks or work with small groups. Some teachers reported using play as a reward for finishing work. Teachers in this study also indicated there are many barriers to play including an emphasis on academic curriculum, school administration and parental expectations.

One question that is often asked is how educators understand what play means in the classroom. There is a common belief that work and play should be kept separate and that play should occur only after work is completed as a reward for work (Ortlieb, 2010). Preservice teachers' understandings of play have been found to have contradictory attitudes toward play. Sherwood and Reifel (2013) interviewed preservice teachers from a teacher education program. The preservice teachers in the study viewed play as important, however they did not see play as essential in the classroom. The preservice teachers also valued more academic types of activities as more meaningful than play activities. They generally suggested that play is more a break from work and a way to burn off excess energy.

Parent Attitudes

Parents may also be a factor in an increased emphasis on academics over play in early childhood classrooms. What parents view as school readiness may differ from what educators view as significant to this end. Kane (2016) found that parents focused on early literacy and early numeracy skills in evaluating preschool curricula. Although parents reported that they felt play was important, they did not see play as being part of a child's learning. Yahya (2016) also found that immigrant parents showed concern in a play-based program. Their beliefs about learning conflicted with the play curriculum used in some American schools.

Children's Considerations

Children are often left out of discussions of what is meaningful about play in early childhood. Although educators are responsible for monitoring children's play and they set limits on children's play in an educative setting, children often subvert the intentions of adult rules in order to assert their agency into a play situation. They may resist the rules imposed by adults and push the boundaries of what is allowed. Wood (2014) suggests that adult educators should be aware of this agency and should be reflective about the power relationships involved in the classroom play setting.

Children's themes for play often subvert the intentionality of teachers. Teachers frequently limit how children can play in the classroom such as by not permitting games that portray violence and war play, and by stifling rough and tumble play (Lewis, 2017; Katch, 2001; Levin & Carlsson-Paige, 2005). Chen (2009) discusses the "underlife" of children's play. This underlife is the themes of media pop culture, racism, and violence that is often expressed in children's play. The underlife is often suppressed by teachers and forced into illicit play.

Kinard, Gainer, and Soto Huerta (2018) describe a scenario played out in a bilingual preschool where a group of boys in a summer program dressed in cardboard armor and declared they were going to war on anyone speaking Spanish. The developers of the program were devoted to social justice and anti-racism so they were dismayed when such hostility was expressed during free play. Although tempted to jump in and confront the children, they initially held back. This led to a discussion and eventual resolution between the children about the meanings they were trying to convey during play. Teachers, confronted with the themes that children take up, often find ways to suppress this play. Teachers have to make difficult decisions about when to intervene in play and when to step back and observe.

Adults Setting the Stage for Play

We have a long history of creating environments where children can play and learn, based on our understanding about the importance of play for young children and the educational environments that educators create for them. These environments have been influenced by the more than a century of scientific research on children's play and learning. Finally, the theoretical links between play and learning are being reinforced by modern research methods that help us to more closely examine the technical aspects of play and learning.

An important aspect of the changing landscape of play is the role of the educator. The educators' role in play and curriculum has been debated and discussed since play was included in academic settings. The debate centers around the idea that play, under many definitions, requires voluntary participation, freely chosen activities, and an emphasis on process over outcome. This definition of play is often in conflict when considering educational settings, which emphasize intentional teaching (Edwards, 2017).

Generally, the role of the teacher is seen as being on a continuum from "hands-off" to direct play instruction. Hands-off teaching suggests that the child's play needs to be trusted to fulfill the needs of the child. On the other hand, adult interventions in play have been found to improve children's learning outcomes (Trawick-Smith, 2012). Although adult interventions in children's play have shown positive outcomes, adults can also become overly didactic when planning play learning activities, which children may resist (Sutterby, 2005).

Van Oers and Duijkers (2013) provide further details about the types of activities teachers can engage in to enhance socio-dramatic play without interrupting it. They suggest there are five strategies: orienting, structuring and deepening, broadening, contributing, and reflecting. Orienting consists of helping children focus on the background in a dramatic play scenario, for example what types of roles there are in a grocery store theme. Structuring and deepening have the educator helping to set the scene and helping to script the activity by asking questions such as "what does the cashier say to the customer?" Broadening involves making connections between play and other activities in the classroom. For example, teachers may find ways for children to contribute to the scenario by selecting props for the dramatic play center or researching what types of products are found at the store. Contributing involves adding materials that meet the needs of the play scenario, like adding shopping lists or pretend money for the children to count. Finally, reflecting involves asking questions of the children that help them expand on their discourse, by getting them to think more about what is going on in the scenario.

Depending on their background and experience, educators often have conflicting perspectives on play. One such area is on intervention in play. Educators in one study were more hands-off in their play intervention in outdoor environments compared to indoor environments. They took more of a supervisory role while in the outdoor environment due to a number of factors including an emphasis on safety. On the other hand, educators found it easier to work with a small group intentionally indoors as their need to supervise was lessened (Leggett & Newman, 2017).

Media and Technology in Play

Media and technology are increasingly part of the play landscape in early childhood education. Play and technology in the classroom has been controversial since the introduction of televisions in the 1960s and personal computers in the late 1980s. The simple computer games available at that time were frequently criticized for encouraging passive play. With the introduction of touch screen technology into phones and tablets, the debate on the role of technology has shifted.

Recognizing that media and technology surround children everywhere they go, the American Academy of Pediatrics has updated its recommendations on technology use for young children. Rather than rejecting technology use entirely, the Academy recommends that adults watch media with children and that they select high quality media that is creative and engaging. They also recommend that technology not replace physical activity and face-to-face social interactions (American Academy of Pediatrics, 2016). NAEYC has also developed a position statement on technology in the classroom (NAEYC, 2012). It recognizes how media is ubiquitous in today's households and schools as well, and also recommends that media use be mediated by adults. NAEYC further suggests that careful introduction of media can have benefits for young children if the media are used as tools to extend learning and allow for social interaction.

Research investigating the effects of technology on the types of play that children engage in has shown varied results; some have demonstrated negative consequences while others suggest a more nuanced perspective. Nuttall and colleagues (2013) found that while traditional toys did encourage more problem solving during play, familiar commercial and digital elements tapped into children's pre-existing knowledge and experiences from home. For example, a play material may be extended by including a known media figure like Thomas the Tank Engine and providing interactions with digital media associated with the figure. In their study, children engaged in higher levels of a number of factors such as metacognition, humor, and mathematical knowledge with the popular media figures and the digital media. The authors' recommendation was to allow commercial and digital play as part of children's cultural context.

Although digital play is an issue that is currently debated in early childhood practice, unfortunately, most research on digital play has either focused on older learners or has not included the growing access to more recent technological innovations like tablets and smart phones (Waller, 2011). Waller suggests that digital play can be transformative in that technology can lead to children being the "experts" of their play and it allows for the development of new forms of play that would not be possible without technology.

This commercialization and emphasis on popular media is concerning to educators. Commercially based media products such as toys based on cartoon characters are a large source of profit for corporations. These toys can limit children's creative play through limiting the possible narratives that can be attached to the toy (Lewis, 2017).

As technology continues to change, educators will also have to continue to update their knowledge and understandings about how to use it in play-based learning. Decisions will have to be made about what technology to include, how much time children will use it, and how it can be equitably distributed.

Alternative Places for Play

We often consider play in early childhood education through the lens of more or less formal educational settings such as Head Start, preschools, and child care centers. Even as barriers to play and curriculum have been identified, many educators are working to create more play opportunities for children, like children's museums and nature preschools. Frost (2010) suggests this is related to a new child saving movement that recognizes the importance of play and sets out to find alternative spaces for it. Efforts are being made to introduce play into settings where play was previously not encouraged. This includes settings that encourage unschooling, or in non-traditional schools such as nature preschools and non-formal educational spaces such as museums, specifically children's museums and summer school programs which are often free of many of the constraints of formal education settings. Unfortunately, many of these opportunities are primarily offered to children of a generally higher socioeconomic class.

Unschooling

Unschooling is a growing trend found in the homeschooling movement, as well as in a number of non-traditional schools. The emphasis of the unschooling movement is that children should learn the significant social and cultural knowledge that directly applies to the real world. Children in the unschooling movement directly learn through their interests and experiences using a democratic process (Ricci, 2011).

Unschooling programs suggest that learning is the learner's responsibility and that forced learning is inefficient because unmotivated learners do not apply themselves to the task. These programs and families embrace "unlimited freedom to play, explore, and pursue one's own interests" (Gray, 2016, p. 78). Children in these programs have access to real tools with which they are allowed to play, such as computers. Adults are discouraged from interfering in children's play (Hewitt, 2014).

In homeschooling and non-traditional schools, there is also the opportunity for cross-age play, which is often not the case in traditional schools. This allows for the passing of knowledge of play and games from one generation to the next. The scaffolding that older players provide to younger players in following rules, maintaining attention, and considerations of strategy, helps the younger player to play at a higher level than if they were left with only same-age play partners. Meanwhile, older players learn to be good guides and have the opportunity to be caring elders. Participation in an unschooling home or school has been correlated with high academic success for children who have the resources to participate in these activities (Gray, 2016).

Nature Preschools

While teachers at many traditional schools struggle to fit play into their schedules, at a new and rapidly emerging type of American school, the entire curriculum is centered on learning outdoors, often using a play-based approach. Nature-based schools, which are especially popular for young children, were initially modeled after European forest kindergarten schools. The first nature preschool in the US is thought to have opened in 1966, and there has been a sharp growth in their numbers recently, from about 24 in 2012 to 250 in 2017 (Bailie, 2012; NAAEE, 2017). The vignette that follows illustrates how a 5-year-old boy at a nature preschool solidifies his learning about animals through play (Kharod, 2017).

At circle time one week, the teacher talked about classifying animals by their diets (herbivores, carnivores, and omnivores); for 5-year-old Grady, these ideas seemed to solidify into understandings as he applied and developed them through play. In one of his favorite games, Dinosaur Babies, he usually was a T-Rex. As Grady and his friend Antonio (a triceratops) pretended to be dinosaurs, they used what they knew about dinosaurs to define their roles ("Are you a plant-eater?") and engaged in behaviors (movements, sounds) that they considered appropriate to their chosen dinosaurs.

The large rocks, open spaces, and trees at their nature preschool provided ample affordances to climb, hide, run, chase, and forage – activities they felt were befitting a baby dinosaur, while they stretched and squealed. Furthermore, Grady used the unstructured time in nature to pause during the game to notice details such as the heights of trees, sizes of leaves, and availability of rocks and sticks in a given habitat. Whether the theme of his pretend play was cops and robbers, cheetahs, or dinosaurs, the natural supplies of the setting supplied the props.

Many researchers agree that children need nature play – the kind that involves spending the blocks of unstructured time outdoors available to Grady and Antonio, not simply participating in organized athletic activity – for holistic wellness and growth (Louv, 2008; Nabhan & Trimble, 1994; Pyle, 2003; Wilson, 2010). The benefits include fitness and health, spiritual growth, and development across multiple domains: cognitive, social-emotional, aesthetic, and physical (Acar & Torquati, 2015; Bell & Dyment, 2008; Faber Taylor & Kuo, 2011; Kellert, 2002, 2012). Children may learn skills and facts through formal teaching, but it is in play that they apply and practice what they learn, make discoveries, and deepen their connection with nature to develop a caring relationship with it (Kharod, 2017). The effects of childhood experiences in nature are known to persist through adulthood (Chawla, 2007), making it all the more important that young children have ample opportunities to learn through nature-based play.

In terms of materials and spaces, nature preschools typically spend from 25 percent to 100 percent of the school day outdoors (NAAEE, 2017), in areas that children perceive as "minimally managed by adults" (Charlton, personal communication, 2018). Nature preschools' curricula vary considerably, partly because more than 70 percent are developed by school staff, who are expected to be knowledgeable and experienced in the areas of environmental and early childhood education (NAAEE, 2017). The variety in curricula also comes from a focus on local places due to a belief that when children build relationships with their local, familiar environment, they develop a deeper and more enduring connection to nature and are more likely to act to protect it in the long run (Heerwagen & Orians, 2002; Kellert, 2002; Pyle, 2003).

Children's Museums

Another non-traditional but high-growth space devoted to play and learning is the children's museum, which emerged during the early 19th century in response to then-new ideas that children learn by doing and that adults should act as facilitators to support them (Mayfield, 2005). In her guide to US children's museums, Cleaver (1992) wrote, "It's not at all a coincidence that this country's first children's museums (in Brooklyn, Boston, Detroit, and Indianapolis) were founded between 1899 and 1925, when Dewey's and Montessori's theories were initially popular" (p. 8). A new wave of growth occurred in the 1960s, spurred by Piaget's ideas about play and children's development and through the work of Michael Spock at the Boston Children's Museum. A group of teachers established that museum in 1913 and invited children not just to interact with its exhibits, but to help create them (Boston Children's Museum [BCM], n.d.). As its director from 1961 to 1985, Spock is credited with having reinvented children's museums as spaces (Herz, 2017; Mayfield, 2005) where objects were taken "out of cases and into children's hands" (BCM, n.d.).

Although "play is a central, defining concept for children's museums" (Luke, Letourneau, Rivera, Brahms, & May, 2017, p. 37), the tensions around play that exist in American society and public discourse have affected how children's museums envision their identities too. While they value learning through play, many feel the pressure of catering to the academic skills and standards that drive public education (Luke et al., 2017). Even as children's museums reinvent themselves to cater to age groups from infants through school-aged children, their popularity remains high – by the end of 2015, the US had more than 500 (Institute of Museum and Library Services, 2015).

Summer School Programs

Another example of attempts to get around strict school-based guidelines with academic curriculums is to have programs outside of school that emphasize play. Examples of these programs include a university-based summer project paired with school children to create a play-based summer program. Kinard, Gainer, and Huerta (2018) describe a bilingual summer program that emphasizes children's play and that challenges traditional ideas about how play based programs should be set up. They describe their work as activist and transformational. The freedom allowed by working in a summer program rather than an academic one allowed them to reorganize classrooms. As part of the transformation, children were free to move from class to class or to the outdoors as it pleased them. This removal of barriers challenged the hierarchy of schools and teachers and children.

Because this program was set up over the summer, the organizers of the program also had flexibility in how classrooms were set up. Instead of following the traditional layout of having centers like blocks and dramatic play, whole classrooms were devoted to one area or another. One classroom was devoted to art, another to dramatic play, another to blocks, and one to storytelling. This over-the-top focus on these content areas was made possible by the fact that the regular curriculum was suspended during the summer.

A similar program set up at another university also centered around how stepping out of the traditional classroom allowed for greater freedom to play and more opportunities for movement. Children engaged in meaningful outdoor play in the natural environment of the university that did not have a focus on fixed playground equipment. Children were encouraged to engage in extended deep play that continued from one day to the next. The documentation of this environment demonstrated that although no central curriculum was followed, the children demonstrated high levels of engagement in meaningful play. This program also framed their purpose around issues of social justice for children who do not have opportunities to play in their traditional academic programs (Durham, 2018).

Areas for Growth

Both nature-based schools and children's museums offer valuable alternate spaces for play-based learning; however, these spaces are often not equally accessible to all American children. The unschooling movement is mostly available to families who are able to financially afford either a non-traditional education or homeschooling. Research clearly shows that children who participate in these places do not reflect the nation's diversity in terms of race, ethnicity, and language, socio-economic background, and special needs (Farrell & Medvedeva, 2010; NAAEE, 2017).

Jarrett, Sutterby, DeMarie, and Stenhouse (2015) have been presenting at the NAEYC conference on play and social justice for many years. The focus on these presentations has been on inequitable access to play based on race and social class. Unequal school and park funding also based on race and social class has led to differences in environments for play as well as opportunities for play. Although these differences have been identified, there has been little movement from a policy perspective to rectify these deficiencies.

Conclusion

There is no doubt that humans are made to play. Understanding what play means for the child and how play might benefit the child is something that continues to be discussed. Play in the classroom continues to be promoted even when challenged by more teacher-directed activities. In addition, the materials for play, especially technology, are changing and will require continued examination to determine the effects on children. Finally, play is being introduced outside of the traditional classroom, so that it can be adapted to all sorts of environments. In all of these aspects a re-examining of play is required.

References

Acar, I., & Torquati, J. (2015). The power of nature: Developing prosocial behavior toward nature and peers through nature-based activities. *Young Children*, 70(5), 62–71.

American Academy of Pediatrics (2016). Media and young minds. *Pediatrics*, 138(5), 1–6. doi:10.1542/peds.2016-2591

Bailie, P.E. (2012). *Connecting children to nature: A multiple case study of nature center preschools* (Doctoral dissertation). Available from ProQuest Dissertations and Theses database. (Order No.: 3546594)

Barblett, L., Knaus, M., & Barratt-Pugh, C. (2016). The pushes and pulls of pedagogy in the early years: Competing knowledges and the erosion of play-based learning. *Australasian Journal of Early Childhood*, 41(4), 36–43.

Bell, A.C., & Dyment, J.E. (2008). Grounds for health: The intersection of green school grounds and health-promoting schools. *Environmental Education Research*, 14(1), 77–90. doi:10.1080/13504620701843426

Bjorkland, D., & Beers, C. (2016). The adaptive value of cognitive immaturity: Applications of evolutionary developmental psychology to early education. In C. Geary & D. Berch (Eds.) *Evolutionary perspectives on child development and education*, (pp. 3–32). New York: Springer.

Bodrova, E., & Leong, D.J. (2015). Vygotskian and post-Vygotskian views on children's play. *American Journal of Play*, 7(3), 371–388.

Boston Children's Museum (n.d.). History. Retrieved from www.bostonchildrensmuseum.org/about/history

Bouffard, S. (2017). *The most important year: Prekindergarten and the future of our children*. New York: Avery.

Brown, F., & Patte, M. (2013). *Rethinking children's play*. London: Bloomsbury.

Chawla, L. (2007). Childhood experiences associated with care for the natural world: A theoretical framework for empirical results. *Children, Youth, and Environments*, 17, 144–170.

Chen, R. (2009). *Early childhood identity: Construction, culture and the self*. New York: Peter Lang.

Cleaver, J. (1992). *Doing children's museums: A guide to 265 hands-on museums*. Charlotte, VT: Williamson Publishing Co.

Dockett, S. (2011). The challenge of play for early childhood educators. In S. Rogers (Ed.) *Rethinking play and pedagogy in early childhood education* (pp. 32–47). New York: Routledge.

Durham, S. (2018). *Unleashing the power of documentation: Making visible the advantages when children just play*. Paper presented at the annual conference for The Association for the Study of Play, Melbourne, Florida.

Edwards, S. (2017). Play-based learning and intentional teaching: Forever different? *Australasian Journal of Early Childhood*, 42(2), 4–11. http://dx.doi.org/10.23965/AJEC.42.2.01

Faber Taylor, A., & Kuo, F.E. (2011). Could exposure to everyday green spaces help treat ADHS? Evidence from children's play settings. *Applied Psychology: Health and Well-Being*, 3(3), 281–303.

Farrell, B., & Medvedeva, M. (2010). *Demographic transformation and the future of museums*. Washington, D.C.: American Association of Museums.

Fowler, C. (2017). Reframing the debate about the relationship between learning and development: An effort to resolve dilemmas and reestablish dialogue in a fractured field. *Early Childhood Education Journal*, 45(2), 155–162. doi:10.1007/s10643-10015-0770-x

Frost, J. (2010). *A history of children's play and play environments*. New York: Routledge.

Gibbons, A. (2013). In the pursuit of unhappiness: The 'measuring up' of early childhood education in a seamless system. *Educational Philosophy and Theory*, 45(5), 502–508. doi.org/10.1111/j.1469–5812.2012.00855.x

Graue, E. (2011). Are we paving paradise? In our rush to promote achievement we've forgotten how five year olds really learn. *Educational Leadership*, 68(7), 12–17.

Gray, P. (2016). Children's natural ways of educating themselves still work: Even for the three Rs. In D. Geary & D. Berch (Eds.), *Evolutionary perspectives on child development and education. Evolutionary psychology* (pp. 67–93). New York: Springer. doi-org.libweb.lib.utsa.edu/10.1007/978-3-319-29986-0_3

Heerwagen, J.H., & Orians, G.H. (2002). The ecological world of children. In P.H. Kahn Jr. & S.R. Kellert (Eds.), *Children and nature: Psychological, sociocultural, and evolutionary investigations* (pp. 29–63). Cambridge, MA: The MIT Press.

Herz, R.S. (2017). Children's museums: A look back at the literature. *Curator: The Museum Journal*, 60(2), 143–150.

Hewitt, B. (2014). *Home grown*. Boston, MA: Roost Books.

Howard, J. (2010). Early years practitioners' perceptions of play: An exploration of theoretical understanding, planning and involvement, confidence and barriers to practice. *Educational & Child Psychology*, 27(4), 91–102.

Institute of Museum and Library Services (2015). *Museum universe data file FY 2015 Q3* [Data file]. Retrieved from: https://data.imls.gov/d/et8i-mnha/visualization

Jarrett, O. (2016). The state of play in the USA: Concerns and hopeful trends. *International Journal of Play*, 5(1), 4–7.

Jarrett, O.S., Sutterby, J., DeMarie, D., & Stenhouse, V. (2015). Children's play opportunities are not equitable: Access to quality play experiences as a social justice issue. *Spotlight on Play*. Washington, DC: National Association for the Education of Young Children.

Johnson, S. (2017). *Wonderland: How play made the modern world*. New York: Riverhead Books.

Kane, N. (2016). The play-learning binary: U.S. Parents' perceptions on preschool play in a neoliberal age. *Children and Society*, 30(4), 290–301. doi:10.1111/chso.12140

Katch, J. (2001). *Under deadman's skin: Discovering the meaning of children's violent play*. Cambridge, MA: Beacon Press.

Kellert, S.R. (2002). Experiencing nature: Affective, cognitive, and evaluative development in children. In P.H. Kahn Jr. & S.R. Kellert (Eds.), *Children and nature: Psychological, sociocultural, and evolutionary investigations* (pp. 117–151). Cambridge, MA: The MIT Press.

Kellert, S.R. (2012). *Birthright: People and nature in the modern world*. New Haven, CT: Yale University Press.

Kharod, D. (2017). *Caring and biophilia in a nature-based preschool: A multiple case study of young children's engagement with nature*. (Doctoral dissertation). Available from ProQuest Dissertations and Theses database. (Order No.: 10681562.)

Kinard, T., Gainer, J., & Soto Huerta, M.E. (2018). *Power play: Explorando y empujando fronteras en una escuela en Texas through a multilingual play-based early learning curriculum*. New York: Peter Lang.

Kuschner, D. (2012). Play is natural to childhood but school is not: The problem of integrating play into the curriculum. *International Journal of Play*, 1(3), 242–249.

Leggett, N., & Newman, L. (2017). Play: Challenging educators' beliefs around play in indoor and outdoor environments. *Australasian Journal of Early Childhood*, 42(1), 24–32.

Levin, D., & Carlsson-Paige, N. (2005). *The war play dilemma: What every parent and teacher needs to know*, 2nd edition. New York: Teachers College Press.

Lewis, P. (2017). The erosion of play. *International Journal of Play*, 6(1), 10–23.

Louv, R. (2008). *Last child in the woods*. Chapel Hill, NC: Algonquin Books of Chapel Hill.

Luke, J.L., Letourneau, S.M., Rivera, N.R., Brahms, L., & May, S. (2017). Play and children's museums: A path forward or a point of tension? *Curator: The Museum Journal*, 60(1), 37–46.

Lukianoff, G., & Haidt, J. (2018). *The coddling of the American mind: How good intentions and bad ideas are setting up a generation for failure*. New York: Penguin Press.

Mayfield, M.I. (2005). Children's museums: Purposes, practices and play? *Early Child Development and Care*, 175(2), 179–192. doi:10.1080/0300443042000230348

Nabhan, G.P., & Trimble, S. (1994). *The geography of childhood: Why children need wild places*. Boston: Beacon Press.

National Association for the Education of Young Children (NAEYC) (2012). *Technology and interactive media as tools in early childhood programs serving children from birth through age eight*. Retrieved from www.naeyc.org/resources/topics/technology-and-media

North American Association for Environmental Education (NAAEE) (2017). *Nature preschools and forest kindergartens: 2017 national survey*. Washington, DC: NAAEE.

Nuttall, J., Edwards, S., Lee, S., Wood, E., & Mantilla, A. (2013). The implications of young children's digital-consumerist play for changing the kindergarten curriculum. *Cultural-Historical Psychology*, 6(2), 54–63.

Ortlieb, E. (2010). The pursuit of play within the curriculum. *Journal of Instructional Psychology*, 37(3), 241–246.

Patte, M. (2012). Implementing a playful pedagogy in a standards-driven curriculum: Rationale for action research in teacher education. In L. Cohen & S. Waite-Stupiansky(Eds.) *Play: A polyphony of research, theories, and issues*, (pp. 67–89). New York: University Press of America.

Pyle, R.M. (2003). Nature matrix: Reconnecting people and nature. *Oryx*, 37(2), 206–214. doi:10.1017/S0030605303000383

Reifel, S., & Sutterby, J. (2009). Play theory and practice in contemporary classrooms. In S. Feeney, A. Galper, & C. Seefeldt (Eds.), *Continuing issues in early childhood education*, (pp. 238–257). Upper Saddle River, NJ: Merrill.

Ricci, C. (2011). Unschooling and the willed curriculum. *Encounter*, 24(3), 45–48.

Rushton, S. (2011). Neuroscience, early childhood education and play: We are doing it right! *Early Childhood Education Journal*, 39, 89–94. doi:10.1007/s10643-10011-0447-z

Sherwood, S.A.S., & Reifel, S. (2013). Valuable and unessential: The paradox of preservice teachers' beliefs about the role of play in learning. *Journal of Research in Childhood Education*, 27, 267–282.

Sutterby, J. (2005). "I wish we could do whatever we want!": Children subverting scaffolding in the preschool classroom. *Journal of Early Childhood Teacher Education*, 25, 349–357.

Trawick-Smith, J. (2012). Teacher-child play interactions to achieve learning outcomes. In R. Pianta, S. Barnett, L. Justice, and S. Sheridan (Eds.) *Handbook of early childhood education*, (pp. 259–277). New York: The Guilford Press.

Van Oers, B., & Duijkers, D. (2013). Teaching in a play-based curriculum: Theory, practice and evidence of the developmental education of young children. *Journal of Curriculum Studies*, 45(4), 511–534. https://doi.org/10.1080/00220272.2011.637182

Vandervert, L. (2017). Vygotsky meets neuroscience: The cerebellum and the rise of culture through play. *American Journal of Play*, 9(2), 202–227.

Vygotsky, L. (1978). The role of play in development. In *Mind in society* (pp. 92–104). (Trans. M. Cole). Cambridge, MA: Harvard University Press.

Waller, T. (2011). Digital play in the classroom. In S. Rogers (Ed.) *Rethinking play and pedagogy in early childhood education* (pp. 139–151). New York: Routledge.

Wilson, R.A. (2010). Goodness of fit: Good for children and for the earth. In J.L. Hoot & J. Szente (Eds.), *The earth is our home: Children caring for the environment* (pp.17–36). Olney, MD: Association for Childhood Education International.

Wisneski, D., & Reifel, S. (2012). The place of play in early childhood curriculum. In N. File, J. Mueller, & D. Wisneski (Eds.) *Curriculum in early childhood education: Re-examined, rediscovered, renewed* (pp. 175–187). New York: Routledge.

Wood, E. (2014). Free choice and free play in early childhood education: Troubling the discourse. *International Journal of Early Years Education*, 22(1), 4–18. doi.org/10.1080/09669760.2013.830562

Wood, E., & Hedges, H. (2016). Curriculum in early education: Critical questions about content, coherence, and control. *The Curriculum Journal*, 27(3), 387–405. doi.org/10.1080/09585176.2015.1129981

Yahya, R. (2016). Bridging home and school: Understanding immigrant mothers' cultural capital and concerns about play-based learning. *Early Years: Journal of International Research & Development*, 36(4), 340–352. doi:10.1080/09575146.2015.1110786

10

A STORY ABOUT STORY

The Promise of Multilingual Children and Teachers and a Framework for Integrated Curriculum

Elizabeth P. Quintero

This is a story about learning from and with teachers, children, and their communities. My ongoing research and pedagogy have a focus on storying. The story of this chapter comes from multilingual children and their student teachers who have led the research documenting stories through integrated curriculum to build new learning (Quintero, 2015; Quintero & Rummel, 2014). The stories of adults and the children with whom they work are from their lived experiences, and they nudge our thinking about aspects of child development and learning. Stories create the spaces for an integrated curriculum – that then allow for more story. And then story becomes the integrated curriculum of the classroom.

Wisdom comes from learners of all ages and backgrounds. Expertise comes from a 3-year-old who explains, "He be-s [sic] mean to me, but I want him to like me." And also through a student teacher who said, "It is important to learn what others have found and concluded. But nothing beats personally working with these kids and firsthand verifying that what one is reading in academia is true." And through a Nigerian woman, who'd escaped from jail in Libya and swam to the Italian shore when the rubber raft sank, who explained, "It's never easy staying alive, learning new languages, and studying with people I don't always like." We all compile our stories, live our lives, in a "curriculum" of life. Children tell stories through pretending and share their "stories" with others. There are authentic riches in the processes and products of this storytelling. We can support this storying and the developing of a curriculum through the storytelling that can build upon the assets, strengths, and riches of communities that have provided the basis for young children's ways of knowing.

In my work as a teacher educator, I have been allowed to observe how as the student teachers interact with, observe, and develop relationships with children. The student teachers and the children exchange stories that emerge differently in each classroom, connecting and weaving with each other in a multitude of ways. This approach focuses on making connections for teacher education students about young children's learning and for young children to guide their own learning. This provides opportunities for inclusivity in pedagogy and reflects young children's lives in context so that they can build upon their own rich family history and use their home languages while in the process of learning English. Curriculum is everything in a child's life. It is the whole picture, and it begins with the earliest memories.

What Is Integrated Curriculum?

Many early childhood specialists, as we work with diverse children and families, are committed to the importance of including multilingual communication and multi-literacies in our work with young children (and those learning to become teachers of these children). We have found time and again in our research that story, as a basis for the framework of an integrated curriculum, provides rich and generative possibilities for learning. This includes all subject matter content supported by a foundation built upon multiple languages, family history, and cultural and political realities. Using story encourages thinking about language, literacy, and learning as dynamic systems that exist in familiar (to the learners) dimensions.

Even in these familiar dimensions of language and literacy, spaces in between two points can create a third space between incongruous polarizations where new intersections become possible. I found "third spaces" (Bhabha, 2004) in early childhood learning by listening to the power of stories with/in integrated curriculum. In my work I have found it key that these spaces encourage opportunities to use families' home languages and varied histories to support learning and literacy in target languages. This also means that the lives and experiences of the children become part of the official curriculum of the classroom.

Integrated Curriculum connects different areas of study, cuts across content areas, and emphasizes unifying concepts. Nelson (2009) considered experience and meanings as they occur in the social and cultural worlds of young children. In the context of each child's individual self-organization, meanings intersect and interact in dynamic, cyclical ways. Dahlberg, Moss, and Pence (2013) note the importance of lived experiences and stress that in order to avoid silencing some learners' voices we must listen to stories that may be different from our own. The integrated curriculum framework allows for the dynamism of story and the third space.

The stories shared in this chapter, of teacher education students and the children and families they worked with, concretize the advice of Dahlberg et al. and an integrated curriculum can provide the structure for this learning. And it is through the stories in the integrated curriculum framework that we have studied that the need for expanded theoretical positions arose. These included key perspectives from outside our traditional early childhood foundations. Guiding perspectives came from theoretical frameworks aligned with current realities for children in the United States and worldwide.

This approach to teaching and building a dynamic curriculum is complex. Yet with a focus on stories, there are openings for meaning-making through multiple subject areas, in multiple languages addressing the past histories and present-day realities of children, families, and student teachers. Story as pedagogy and research enables all participants to be researchers; the student teachers and the children join in our "complicated conversation" (Pinar, 2004) that is integrated curriculum. This is important because the research is generated by the storytellers living their lives. No voices are silenced. I see it as Freire's (1985) insistence on the responsibility for participation in critical pedagogy. Learners of all ages, all histories, and all levels of education have stories to tell from which everyone can learn. Story in early learning, and the holistic weaving of context, culture, affect, and cognition, are necessary for learners of all ages to be the masters of their own learning journeys. This premise illustrates the three tenets of critical theory: participatory responsibility, multiple sources of knowledge, and transformative action (Freire, 1985). This premise has led us – while standing on the foundational importance of critical theories, and child development theories – to a study of integrated curriculum through additional theoretical frameworks.

This research, built on story, has led to three important theoretical perspectives that have shaped and influenced the approaches to integrated curriculum that I see as key to an inclusive and generative learning environment for all young children – and student teachers. These perspectives are: 1) a focus on family history, including Conocimiento Theory (Anzaldúa, 2002) and critical perspectives of place; 2) the disruption of outdated child development theories (Nelson, 2009); and, 3) the overlapping attention to cultures and languages through integrated curriculum and stories leading to Matters of Concern (Latour, 2004).

In our work, as university students study in their teacher education program, the importance of story in learning is stressed. Student teachers reflect on their own family history to emphasize the meaning-making involved in learning. Student teachers also listen to children through their pretend play which reveals their own stories about their ongoing making sense of the world. Multicultural children's literature also puts stories at the center of integrated curriculum. And children writing their own stories in narrative form (in their home languages and in target languages) becomes a way to generate meaningful integrated learning. Multiple studies on this work (Quintero, 2015; Quintero & Rummel, 2014) have documented richness of collaborations among researchers, teachers, and children.

The stories highlighted here include family history and current lived experience, told through multiple languages, with a mixture of fact and legend. All learners are informed by fact and fiction, and children are experts at using fantasy to analyze reality in their worlds. Data are enriched by the very nature of who our participants are, where they live and work, and the number of them who have experienced migration. Whether families migrate from one country to another seeking a better life, fleeing violence and war or famine, children are living their lives amidst a reality of struggle. Many participants, both children and adult student teachers, are living and studying in the Global North (the United States), and they brought with them generations of family history, knowledge, linguistic backgrounds, and lived experiences from the Global South (Mexico, Central and South America, the Philippines, Southeast Asia, the Middle East). Their stories have created a third space (Bhabha, 2004) where choice between one language and another isn't necessary and where historical experiences can be built upon. What appears in the third space is informative, inclusive, and inspiring. This third space is integrated curriculum at its finest. We listen to children and student teachers use their own languages and ways of thinking in order for the integrated curriculum to be generative and authentic.

Carrying Our Roots: A Third Space through Integrated Curriculum

A beloved poet showed us ways personal and community stories can engage learners in integrated study of life, through multiple languages. The late poet and elementary school teacher Francisco X. Alarcón (2005) explained experiences of multinational, multilingual learners through his poetry. He was born in Los Angeles, California, and he considered himself "bi-national." Throughout his life he spent time in both Mexico and the United States with extended family and friends. His poetry was inspired by stories he heard from his grandmother and by experiences he had growing up. He highlighted these important aspects of his life in his bilingual poetry for children. In one poem he uses metaphor to show the importance of family history. He wrote, "I carry my roots with me all the time/Rolled up I use them as my pillow" (2005, p. 3). He always wrote and presented his poetry in both Spanish and English. This approach to learning, life, loved ones, and struggle is reflected through student teachers' and children's stories. The idea of "carrying our roots" from one world to another creates a third space where the "roots" become a metaphorical "pillow" to enlighten us throughout our lives.

In my pedagogy, early childhood student teachers begin studying integrated curriculum by focusing on their own family histories. One student remembering her metaphorical "pillow" of her family roots, wrote a journal entry about ways that factual autobiographies of her elders and folktales from their home country were meaningful to her.

> I remember that my family had a lot of books, but not children's books. My grandfather and I had very good relationship and we are still very close. When I was young, we used to live together as a big family. It was always the nighttime, when I was going to bed, he told me the folktales. He didn't have a book. It was folktales that he knew from a long time ago. Those stories were amazing. I imagined all the characters, and I imagined all the

happenings that came out of my grandfather's mouth. While I was thinking about the story, I fell into sleep and dreamed about it.

On the other hand, my grandmother used to tell me her real-life stories. For her, it was real, but for me, it was a tale. She lived in a completely different society from mine. She talked about her house, school, family, marriage, and the Korean war. It was all about her. However, it was also a culture and history lesson for me. Every night, I begged for a story from them. Oftentimes they said, "I already told you about that story, didn't I?" I replied, "Yes, but that's okay, I can listen one more time. . . ." I still remember every single story and moment that we shared.

(Quintero, 2009, p. 83)

The student teacher, through her memories of family stories, put together factual, historical stories with ancient cultural legends from her Korean family history to realize how the stories influenced and supported her learning as a young child.

In pedagogy with integrated curriculum, as I mentioned earlier, I rely on Pinar's (2004) idea of curriculum as a complicated conversation.

> The complicated conversation that is the curriculum requires interdisciplinary intellectuality, erudition, and self-reflexivity. This is not a recipe for high test scores, but a common faith in the possibility of self-realization and democratization, twin projects of social subjective reconstruction.
>
> (p. 8)

"Complicated conversations" frame the discussions in our university classes, and later, the research questions, and finally, the patterns of interrelated themes of research findings. As stated earlier, all our stories are complicated and at the same time factual and metaphorical. When we have space to give and receive the stories, meaning-making is authentic. Integrated curriculum, through personal story through multicultural literature, and through children's use of multilingual narrative in writing, encourages all areas of curriculum while we intentionally strive for "self-realization and democratization" (Pinar, 2004, p. 8). In other words, the student teachers and children become researchers by informing us of their histories and cultural ways of knowing. This becomes our integrated curriculum – both for the adult student teachers in their university class and for the children whom they work with.

Both the student teachers and the children are encouraged to use their home languages in their learning. Sociolinguistic research, and now neuroscience (Kuhl, 2014), verifies that the brains of babies and young children can support multilingual development. Kuhl's research confirms that all ages of multilingual learners have cognitive gains and more cognitive flexibility than monolingual learners. People who reside on geographical borders where two, three, or more languages are spoken learn all the languages. Often, they learn each language separately and sometimes code-switch between the languages. The acquisition of multiple languages happens "unevenly" and with different timing, but acquisition is always progressing. Integrated curriculum that is story-based is flexible in ways to support literacy skills in two or more languages. Furthermore, when families and children have histories in one philosophical tradition and then migrate to a different place with different traditions, they choose to keep the learning from their past while learning new traditions. These differing histories and lived experiences come to light in many ways through stories shared within integrated curriculum.

Also, stories problematize some aspects of deficit conceptions of children and families and the resulting learning experiences for them (Hérnandez-Ávila & Anzaldúa, 2010; Nelson, 2009; Quintero & Rummel, 2014). These conceptions of children and families influence the institutional systems, the pedagogies, and daily life realities of all learners. This is especially true for learners who are immigrants and those who are currently migrating through uncertain global landscapes. Stories in integrated curriculum provide for inclusion of positive aspects of unfamiliar cultures and lived experience so the information can be respected and learned from – without being framed in a deficit model. Stories from my work reveal patterns of findings that provide information for educators in a world of changing demographics.

Contexts and Stories

Contexts are crucial to explaining the complex conversations of stories and integrated curriculum. In my research, stories have been generated by early childhood teacher education students and the children they work with in early childhood programs in California. Many adult students and children are bi-national (Quintero, 2015), and their histories and current lived experiences reflect communities around the world where intergenerational participants of two or more cultures and language groups with different economic and political histories find themselves living and learning together.

Teacher education students described here were in an early childhood studies program student teaching with children (ages 4 to 8) in preschools and primary schools (pre-Kindergarten to third grade). More than half of the student teachers described were first generation college students, and a large percentage of them from families and communities of migrant farmworkers in California (Quintero, 2015). These participants have truly lived bi-culturally with loved ones located in Mexico and Central America.

Similar to the student teachers, many children in early education programs in our county are from Mexico and Central America, and many are Mixtec, an indigenous group from Oaxaca, Mexico. Mixtec children come to preschool speaking their home language of Mixteco. They are learning Spanish as a second language in their communities, and then learn English as a third language when they come to school. These children truly carry their roots with them at all times.

Sadly, their parents caution them not to talk at school using their home language because of the fear of racism and discrimination. This has the unintended consequence of delegitimizing the richness and foundation of children's home experiences, leaving this unavailable.

Participants now living in the Global North were, of course, influenced by experiences with located study, knowledge, policy, and politics of their new home. Yet, there are examples of influence coming from the Global South through family histories, multiple sources of knowledge (Freire, 1985), and examples of transformative actions that were reflected the work of Latina/o artists whose work we had studied for years (Anzaldúa, 2002; Hérnandez-Ávila & Anzaldúa, 2010). These knowledges continually appear in our complex findings in the teacher education students' and children's stories. The complexities of the findings over the years have pushed me to consider research questions that include:

In what ways do children and student teachers – across generations and roles – create, build upon, and reinvent each other's stories to make new meanings considering family history, multigenerational knowledges, and experiences with critical conceptions of place that are important curricular considerations?
and
In what ways do the children's and teacher education students' stories offer new possibilities for language and literacy to connect Global South knowledges to the Global North contexts to enrich pedagogical practice through story and a welcoming of multiple languages and literacies, family history that create a rich third space for understanding and honoring lived experiences?

These research questions, over time, have uncovered rich findings that have led to new theoretical journeys. The idea of "carrying our roots" from one world to another has created a third space where the "roots" become a metaphorical "pillow" to provide comfort and enlighten us throughout our lives. My evolving theoretical stances to early childhood work with children and families is based upon the third space that combines aspects of the Global South and the Global North, which always influences our pedagogy. The findings from years of this work are a compilation of stories based on intergenerational influences of family and community, the pedagogical realities of integrated curriculum as a third space to hear the voices often silenced of people among us. And the complicated conversations are influenced by historical, pedagogical, sociological realities.

Family History and Theoretical Musings

Theoretical support for third space and story as integrated curriculum emerges clearly through family history. Nelson (2009) insisted that meaning-making and memory in children reveal that children are not developing in an individual way in a predicted sequential journey, but that children are components of an integrated system. This integrated system includes family and community. Nelson (2009) said:

> Meaning is in the mind and the brain; it is also in the body that recognizes familiar things and places. Meaning comes to reside in the child, but it also resides in the social world, in the affect-laden interactions with caretakers and others, in the symbols and artifacts of the culture, in the language spoken around the child.
>
> *(p. 10)*

For example, a student teacher who had just met the children in her class six weeks earlier, noted that the children blithely jumped from an excitement about fantastical superheroes to heroic family members. She wrote:

> There is continuing interest in superheroes in the classroom, especially through the costumes children wore during Halloween. In addition to this continued interest, there is also an increasing display of pride for their culture. About half of the students in my classroom are Latinos. They can communicate in Spanish, and a lot of them are very proud of their culture, families, and language abilities.
>
> For example, when the class was doing an art activity, a boy chose three unique colors for his sea creature. He told his friend: "I'm going to color my shark with the color of the Mexican flag because that's where my mom was born. I was born in Oxnard." The same boy turned to me a few minutes later and told me, "I can speak two languages. English and Spanish, " which prompted another child in the table to say, "I can speak Spanish too!"
>
> *(Ventura, 2018)*[1]

She reflected about ways she saw the children's families and community heroes in this third space:

> This lesson connects the in-class experiences of children's interest in superheroes to their curiosity about real life heroes. This also connects with the lesson they've explored about Latino history and culture in their own community.
>
> *(Ventura, 2018)*

Those of us working with our "roots rolled up" as a pillow each night (Alarcón, 2005, p. 3) consider "reconceptualizing work with renewed understandings of place, as grounded and relational, and as providing roots for politics that are deeply specific to place, and yet deeply connected to other places" (Tuck & McKenzie, 2015, p. 29). In California, as in many places around the world, there are layers of exploitation with complicated historical (documented and not documented) antecedents (Hinkinson, 2012). Place is where we are, where we have been, and where we are going. What is our "place" within these places? Imagine the children who've traveled from Central America in terrible circumstances, with family or without, and end up in Texas or California. There are many aspects of reality and meaning-making going on, both horrible and hopeful. Issues surrounding critical conceptions of place are an important aspect of family history for many children today.

Another student teacher, Lea, had been working for a few months in an elementary school with 8-year-olds. She was pushed to think of family history and current realities in terms of place as it relates to all dimensions of life, especially as it all relates to the 8-year-olds she met in student teaching. The school serves the most economically challenged families in the city with a large population of children from the migrant Mixtec community. The student teacher was jolted by her own initial impressions of the children. She is bilingual (Spanish/English); her family was originally from Mexico and has lived in California for several generations. She reflected:

> I looked back on my notes from day one and realized how much I have learned from students in these past weeks. I realized that I had written in my notes on the first day that some children lack energy and motivation to engage in classroom activities and learning. I have realized now that this is because most children don't get the sleep they need at night or have peace and quiet at home. Some of them share a home with other families, and this affects how they function at school.
>
> I realized that I'd been so fast to judge them in the beginning and now I empathize with them. I found out just last week that one of the students is currently homeless and his family sleeps in their car.
>
> *(Reyes, 2016)*

Thinking about learning contexts within the Global South and Global North and our lived experiences, always carrying our roots, has led to revisiting Gloria Anzaldúa. In Conocimiento Theory, Anzaldúa highlights transformative elements of her theories of mestizo consciousness and la facultad (mental ability). "Like mestizo consciousness, conocimiento represents a non-binary, connectionist mode of thinking; like la facultad, conocimiento often unfolds within oppression and entails a deepening of perception" (Keating, 2009, p. 320). So, families in the home and teachers and children in schools should not be required to separate their heads from their hearts, separate their thinking, speaking, and writing in to one language or another, and most importantly, to sacrifice one aspect of learning in order to learn something else in the required curriculum. When we employ stories in the integrated curriculum, we create the third space where this duality of two languages and aspects of affect and cognition can flourish together.

Another student teacher, Ilia, in the same school revealed how conceptions of place connected to family history and languages.

> In my small group (in a kindergarten classroom) I wanted to focus on family story, and bookmaking. I began by sharing that my mother had come to California two months before I was born, and that many of my cousins still live in Mexico. I hoped to get to know the students better and thought maybe they would share their stories if I shared mine.
>
> When I asked if anyone had family members that lived or currently live in a different location from our city, one student shared with me that her father is in Mexico. I thought this was interesting because this child refuses to speak Spanish at times and seems to be ashamed of her Spanish language.
>
> And there were two other students who are not very outspoken and didn't share as much about their family. But to make sure they wouldn't feel left out, I made sure that everyone got a turn to talk about family. I did this by asking them each a few specific questions in Spanish individually. I did see that they became more engaged when I asked the questions in Spanish. I finally got a response from one of these students who shared with me that her grandparents lived in Mexico. That sounds like a small thing, but I had been working with these students for six weeks and this was the first time this girl had mentioned her own family.
>
> (Santos, 2015)

This adult sharing her own personal stories about family and place is intentional, a way to invite the children to share their stories. It also illustrates overlapping of several categories of findings (Quintero, 2015; Quintero, 2009). Sadly, for decades outdated thinking with deficit perspectives has persisted, highlighting the irony that exists for children when they perceive that all learning must be done in English, no matter what home languages families speak. What we saw was that the student teachers and children had barriers in their lives, yet many were bilingual, had rich family histories, and used stories in Spanish to support their own learning.

Giving and receiving stories opens up new spaces through which to consider information in curriculum. This idea of creating a third space with stories brought us to analyze more deeply learners' experiences. Another example of a teacher education student addressing this was from Fátima, a Latina from East Los Angeles. Fátima explained her work in California with learners from the Mixtec community (discussed earlier in this chapter) in a variety of settings, from infant/toddler programs to tutoring programs in middle and high schools. Fátima was appreciative that both the Spanish language of her ancestors in Mexico and the English of her school, state, and country were both honored in her family home and community. And she wrote that she immediately was sensitive to 4-year-olds struggling with learning a third language. She noted:

> Working with migrant students, ages 3 to 18 from the Mixtec community, has been an experience unlike any other. When I was focusing solely on the younger ages in preschool, I witnessed children struggling to identify a language to speak. The English of some teachers was the third language they'd been introduced to—after Mixteco and Spanish. What is going to happen to them when they enter the elementary years and are expected to read a language that no one in their home speaks?
>
> *(Muñoz, 2013)*

She acknowledged, "I am the oldest in my family (so I could help my siblings) but here, I wonder who these kids go to for help? How are parents supposed to be involved parents if this language barrier stops them?" (Muñoz, 2013).

Unfortunately, schools and programs still often call for special education diagnoses for children who are "developmentally delayed in speech and language" when the child is learning to internalize three languages – at age 4. Teachers must understand that language acquisition can take time to become complete, and unfortunately many educators are not educationally prepared to deal with this complexity.

The same student teacher documented a conversation between herself and a high school student she was tutoring from the Mixtec community. The excerpt further highlights family circumstances relating to Conocimiento Theory and critical conceptions of place in our work:

> A tenth grader approached me asking about my own living situations. "Maestra, usted vive sola?" (Do you live alone?) she asked. I said I had a roommate, then I had to explain what a roommate was, and that yes, I take care of my personal things.
>
> She asked if I missed my family, and specifically she asked if I missed my mother. At the moment this wasn't awkward; later I made the connection. A while later she told me that she had lived in Mexico while her mother lived and worked in California. This young girl, while in Mexico, had to go to school, work, and maintain a home for her eight younger siblings. Three years ago, her mother brought her to California, and here she is. She is a straight "A" student speaking English very well, soaking in academic information, and was well on her way to college and to being a success story.
>
> But. . . now, she is being taken out of my program. Worse than that, she is being taken out of school. Her mother is moving her to Las Vegas with no plans to enroll her in school.
>
> *(Muñoz, 2013)*

Muñoz's final thoughts about migrant students show stories in a third space where family history, place, and Conocimiento Theory are at the forefront – where the student teacher is able to pull strength from her family history and two geographical "spaces" to support her own critical learning and support her students. Muñoz wrote,

Reading articles about some things like teaching methodology makes us knowledgeable; it is important to learn what others have found and concluded. But nothing beats personally working with these kids and first hand verifying that what one is reading in academia is true.

(Muñoz, 2013)

Many decades separate her experience from my own, but her story and mine are aspects of this *knowing*. This student teacher is internalizing the potential of the third space in integrated curriculum.

Many scholars worry that our work in the Global North seldom includes aspects of theories, philosophies, and practices that have been long ingrained in childrearing, daily life, and scholarship from the Global South. We see this absence reflected in the theories of child development and curriculum development in the Global North. Our thinking led to Anzaldúa's Conocimiento Theory of consciousness that includes all dimensions of life, both inner – mental, emotional, instinctive, imaginal, spiritual, bodily realms – and outer – social, political, lived experiences (Hérnandez-Ávila & Anzaldúa, 2010). And in turn, this more expanded theoretical focus led to overlapping complexities of family history and place led to questions about theoretical stances upon which early childhood work stands.

Scholars in early childhood circles are realizing the impact of Nelson's (2009) research and its influence on our knowledge of young children's learning and language. Bruner (2004) described Nelson as a "contextual functionalist" studying "the contexts that give human acts their meaning" while investigating the functions that these acts play in longer-term scenarios. Nelson (2009) provided alternatives to traditional developmental theory that focused on presumed innate abilities and assumptions of child and adult forms of cognition and static stages of development. Her data provides new perspectives about meaning-making through language, literacy, and experience. She argued that children are members of a community of minds, striving not only to make sense of the world, but also to share meanings with others. Nelson (2009) stressed that children are "components of an integrated system" (p. 186) and she maintained, "stories bear directly on the problems of different minds, different selves, and different times that are central to the child's emerging understanding of the world" (p. 172). At the same time, individual meaning-making is integrated in to the contextual world of people, places, and events in the child's life.

This theoretical framework supports our integrated curriculum through a third space of participants' stories and the stories of many families around the world, as their lives transition from one continent to another. We see that they do proudly carry their roots to new contexts, and that this can effectively be the basis for curriculum. Often the stories of the children and teachers become the "third space" that is a special communalized combination of Global North and Global South influences. In our changing world shouldn't curricula support communalized knowledges? I think it is urgent, and perhaps the only way to bring educational possibilities and access to all children.

Nelson's (2009) theory that children are members of a community of minds, striving not only to make sense, but also to share meanings with others, is seen in the story of Fernando. A student teacher related this story, highlighting issues of traditional child development theory, home language, pedagogy, and imagination. Fernando was a preschooler in California. Many children were Spanish-speaking and just learning English for the first time; the school didn't promote support of home language in the classroom. The student teacher, Pam, herself a bilingual California native, was in a sensitive position of trying (subversively) to support the 4-year-old's use of his home language. She wrote a lengthy journal story about Fernando, the situation, and his potential. The vignette points to a child who is developing in complex ways in spite of the misconceptions of many of his teachers who find it easier to request a diagnosis from special education than to really listen to the potential of the child. She wrote:

> I am assigned to sit with 4-year-old Fernando who is unable to sit still on the rug during literacy time. Since he is unable to "control his behavior", and sit quietly crossing his legs (that all children are requested to do) Fernando must sit in a chair. Fernando shows interest in my notebook as soon as he notices I am writing notes. He wants to write his name. I said, "Fernando, you may write your name as soon as we go out and play. Let's listen to Teacher right now."
>
> "Yo escribo mi nombre?" (I write my name?), he asks me in Spanish. "Si, despues que salgamos a jugar afuera" (Yes, after we go to play outside), I answer him back in Spanish. "Okay, Teacher. Gracias." He turns to listen to his other teacher.
>
> As soon as we are outside during playtime, Fernando runs up to me, "Teacher Pam, yo hago homework" (Teacher Pam, I do homework). "You do your homework?" I ask. "No! Tu homework!" (No, your homework!). He wants to do my homework? I give him my notepad, unsure what he means. He begins writing. He writes, then looks up, looks around, then writes some more.
>
> *(Mata, 2013)*

Pam then reflected on what she had learned about the child, his learning context, and about herself as a professional:

> My new friend, Fernando, cannot manage to sit still with his peers, but he'd been observing me and noticed I take notes. It seems that our friendship and what he's noticed me doing (writing) have become important to him, and he can communicate it all with me in his home language. I don't see the "developmental delays" his teachers have mentioned.
>
> *(Mata, 2013)*

Fernando's developmental assessment by his teachers was in contradiction with Nelson's theory and the student teacher's analysis of her experience with Fernando. A social relationship had developed between an adult who did speak his home language and was willing to allow his language context to open a third space for their learning relationship. The child keenly observed his new friend involved in an activity that was important to her (taking notes), and he showed focused interest in using literacy through his pretending.

There are many stories from other participants that relate to research on language acquisition specifically and child development more broadly. There is consensus from neuroscientists and sociolinguists (Kuhl, 2014; Nelson, 2009) supporting dual language opportunities for learners. The research supports ideas of the third space and integrated curriculum. This social understanding between the self and others identified by Nelson suggests that story can be a third space that naturally accommodates many cultures and many languages in our meaning-making not only in families from the earliest experiences in life, but also in school. This encourages multidirectional learning among generations and across school and home contexts.

To Matters of Concern

Third space stories allow for the expression of care for our loved ones, known and not yet met, and this caring can also then be reflected in the curriculum and as the basis for learning. Theoretical support here comes from a body of work not often referenced in early childhood which is Latour's (2004) "Matters of Concern" theory. This theory urges researchers to consider a multiplicity of realities, or "worlds" for each actor's agency and inspiration for action. Documenting this action involves a strong dedication to relativism, which is important because "The relativist takes seriously what [actors] are obstinately saying" (p. 232).

Lea, mentioned previously, who works with 8-year-olds at an elementary school with many Mixtec children, analyzed Latour's relativism and multiple realities affecting children's engagements with their teachers:

> During my time at the elementary school, I observed that it is a low-income school. I observed that many students in the classroom can barely speak English and write simple sentences (in any language), which is unfortunate. I observed that the school's principal imagines particular goals for students and the teachers to meet, but the teachers set different ones.
>
> I think overall what is important is that the students see this school as a second home, a place where many find comfort, love, and their basic needs met. In the beginning of my days in the classroom I asked my cooperating teacher, Mrs. Reza, what the philosophy of the school is. She said, "that every child be college-ready by the end of their years at this school." Her own philosophy is different. She said her philosophy is "believing that if she

tries her best at teaching then her students will try their best at achieving." And I can see that she truly cares about her students. I can see this by the way students from her previous classes come into her class and run up to her in the halls. That is the type of teacher I want to be – a teacher everyone remembers because of the caring she gave them. She did more than just teach them the required knowledge, she actually cared.

(Reyes, 2016)

The emphasis on the stories in the third space of integrated curriculum allows for teachers who care deeply to support students who face multiple challenges. This use of stories, along with the teachers' sensitivity to children's strengths as well as struggles, especially in a school that is consistently pressured to focus on reading scores (in English), is an example of Matters of Concern.

Implications and Final Thoughts

Over a long career of studying early childhood learning, languages, and literacies, I have seen that stories are ways to document, learn from, and generate understanding in multilingual contexts in diverse, even crisis, situations. The student teachers and children with whom we have worked show that children and families, when supported, share stories that create a third space for new kinds of learning and understanding that would not be otherwise available.

What is still seen in classrooms and in the dominant discourse around language learning is a deficit perspective couched in the outcome of "achievement gaps." The need for counternarrative, or alternative stories, arises from the dominant narrative, about certain people and who they are (Moss, 2015). Dominant narratives perpetuate one way of telling a story, and marginalizing all other stories. A third space to share each other's stories is a way to encourage an important counternarrative. The use of story supported by integrated curriculum supports the possibility of counternarrative becoming a foundation for learning and for allowing children (and student teachers) to use their assets in the learning endeavor. The hope is that this work in the United States with student teachers and children can connect to broader work with world migration. It can set the stage for broader and more inclusive cultural understanding, and for a more open realm of what education can mean for communities.

In a story that mixes the historical struggle of indigenous people in southern Mexico and folklore, Subcomandante Marcos (leader of the Zapatista rebels in southern Mexico) listens to elder Antonio, telling a story about Zapata, who was of indigenous ancestry and led the Mexican Revolution. Antonio says, "But it is also not about Zapata. It is about what shall happen. It is about what shall be done" (Ortiz, 2001, p. 51). Antonio explained that there is wisdom in asking questions while walking, struggling towards transformative action. He says that true men and women "are never still" (Ortiz, 2001, p. 51).

May we never be still and may stories of children, families, and teachers never be silenced.

Note

1 Journal quotations were taken from data collected as part of a previous research project with IRB oversight at CSU – Channel Islands. The quotations were from journals produced by student teacher participants in the project and permission was granted by the participants for their use. Pseudonyms were used in order to protect the confidentiality of the participants.

References

Alarcón, F.X. (2005). *Poems to Dream Together/poemas Para Sonar Juntos: Poemas Para Sonar Juntos*. San Francisco, CA: Lee & Low Books.
Anzaldúa, G. (2002). Now let us shift . . . the path of conocimiento . . . inner work, public acts, in G. Anzaldúa & A. Keating (Eds.), *This bridge we call home: Radical visions for transformation*. New York: Routledge, pp. 540–578.
Bhabha, H.K. (2004). *The location of culture*. Abingdon: Routledge.
Bruner, J. (2004). Katherine Nelson: Contextual functionalist, in J.M. Lucariello, *The development of the mediated mind: Sociocultural context and cognitive development*. New York: Psychology Press, pp. 239–244.
Dahlberg, G., Moss, P., & Pence, A. (2013). *Beyond quality in early childhood education and care: Languages of evaluation*. New York: Routledge.
Freire, P. (1985). *The politics of education*. Granby, MA: Bergin & Garvey.
Hérnandez-Ávila, A., & Anzaldúa, G. (2010). Interview. In A.C. Elenes (Ed.), *Transforming borders: Chicana/o popular culture and pedagogy*. Lanham, MD: Lexington Books.
Hinkinson, J. (2012). Why settler colonialism? *Arena Journal*, 37/38(1), 1–39.
Keating, A.L. (Ed.) (2009). *The Gloria Anzaldúa reader*. Durham, NC: Duke University Press.
Kuhl, P. (2014, January). How babies learn language: Q&A with Patricia Kuhl. *Cognitive Neuroscience Blog Archive*. Retrieved from www.cogneurosociety.org/cns-2014-blog-coverage/
Latour, B. (2004). Why has critique run out of steam? From matters of fact to matters of concern. *Critical Inquiry*, 30(Winter 2004), 225–248.
Mata, J. (2013). Unpublished research journal. Camarillo, CA.
Moss, P. (2015). Time for more storytelling. *European Early Childhood Education Research Journal*, 23(1), 1–4.
Muñoz, F. (2013). Unpublished research journal. Camarillo, CA.
Nelson, K. (2009). *Young minds in social worlds: Experience, meaning, and memory*. Cambridge, MA: Harvard University Press.
Ortiz, S. (2001). Essays. In *Subcomandante Marcos, Folktales of the Zapatista revolution*. El Paso, TX: Cinco Puntos Press.
Pinar, W.F. (2004). *What is curriculum theory?* Mahwah, NJ: Lawrence Erlbaum Associates.
Quintero, E.P. (2009). *Critical literacy in early childhood education: Artful story and the integrated curriculum*. New York: Peter Lang.
Quintero, E.P. (2015). *Storying learning in early childhood: When children lead participatory curriculum design, implementation, and assessment*. New York: Peter Lang.

Quintero, E.P., & Rummel, M.K. (2014). *Storying, a path to our future: Artful thinking, learning, teaching, and research*. New York: Peter Lang, Series on Critical Perspectives in Qualitative Research.
Reyes, L. (2016). Unpublished research journal. Camarillo, CA.
Santos, I. (2015). Unpublished research journal. Camarillo, CA.
Tuck, E., & McKenzie, M. (2015). *Place in research: Theory, methodology, and methods*. New York: Routledge.
Ventura, C. (2018). Unpublished research journal. Camarillo, CA.

11

CHANGING THE DISCOURSE

The Capability Approach and Early Childhood Education

Cary A. Buzzelli

The Capability Approach (CA) puts at its center individuals' agency, well-being, and freedom. Individuals are agents acting on their own behalf who should have the freedom to pursue activities and make choices that contribute to their well-being. Sen outlines CA as:

> a moral approach that sees persons from two different perspectives: *well-being* and *agency*. Both the "well-being aspect" and the "agency aspect" of persons have their own relevance in the assessment of states and actions. Each aspect also yields a corresponding notion of freedom.
>
> (1985, p. 169, italics in original)

These principles are captured in Sen's often-quoted statement that individuals have the freedom "to choose the lives they value and have reason to value" (1992, p. 81). In Sen's view, this is necessary for individuals to flourish.

The purposes of this chapter are to present the key concepts of CA and to consider the implications CA has for changing the discourse in early childhood education. This chapter is divided into two major sections and proceeds as follows. In the first section, I present a brief overview of CA. This is followed by a discussion of three models of education (Robeyns, 2006a). For each model, Robeyns addresses the goals and purposes of education, comparing CA to two other possibilities. The second major section then considers how CA can change the discourse in early childhood education. Here I examine the implications of CA for curriculum, teaching, and assessment. By proposing a new way of conceptualizing early childhood education, CA poses a number of challenges to early childhood professionals. These are presented as a series of "what if" questions.

The Capability Approach

Sen developed CA with the goal of providing another means of assessing the well-being of individuals living across a continuum of circumstances. The main purpose was to develop a way to assess individual well-being based on information gathered from indicators that reflected the health, educational, economic, social, political, and cultural circumstances in which individuals lived, rather than a single economic measure.

Sen believed that the assessment of individual well-being should be based on not only what individuals are able to do and be, but also on the freedoms individuals have to expand the capabilities they have. Sen uses the term "functionings" to describe an individual's skills, knowledge, and the abilities. Examples include being literate because of having the opportunities to learn to read and the availability of reading materials, or being in good health as the result of proper nutrition and medical care. Capabilities are the range of freedoms individuals have to expand their skills, knowledge, and abilities allowing them "to lead the kind of life they value – and have reason to value" (Sen, 1999, p. 18).

Sen (1999) refers to several kinds of what he calls instrumental freedoms that "contribute, directly and indirectly, to the overall freedom people have to live the way they would like to live" (p. 38). These align with a number of the indicators of well-being mentioned previously. By economic freedoms and opportunities, Sen means that individuals can "utilize economic resources for the purpose of consumption, or production, or exchange" (p. 39). Careful consideration is paid to two important aspects of economic freedom. The first is that the measurement of increases in economic freedom and productivity be assessed in ways that include individuals and/or families as well as aggregate measures at the national level such as gross domestic product (e.g., GDP). Secondly, attention is given to how the increases in economic growth are distributed: do all share equally in economic growth or are the benefits accruing for a small number of elites?

Social freedoms and opportunities include a variety of "arrangements that society makes for education, health care and so on, which influence individuals' substantive freedom to live better" (1999, p. 39). While Sen says that these are important for individuals and their own quality of life they also are needed so individuals are able to participate more effectively in political and economic activities. For example, being literate gives individuals the freedom to engage in many activities that enhance one's own life. However, literacy also is needed to engage in some economic, social, and political activities important for one's own well-being and that of others.

The final type of freedom considered are political freedoms, which for Sen include civil rights. Political freedoms are freedoms to participate in and vote for the election of those who shall govern and in the determination of the principles and laws that all will abide by. Also, necessary are freedoms that allow for the press and individuals to criticize the government and to engage in political dialogue. Sen discusses these and other freedoms at length regarding their fundamental roles in supporting human flourishing and development (1999, 2009), and as related to social justice. More detailed descriptions of CA, its development, and fundamental tenets can be found in Alkire and Deneulin (2009), Biggeri and Santi (2012), Biggeri, Ballet, and Comim (2011), Deneulin (2014b), Deneulin and Shahani (2009), Nussbaum (2000, 2011), Robeyns (2005, 2006b), Sen (1985, 1997, 1999, 2009), and Walker and Unterhalter (2007).

CA and Education

Education for Sen is crucial for human flourishing and it plays an important role in CA and human development. Yet, Sen has written little specifically addressing education (Unterhalter, 2009). Sen does not provide guidelines about curriculum or teaching methods. Rather, as is characteristic of his stance in CA, he believes that the central aspects of education such as curriculum and teaching be decided upon through democratic discussions among community members. However, Sen is adamant that education be universal and that education be focused on teaching critical thinking. In sum, at the heart of Sen's view of education is that it should expand the development of individuals' capabilities and the extent to which they can lead lives that they value and have reason to value (1985, 1987, 1990, 1997, 1999). To understand further how a CA approach to education differs from other models of education we turn to the work of Ingrid Robeyns.

Robeyns (2006a) presents three models for understanding the role of education in human development. The three models are human capital theory, human rights discourse, and the capabilities approach. For each model, Robeyns outlines its core values and purposes. She also presents, for each model, its strengths and shortcomings.

Robeyns first describes the human capital model of education that draws on the work of economists Gary Becker (1964, 1976, 1993) and Theodore Schultz (1963). Both posit that education is a form of capital used to increase economic growth and productivity. Through education individuals gain knowledge and skills that increase their capital in the form of resources they bring to the workplace. Increases in one's human capital can lead to more opportunities for employment and to a higher standard of living. It follows that a more highly skilled workforce results in higher economic productivity and growth. In sum, the purpose of education is to increase human skills and capital that contribute to economic development, productivity, and efficiency.

Robeyns' (2006a) critique of this model of education is that it is "*entirely* instrumental: it values education, skills and knowledge *only* in so far as they contribute (directly and indirectly) to expected economic productivity" (p. 73, italics in original). Thus, according to human capital theory, the knowledge, skills, and dispositions that offer no immediately discernable increases in economic productivity have no investment value. Because the human capital model offers an instrumental role for education, it narrows the value of education in the lives of individuals. Robeyns notes that when individual agency is seen only in the capacity for economic gain, individuals' agency toward goals and activities plays an instrumental role as a means to an end. The role of agency for gaining what individuals value and have reason to value, that is, seeing agency as an end in and of itself, is lost.

The second model based on a human rights discourse takes a different perspective. Education is seen as "a human right that should be guaranteed to all. . . every human being, including every child, is entitled to a decent education, even when one cannot be sure that this education will pay off in human capital terms" (Robeyns, 2006a, p. 75). Education becomes a fundamental right with both instrumental and intrinsic value for all. Education contributes to individuals' well-being beyond instrumental and economic purposes. This view, however, is not without shortcomings. For one, Robeyns asks, if education is a right, is it a legal right or a moral right? That both rights can co-exist results in complex and difficult-to-answer questions. For example, declaring education a human right begs the question of which level of government has the obligation and responsibility of guaranteeing it. Alternatively, if education is a moral right, it becomes the obligation of all, and all should be committed to its guarantee. The result is that if seen as a legal right, the responsibility for procuring that right is vague at best, and if seen as a moral right, then all are called to fulfill this obligation. In sum, education cast as a human right presents contradictory messages about the obligations and responsibilities of individuals, governments, and society for its guarantee.

Robeyns' comparison of these two models leaves us with the following. From a human capital perspective, the goals and purposes of education focus narrowly on economic productivity. From a human rights perspective, while stating a clear guarantee to education, left vague is the responsibility for ensuring the right.

It is the third model of education, the human capability approach, which Robeyns sees as having both instrumental and intrinsic value for individuals and society. Comparing the human capital model to the human capability approach, Sen (1999) says both focus centrally on individuals. However, a crucial difference is that "the yardstick of assessment focuses on different achievements" (p. 293). As noted previously, the focus and objective of human agency in the human capital perspective is on increasing economic productivity, whereas the human capability perspective focuses on providing individuals with the freedoms and opportunities to make choices they value about how they want to live their lives. For Sen, the distinction between instrumental and intrinsic value of education parallels the distinction between means and ends; "human beings are not merely means of production, but also the end of the exercise" (p. 296). He says, "The acknowledgement of the role of human qualities in promoting and sustaining economic growth – momentous as it is, tells us nothing about *why* economic growth is sought in the first place" (p. 295, italics in the original).

Thus, the human capital model sees individuals as means to the ends of increasing economic efficiency and productivity, whereas in CA individuals are seen as an ends, that end being "to lead the kind of life they value and have reason to value" (Sen, 1999, p. 18). Likewise, Martha Nussbaum (2011) believes that when considering freedom in relation to an individual's well-being, it is crucial to view the opportunities available to each individual to enhance well-being rather than considering some overall or total measurement. Focus is on the individual as an end. In sum, the human capability model of education directly addresses both the instrumental and intrinsic value of education and, in doing so, makes the important moral connection between them. This moral connection is discussed later on.

CA and Early Childhood Education

Robeyns makes the case that the human capability model offers a radically different perspective on children's learning and development from the human capital and human rights models. To date, there are few studies in early childhood education which have used CA as a theoretical framework (e.g., Adair, 2014; Adair & Colegrove, 2014; Buzzelli, 2015a, 2015b; Ballet, Biggeri, & Comim, 2011; Biggeri, Ballet, & Comim, 2011; Colegrove & Adair, 2014). By focusing specifically on the implications of CA for early childhood education, these studies demonstrate how the incorporation of CA can change the discourse in early childhood education. The second section of this paper, then, examines how engagement with CA offers rich possibilities for changing the discourse of early childhood education. The possibilities CA poses are presented in a series of "what if" questions meant to engage early childhood professionals in a new discourse with CA.

Changing the Discourse in ECE

To begin examining how CA can change the discourse in early childhood education, we return to the quote that began this article. My purpose here is to examine the "what if" questions following Sen's central notions of CA, namely that it offers "a moral approach that sees persons from two different perspectives: *well-being* and *agency*" and "each also yields a corresponding notion of freedom" (Sen, 1985, p. 169). At the end of each "what if" section I discuss the implications for changing the discourse in ECE.

What If . . . CA Provides the Normative Language for a Moral Perspective on Children's Development and Learning for Early Childhood Professionals?

The moral approach to development that Sen proposes sees children from the perspectives of their agency and well-being with both related in important ways to freedoms. For Deneulin (2014a) CA offers a normative language that "offers a framework to judge a situation, and that judgement leads to a certain type of action to transform that situation" (p. 47). Deneulin seeks a definition of development grounded in a moral framework. To do so, she turns to the work of Denis Goulet (1971, 1995, 1997) in development ethics. For Goulet (1997) questions about development focus on values, attitudes and self-defined goals, that development must support for individuals to become "more human and more developed. . . enabled to *be* more" (p. 1167, italics in original). Deneulin combines Goulet's development ethics with CA for a definition of development that considers opportunities individuals have to choose lives they value and have reason to value, and importantly also assesses if the social, political, economic, and cultural realities in which they live enable them to make those choices.

Deneulin's definition illustrates how CA provides a normative language which can frame how early childhood professionals view children and their emerging abilities. Basing practice on this normative language means early childhood professionals must be carefully attuned to and scrutinize curriculum, teaching methods, and assessment practices: Do learning activities allow children freedom to pursue interests to their fullest while acknowledging the moral and legal responsibilities of teachers to determine boundaries of children's freedoms in pursuit of their own well-being? Thus, this first "what if" presents a new normative language for early childhood education.

Implications and Speculations for Further Investigation

From the outset, CA casts early childhood education as a moral endeavor with implications as moral principles for guiding early childhood professionals in their practice (Buzzelli, 2015a, 2015b, 2018). The decisions teachers make are moral decisions because they are based on their values and, importantly, because they influence who children become as learners and as individuals (Buzzelli, 2018, 2019; Buzzelli & Johnston, 2002; Hansen, 1999). Considering CA as a moral language for early childhood professionals moves the moral dimensions of teaching front and center in our practice.

Teachers of young children make countless moment-by-moment decisions that demand walking a fine, moral line between giving children the freedom to exercise their agency while at the same time providing the structure and guidance to nurture their well-being. Nurturing and supporting the well-being of young children requires that children be active agents in the process. Yet, young children are emotionally, cognitively, morally, and legally unable to set boundaries on the extent of the freedom they should have in doing so. Balancing freedom, agency, and well-being while respecting young children as individuals requires that teachers be morally and intellectually attentive to their learning and development (Hansen, 1999). Yet, such attentiveness creates tension with constantly taking into account teachers' moral, ethical, and legal responsibilities while providing for children's well-being and agency within a range of freedoms.

Sen's notion of well-being in CA challenges early childhood professionals to broaden our understanding of what well-being means and how to nurture it in young children. Well-being, for Sen, includes those goods and resources a person has, that is, primary goods in Rawlsian terms (Rawls, 1971, 2001), but crucially also must include the personal characteristics and opportunities to convert those primary goods in pursuing and attaining personal goals. Well-being includes the substantive freedoms, in CA terms, the capabilities to choose a life that one values and has reason to value.

Allowing children to pursue their own interests has long been a central element in a number of early childhood curriculums and frameworks in the US and abroad (e.g., NAEYC's DAP, the Project Approach, Reggio Emilia, *Te Whariki*, among others). However, new in CA is the concept of conversion factors. Conversion factors are those aspects in the environment that facilitate how an individual can use the goods, resources, and opportunities available for pursuing one's own aspirations and goals (Deneulin, 2014a; Hart, 2012). Conversely, factors in the environment can function as physical, psychological, sociological, and cultural barriers preventing individuals from pursuing or attaining valued goals. The concept of conversion factors challenges teachers to be attentive to situations and factors, be they educational, economic, societal, cultural, or of another source, that can hinder or prevent children from converting their resources and opportunities into valued outcomes.

Attentiveness to conversion factors requires that early childhood professionals negotiate a delicate dance among the competing demands of the conflicting values, priorities, and resources spread across their commitments to young children, their families, colleagues, and self. Crucial here, too, are the legal and moral responsibilities one has as a teacher.

It is here, as a moral language for early childhood professionals that CA highlights an important distinction between professional ethics and a personal moral stance. While teacher education programs introduce students to the NAEYC Code of Ethical Conduct (National Association for the Education of Young Children, 2011), introducing students to the moral language of CA is a much different matter. Firstly, professional codes of ethics outline the ethical standards for individuals as professionals. The moral language of CA provides professionals with guidance about their own standards as individuals. Put differently, when faced with an ethical dilemma we can look in the code of ethical conduct; when faced with a moral dilemma we look in the mirror. These are different sources of information for guidance. Again, for the former, we can review how our behavior is guided by and consistent with an ethical code of conduct. For the latter, we examine how our behavior is consistent with and acts out our deepest beliefs, values, and personal moral standards. Both are important but they are different; and this difference is a significant implication of CA for early childhood professionals.

In sum, the moral language of CA forces us to look deeply into our own biases and prejudices for how they may prevent us from becoming aware of factors in the environment, again broadly conceived, that influence children's ability to convert resources and opportunities provided them into their valued goals. This is a challenge to confront not only what may be inside our hearts and minds, but also what may, or may not be, but should be, in our programs, policies, neighborhood schools, child- and family-serving agencies, and communities. Such scrutiny seeks to locate sources and causes of inequalities of educational opportunity hidden from view in unexamined biases and prejudices. CA's moral language calls us to confront and remedy them, acknowledging that this is challenging and daunting work.

When teaching takes on moral significance an important distinction is made between the ways children and their emerging abilities are conceptualized. Using the moral language of CA we now turn to an examination of the two competing views.

What If . . . Based on CA, Children's Abilities Are Conceptualized as Capabilities Rather Than as Commodities as in a Human Capital Perspective?

The human capital approach to development and education sees children's skills, knowledge, and abilities as commodities for use toward economic productivity. Education has an instrumental value for the individual, the economy, and society. Alternatively, CA views children's abilities as capabilities, which according to Sen (1984) are not goods or commodities but rather, "as a feature of a person in relation to goods" (pp. 315–316). Education has both instrumental and intrinsic value. The distinction Sen makes between the instrumental and intrinsic value of education is the basis for the connection he makes between the means and ends of education.

Sen has concerns about how the human capital approach views education and children as individuals and learners. His first concern is that conceptualizing education as instrumental turns it into a commodity with only economic value. The goals and purposes of education become increasing individuals' contribution to economic productivity. As such, education has no intrinsic value.

Secondly, when education is a commodity it is measured as a commodity, namely by the numbers. Numbers commonly used in early childhood are children's readiness scores, scores on standardized tests used for state and federal accountability. Likewise, the Organization for Economic Co-operation and Development (OECD) has recently launched the International Early Learning and Child Well-being Study (IELS; OECD, 2018). The stated goal of the project is to provide participating countries with data on children's development and learning. The data on outcomes and practices can be shared among countries with the goal of improving the well-being of all children. Yet, while the information gathered from the study will provide important information on how individual countries address children's development and learning, too often overlooked is the limited information given by the scores. Information from scores must be used judiciously and along with other information gathered through other means lest it is over-interpreted. Suffice it to say that while scores do tell us something, they are often read as telling us more than in fact they can and do.

A third concern for Sen is how the lack of connection between the instrumental and intrinsic value of education resulted in a separation of the means from the ends of education. Sen sees the logical and historical roots of this separation in the severing of ethics from economics (1987).

The connection of ethics to economics links the activities individuals engage in with the meaning that the activity has in their lives and with their worth and dignity as persons. Put in educational terms, education must have an instrumental value – that people learn stuff and master skills – but education also must have an intrinsic value for each individual. That intrinsic value is that education should feed our own goals, purposes, and interests. In CA, then, the means of education, its instrumental value, is not and cannot be separate from the goals and ends of education and its moral vision.

Implications and Speculations for Further Investigations

When education has both instrumental and intrinsic value, when the means of education connect logically and morally to the ends of education, teaching is a moral endeavor and not merely a technical activity. Teaching as a moral endeavor requires the constant consideration of the moral values inherent in the work (Buzzelli & Johnston, 2002; Hansen, 1999, 2001; Schwandt, 2002, 2005, 2007, 2013). This has important implications for early childhood professionals.

A first implication is the acknowledgment by teachers that curriculum, teaching methods, and assessment practices must connect logically and morally to their own beliefs, values, and goals, and those of their programs. Crucial here is ensuring that the fundamental goals of early childhood practices provide children with opportunities for becoming, in the words of Goulet, "more human and more developed... enabled to *be* more" (1997, p. 1167, italics in original).

One goal of early childhood education, preparing children for successful achievement in kindergarten and primary grade settings and beyond, is certainly commonly held and highly desirable. These were some of the goals of the early intervention programs that appeared in the 1960s, including Head Start and later Follow Through, and are now part of the justification for universal pre-K programs. The intent, then and now, is addressing inequalities of educational opportunity. Yet, it is important to question if too much emphasis was and is placed on early childhood programs ameliorating the pervasive the effects of poverty on children and families. Head Start was a multi-pronged approach of which the educational part was one component; however, that one component quickly became the standard by which Head Start was assessed. The effectiveness, and in human capital terms, the cost-benefit value of Head Start and other early childhood programs, was measured solely by children's eventual educational attainment (e.g., Heckman, 2008; Heckman, Grunewald, & Reynolds, 2006), which while important, is only part of children's well-being. The central focus of CA *is* well-being and agency within the contexts of freedoms. Education is a part of well-being.

Likewise, when children's scores on readiness tests and classroom rating scales measures (e.g., Early Childhood Environment Rating Scale [Harms, Clifford, & Cryer, 2004], etc.) become measures of quality, programs can take on instrumental rather than intrinsic value (Moss, 2008). Scores become proxies for relationships and interactions; numbers belie the complexity, depth, richness, authenticity, and intimacy of quality caregiving and teaching that teachers provide. The IELS, previously mentioned, intends to assess program quality and effectiveness and make data available to countries for program improvement purposes. However, critics warn of that data being used for cross country comparisons and international rankings. They note that this is the most recent example of how early childhood practices become more about how children score, than on how they are currently living and who they are becoming as people (Moss et al., 2016; Moss & Urban, 2018). Similarly, when teacher evaluation is based on children's test scores, as it is in some public school systems in the United States, rather than on other means of assessing the quality of teaching, a very narrow slice of what children know and can do becomes the measure of teacher quality and program quality, and consequently the purposes of education.

Regarding assessment from the CA perspective, it should be an analysis of what children can do, what they cannot do, and what they are prevented from doing. For this reason, assessment practices must specifically take into account the presence and absence of conversion factors. When development is about freedom and agency, our assessment practices must consider the range of children's abilities, the range of opportunities available to engage in valued activities, and the environmental factors that support, or importantly, act as barriers to children expanding their capabilities. Put differently, we should learn as much from assessment practices about how the environment does or does not support children's learning, as we learn about what children can do or cannot do (Buzzelli, 2018; Carr & Lee, 2012).

In sum, because CA seeks to expand individuals' freedom, its normative language and moral perspective moves early childhood education toward a broader vision for supporting children's well-being and agency and the types of freedom needed to do so. In Sen's words, "Expanding freedoms that we have reason to value not only makes our lives richer and more unfettered, but also allows us to be fuller social persons, exercising our own volitions and interacting with – and influencing – the world in which we live" (Sen, 1999, pp. 14–15). This statement rests upon the crucial connection CA makes between ethics and economics. In doing so, CA makes a number of moral claims. The first claim acknowledges the inherent dignity and worth of all individuals. The second follows on claiming that education does have, and must be seen as having, intrinsic value. As a result then, the third claim is the recognition that individuals always be treated as ends in themselves and not merely as means to an end.

What If . . . CA Provides the Moral Framework for Curriculum Development, Teaching Methods, and Assessment Practices That Address Equality of Educational Opportunities for Children?

Jennifer Keyes Adair was the first researcher in early childhood education to consider the implications Sen's notion of agency has for early childhood professionals. Adair defines agency as children "being able to influence and make decisions about what and how something is learned in order to expand capabilities" (2014, p. 219). Agency gives children opportunities for "using their curiosity as motivation and inspiration for inventing, planning, designing and problem solving" (p. 219).

A series of studies (Adair, 2014; Adair & Colegrove, 2014; Colegrove & Adair, 2014) examined how Mrs. Bailey, a teacher in whose class were many children of Latino immigrants, made significant changes to her curriculum, teaching methods, and assessment practices in ways that supported children's agency and participation in their own learning. In Mrs. Bailey's classroom, children engaged in project learning in which they could design and carry out extending learning activities based on their own interests. Often daily, children had time to work on their learning projects. Their work included, choosing a topic, the methods for learning about their topic, and the ways they could demonstrate what and how they learned in conducting their project. Children could work individually or with peers.

To make these changes, Mrs. Bailey had to change her views about teaching. Mrs. Bailey expressed concern about giving children more agency and about not being able to "'let go' and 'not be so controlling'" (Adair & Colegrove, 2014, p. 84). Likewise, her views on assessment changed from seeing assessment as being a single indicator of learning, namely benchmark scores, over which adults had control, to a broader range of assessment practices that shared agency with children (Adair, 2014; see also Buzzelli, 2018, Schwandt, 2002, 2005). By giving children agency in their learning, Mrs. Bailey supported children in expanding their capabilities. In Mrs. Bailey's room, agency was conceptualized as expanding children's capabilities.

Findings from these studies are significant for several reasons. Firstly, Colegrove and Adair (2014) note that increases in children's agency lead to greater learning and depth of knowledge. Secondly, conceptualizing agency as expanded capabilities counters assumptions about deficits commonly held about children of marginalized groups such as children of immigrant families and English language learners. Indeed Adair (2014) says that deficit assumptions "become justifications for offering children from these communities bland, repetitive, task-oriented learning experiences, while their privileged counterparts have dynamic, agency-supporting experiences" (p. 231).

In sum, the CA perspective of seeing children as agents of their own learning shifts curriculum planning and teaching methods toward expanding children's capabilities and freedoms. Additionally, giving children agency in assessment and evaluation changes those from something "done" to children to a dialogical process through which children and teachers engage with one another in examining what children know and understand (Buzzelli, 2018; Schwandt, 2002, 2005).

Implications and Speculations for Further Investigations

In his groundbreaking lecture of the same title, Sen asks, "Equality of What?" (Sen, 1980). Sen answers his question outlining how there should be equality of freedoms so that individuals can expand their capabilities. Striving for equality of basic freedoms is necessary so people can "live lives they value and have reason to value." Answering the "Equality of What?" question has far-reaching implications for early childhood education. It proposes that we envision education and development as providing children increased opportunities to expand their capabilities.

Children can encounter difficulties converting resources for expanding their capabilities due to a range of social, economic, political, environmental, and other factors that can influence development and learning (Robeyns, 2005; Sen, 1992; Vaughan, 2015; Walker & Unterhalter, 2007). As noted previously, early childhood professionals must attend to conversion factors and the central role they play for children in converting resources and opportunities available to them into expanded capabilities that enhance their well-being. For Deneulin (2014a) conversion factors are of moral significance in CA regarding individual's development:

> As far as moral judgement is concerned, one needs to focus on the ends and whether the means further the ends, whether people have opportunities to function well and exercise agency with the resources or income they have.
>
> *(p. 29)*

The changes Mrs. Bailey made to her curriculum, teaching methods, and assessment practices are an example of conversion factors because they removed the obstacles of a narrow curriculum and an overreliance on standardized assessments of benchmarks that prevented children from using their agency to pursue their own interests and learning. By removing these barriers, Mrs. Bailey enabled children to convert the school experiences and resources, in this case the learning opportunities of a project-based curriculum, into expanding capabilities. The notion of conversion factors is a means for teachers, policy makers, and others to examine when, where, and how barriers present in children's experience prevent them from converting educational opportunities into expanded capabilities. A focus on conversion factors means we must look past a particular curriculum or framework since in and of themselves they cannot guarantee that implementing them will expand children's capabilities. The same is true of teaching and assessment practices. CA forces early childhood professionals to ask these questions: How do my curriculum, teaching, and assessment practices expand children's capabilities? What factors are in place to help children convert resources and opportunities into expanded capabilities? What factors in my classroom or beyond hinder children from converting resources and opportunities for expanded capabilities? When addressing these questions, we must examine our beliefs and values that are the moral grounding for our practice. Such an examination can push to the very core of one's beliefs about who one is as a teacher and person (Hansen, 2001; Schwandt, 2002, 2005).

The moral significance of CA is that it can move us away from simplistic and binary good/bad, right/wrong statements about a curriculum or practice, to a place of using a moral lens and moral criteria when examining our practices, classrooms, and the conditions of children's lives. Adair and Colegrove (2014) note how this is often the case in classrooms of children of marginalized communities. Examining conversion factors can bring to light how social, cultural, political, and economic arrangements influence the freedom and ability children and their families have to convert the resources and opportunities available "to achieve valuable combinations of human functionings – what a person is able to do or be" (Sen, 2005, p. 153). At its core, locating and addressing barriers to learning by consideration of conversion factors is an issue of equity and equality of educational opportunity.

Summary

Sen offers CA as a moral approach that focuses on individuals' well-being and agency. For individuals to attain well-being through their own agency they must have the requisite freedoms to do so. These ideas are at the core of CA. Related to early childhood education, the focus on well-being, agency, and freedom provides the grounding for creating curriculum teaching methods and assessment practices so all children can experience an education that, to paraphrase Sen, "they value and have reason to value" (1992, p. 81). In short, education must allow children to expand their capabilities. To do so, we must create sites of equality of educational opportunity. CA presents a paradigm for doing just that because through it we can examine the social, political, economic, and cultural influences on early education with the goal of creating sites for equal educational opportunities for all children. To quote Sen one last time, "it is a moral approach" (1985, p. 169).

References

Adair, J.K. (2014). Agency and expanding capabilities in the early grades: What it could mean for young children in the early grades. *Harvard Educational Review*, 84(2), 217–241.

Adair, J.K., & Colegrove, K.S. (2014). Communal agency and social development: Examples from first grade classrooms serving children of immigrants. *Asia-Pacific Journal of Research in Early Childhood Education*, 8(2), 69–91.

Alkire, S., & Deneulin, S. (2009). A normative framework for development. In S. Deneulin & L. Shahani (Eds.), *An introduction to the human development and capability approach: Freedom and agency* (pp. 3–21). Oxford: Earthscan and International Development Research Centre.

Ballet, J., Biggeri, M., & Comim, F. (2011). Children's agency and the capability approach: A conceptual framework. In M. Biggeri, J. Ballet, & F. Comim (Eds.). *Children and the capability approach*, (pp. 22–45). New York: Palgrave Macmillan.

Becker, G.S. (1964). *Human capital: A theoretical and empirical analysis with special reference to education*. New York: National Bureau of Economic Research; distributed by Columbia University Press.

Becker, G.S. (1976). *The economic approach to human behavior*. Chicago: University of Chicago Press.

Becker, G.S. (1993). *Human capital*. Third Edition. Chicago: University of Chicago Press.

Biggeri, M., Ballet, J., & Comim, F. (2011). (Eds.). *Children and the capability approach*. New York: Palgrave Macmillan.

Biggeri, M., & Santi, M. (2012). The missing dimensions of children's well-being and well-becoming in education systems: Capabilities and philosophy for children. *Journal of Human Development and Capabilities*, 13(3), 373–395.

Buzzelli, C.A. (2015a). The capabilities approach: Rethinking agency, freedom and capital in early education. *Contemporary Issues in Early Childhood*, 16(3), 203–213.

Buzzelli, C.A. (2015b). How human capital theory sells early education short: Revaluing early education through the capabilities approach. In D. Lightfoot & R. Peach (Eds.), *Questioning the discourses of human capital in early childhood education: Reconceptualizing theory, policy and practice*, (pp. 215–230). New York: Palgrave.

Buzzelli, C.A. (2018). The moral dimensions of assessment in early childhood education. *Contemporary Issues in Early Childhood*, 19(2), 1–13.

Buzzelli, C.A. (2019). The capabilities approach: A new perspective on enduring and critical questions. In C. Brown, M. McMullen, & N. File (Eds.), *Wiley Blackwell Publishing handbook of early childhood care and education*, (pp. 683–704). Oxford, UK.

Buzzelli, C.A., & Johnston, B. (2002). *The moral dimensions of teaching: Language, culture and power in classroom interaction*. New York: Routledge Falmer.

Carr, M., & Lee, W. (2012). *Learning stories: Constructing learner identities in early education*. London: SAGE Publishing.

Colegrove, K.S., & Adair, J.K. (2014). Countering deficit thinking: Agency, capabilities and the early learning experiences of children of Latina/o immigrants. *Contemporary Issues in Early Childhood*, 15(2), 122–135.

Deneulin, S. (2014a). *Wellbeing, justice and development ethics*. London: Routledge.

Deneulin, S. (2014b). Constructing new policy narratives. In G.A. Cornia & F. Stewart (Eds.) *Towards human development: New approaches to macroeconomics and inequality*, (pp. 45–64). Oxford: Oxford University Press.

Deneulin, D., & Shahani, L. (2009). (Eds.). *An introduction to the human development and capability approach: Freedom and agency*. Oxford: Earthscan and International Development Research Centre.

Goulet, D. (1971). *The cruel choice: A new concept in the theory of development*. New York: Atheneum.

Goulet, D. (1995). *Development ethics: A guide to theory and practice*. London: Zed Books Ltd.

Goulet, D. (1997). Development ethics: A new discipline. *International Journal of Social Economics*, 24(11), 1160–1171.

Hansen, D.T. (1999). Understanding students. *Journal of Curriculum and Supervision*, 14(2), 171–185.

Hansen, D.T. (2001). *Exploring the moral heart of teaching: Toward a teacher's creed*. New York: Teachers College Press.

Harms, T., Clifford, R., & Cryer, D. (2004). *Early Childhood Environment Rating Scale: Revised Edition.* New York: Teachers College Press.

Hart, C. (2012). *Aspirations, education and social justice: Applying Sen and Bourdieu.* London: Bloomsbury Publishing.

Heckman, J., Grunewald, R., & Reynolds, A.J. (2006). The dollars and cents of investing early: Cost-benefit analysis in early care and education. *Zero to Three,* 26(6), 10–17.

Heckman, J.J. (2008). Schools, skills and synapses. *Economic Inquiry,* 46(3), 289–324.

Moss, P. (2008). Sociocultural implications for assessment. In P. Moss, D. Pullin, J.P. Gee, E. H. Haertel, & L.J. Young, (Eds.). *Assessment, equity and opportunity to learn,* (pp. 222–258). Cambridge: Cambridge University Press.

Moss, P., Dahlberg, G., Grieshaber, S., Mantovani, S., May, H., Pence, A., & Vanderbroeck, M. (2016). The Organisation for Economic Co-operation and Development's International Early Learning Study: Opening for debate and contestation. *Contemporary Issues in Early Childhood,* 17(3), 343–351.

Moss, P., & Urban, M. (2018). The Organisation for Economic Co-operation and Development's International Early Learning Study: What happened next. *Contemporary Issues in Early Childhood,* 18(2), 250–258.

National Association for the Education of Young Children (2011). *Code of ethical conduct and statement of commitment.* Washington, DC: NAEYC. Retrieved from www.naeyc.org/sites/default/files/globallyshared/downloads/PDFs/resources/position-statements/Ethics%20Position%20Statement2011_09202013update.pdf

Nussbaum, M. (2000). *Women and human development: The capabilities approach.* Cambridge: Cambridge University Press.

Nussbaum, M. (2011). *Creating capabilities.* Cambridge: Belknap Press.

Organization for Economic Co-operation and Development (OECD) (2018). *Early learning matters.* Paris: OECD.

Rawls, J. (1971). *A theory of justice.* Cambridge, MA: Belknap Press of Harvard University.

Rawls, J. (2001). *Justice as fairness: A restatement.* Cambridge, MA: Harvard University Press.

Robeyns, I. (2005). The capability approach: A theoretical survey. *Journal of Human Development,* 6(1), 93–114.

Robeyns, I. (2006a). Three models of education: Rights, capabilities, and human capital. *Theory and Research in Education,* 4(1), 69–84.

Robeyns, I. (2006b). The capability approach in practice. *Journal of Political Philosophy,* 14(3), 351–376.

Schultz, T. (1963). *The economic value of education.* New York: Columbia University Press.

Schwandt, T. (2002). *Evaluation practice reconsidered.* New York: Peter Lang.

Schwandt, T.A. (2005). The centrality of practice to evaluation. *American Journal of Evaluation,* 26(1), 95–105.

Schwandt, T.A. (2007). Expanding the conversation on evaluation ethics. *Evaluation and Program Planning,* 30(4), 400–403.

Schwandt, T.A. (2013). On the mutually informing relationship between practice and theory in evaluation. *American Journal of Evaluation,* 35(2), 231–236.

Sen, A. (1980). Equality of what? in S. McMurrin (ed.), *The Tanner lectures on human values,* (pp. 196–220). Salt Lake City: University of Utah Press and Cambridge University Press.

Sen, A. (1984). *Resources, values, and development.* Cambridge, MA: Harvard University Press.

Sen, A. (1985). Well-being, agency and freedom: The Dewey lectures 1984. *Journal of Philosophy,* 62(4), 169–221.

Sen, A. (1987). *On ethics and economics.* Malden, MA: Blackwell.

Sen, A. (1990). Justice: Means versus freedoms. *Philosophy and Public Affairs*, 19(2), 111–121.
Sen, A. (1992). *Inequality reexamined*. Oxford: Oxford University Press.
Sen, A. (1997). Human capital and human capability. *World Development*, 25(12), 1959–1961.
Sen, A. (1999). *Development as freedom*. Oxford: Oxford University Press.
Sen, A. (2005). Human rights and capabilities. *Journal of Human Development*, 6(2), 151–166.
Sen, A. (2009). *The idea of justice*. New York: Allen Lane/Penguin Books.
Unterhalter, D. (2009). Education. In S. Deneulin & L. Shahani (Eds.) *An introduction to human development and capability approach*, (pp. 207–227). London: Earthscan.
Vaughan, R.P. (2015). Education, social justice and school diversity: Insights from the Capability Approach. *Journal of Human Development and Capabilities*, 17(2), 206–224.
Walker, M., & Unterhalter, E. (2007). The capability approach: Its potential for work in education. In M. Walker & E. Unterhalter (Eds.) *Amartya Sen's capability approach and social justice in education*, (pp. 1–18). New York: Palgrave.

12

COUNTERING THE ESSENTIALIZED DISCOURSE OF CURRICULUM

Opening Spaces for Complicated Conversations

Andrew J. Stremmel, James P. Burns, Christine Nganga, and Katherine Bertolini

We have heard teachers, teacher educators, and teacher candidates define curriculum in various ways: as the textbook, the standards, pacing guides, scope and sequence charts, and even the test itself. Those conceptualizations convey an understanding of curriculum as something given to teachers to "deliver" to students. The problem with this view is that curriculum is something outside the child, something that is predetermined and prepackaged for easy consumption by some policymaker, academic scholar, or expert. Such technical/ends-means notions of curriculum represent an undemocratic and seriously flawed approach to pedagogy and defeat an essential principle of education: that it is worthy in its own right (Dewey, 1960; Holt, 1990; Stenhouse, 1975). What we hope to articulate in this chapter is a re-understanding of curriculum for children that reaffirms the humanizing potential of education to create community, to support teachers and children to listen, think, and speak mindfully and respectfully, and to be catalysts for change, even at the smallest level. This curriculum engages children to see themselves as agents, who can change their futures, solve their problems, live with hope and imagination, as they create a sense that things can be otherwise. Such a curriculum begins with the notion that good teaching starts with seeing our students as fully human.

In the following pages, we contextualize the present state of curriculum in the paradoxical time and place in which the curriculum studies field currently exists. The bureaucratic rationalization of curriculum established by Tyler (1949) – setting objectives, planning and organizing educational experience, and assessment – has seduced the common sense of the education establishment (Kumashiro, 2008). We propose that Tyler's "rationale" forms a system of governmentality and a regime of truth (Foucault, 2007, 2008) that effects power through the bodies of teachers and children alike. That power seeks the formation of a fabric of disciplinary habits (Foucault, 1977/1995) to create docile, compliant, governable subjects. The reconceptualization of curriculum studies (Pinar, Reynolds, Slattery, & Taubman, 1995), however, has also created many trajectories into curriculum scholarship and theorizing. In problematizing curriculum as a common core of predetermined, assessable official knowledge (Apple, 2001), curriculum theorists attempt to conceptualize dialogic spaces that speak to "a world children know" (Grumet, 1988, p. 171).

We then discuss a curriculum of possibilities based on the notions of relationships, a strong and positive understanding of the child, and the child's process of becoming. We ground our work in the organizing principle of the reconceptualized curriculum studies field as "an extremely complicated conversation" in which "the field has attempted to 'take back' curriculum from the bureaucrats, to make the curriculum field itself a conversation, and in so doing, work to understand curriculum" (Pinar et al., 1995, p. 848). In that spirit, we do not intend to prescribe the "how to" of curriculum. Rather, we critically analyze what has been done in the name of curriculum, and encourage readers to continually question and think differently about it. Like Grumet (1988), we invite teachers, teacher educators, and students to bring their subjectivities with them into the conversation to create aesthetic spaces in which we can truly experience the world. What kind of curriculum, then, could we develop that would support both a view of the child as active, competent, communicative, and social and the view of learning as the development of personal meaning, hope, understanding of self and others, caring, social justice, and possibility?

We believe that curriculum should create spaces for dialogue and inquiry, relationships and partnerships, spaces where children can take initiative and uncover humanizing possibilities (Freire, 1970; Greene, 1988) and teachers can facilitate learning in the encounter of togetherness between adults and children (Rinaldi, 2004; van Manen, 1991). In a democratic society it is within these spaces that children and adults "can be provoked to reach beyond themselves and be empowered to think about what they are doing, to become mindful, to share meanings, to conceptualize, and to make sense of their lived experience" (Greene, 1988, p. 12). Unfortunately, we are seeing less of this in our increasingly techno-fundamentalist (Vaidhyanathan, 2018), standardized, privatized, and consumerist society, where the dominant discourse remains effectiveness, proficiency, efficiency, and excellence narrowly defined and one-dimensional. Even in early childhood education, once the landscape for play and active learning and the development of social skills and relationships, we are seeing increasing evidence of a return to direct instruction, more time with workbooks and performance-based curriculum (Christakis, 2016).

Reducing curriculum to a stifling pedagogy of memorization, teaching to the test, and classroom practices that celebrate mindless repetition and conformity is what we (Stremmel, Burns, Nganga, & Bertolini, 2015) have previously referred to as an "essentialized" audit culture. This culture, which pervades the education system in the United States, devalues and deskills teachers. We believe that teachers cannot care about children without caring about the economic, social, and political world from which they come and to which they go. However, as Giroux (2012) and others (Ayers, 2016; Palmer, 1998; Schubert, 2012) have noted, the things that children are being taught in schools typically bear no relation to the world in which they live. In the following section we offer a more detailed account of essentialized curriculum, our re-understanding of curriculum (Pinar, 2006), and then offer the possibilities we envision. However, we underscore that these possibilities are not prescriptive but our efforts to envision curriculum as a verb rather than predetermined performance tasks – an invitation to participate in the ongoing quest to open spaces for complicated conversations.

What Has Curriculum Become?

The curriculum studies field currently occupies a paradoxical historical moment. On the one hand, the field's reconceptualization, begun in the 1970s, has broadened curriculum scholarship and theorizing as a subjective, historicized, internationalized field of intellectual inquiry open to myriad theoretical frameworks and modes of representation (Pinar et al., 1995). On the other hand, the reconceptualization occurred simultaneously with the rise of the long-term neoliberal project. Politicians, policymakers, and many in the education establishment have become enthralled to audit culture, logics of corporate management and accounting practices that disaggregate every aspect of teaching and learning into discrete, quantifiable, auditable metrics of accountability (Shore & Wright, 1999, 2000; Taubman, 2009). Exemplified by practices such as value-added measures (VAM) of teaching effectiveness, audit culture in education has framed teaching as the "facilitation" of learning as measured by standardized assessments (Pinar, 2012). Most insidiously, audit culture comprises a rationalizing system of surveillance through which teachers and their students form a self-auditing and more easily governable subjectivity (Shore & Wright, 1999, 2000).

The "historic mistake" through which curriculum was conjoined with teaching has thus located the responsibility for "social engineering at the site of the teacher" (Pinar, 2006, p. 110) and positioned the teacher as singularly accountable for both social transformation and student learning outcomes (Kumashiro, 2008, 2012; Taubman, 2009). Proposals that support the systematization of curriculum, instruction, and assessment are not new. From the social efficiency and life-adjustment movements (Hofstadter, 1962; Kliebard, 2004; Pinar, 2012) to the "Tyler Rationale" (Tyler, 1949) and its rebranding as "backward planning" (Wiggins & McTighe, 2005), the notion of curriculum as lived experience and academic study has historically struggled against instrumental conceptions of curriculum as systematic protocols. Instrumental schooling effects disciplinary power through the bodies of teachers, education professors, and children through sophisticated political technologies of the body (Foucault, 1977/1995). Techniques of constant compulsory surveillance, obsessive measurement, data collection, and assessment form compliant governable subjects and position curriculum as a means to an end, the compliment of the capitalist obsession with practical effects (Pinar, 2006).

The conditions of possibility through which our contemporary curricular problem emerged – the degradation of education into standards, assessment, systems management, and the "engineering of understanding" (Wiggins & McTighe, 2005) through the Pavlovian replication of predetermined performance objectives – is expressed by the "Tyler Rationale." Tyler's "small book" (1949, p. 1), originally a syllabus for his course "Basic Principles of Curriculum and Instruction," solidified the rationalization of curriculum, teaching, and testing and formed the regime of truth that has haunted education since. The Tyler Rationale's curricular instrumentalism fits well with the habituation of students and teachers to prevailing modes of power. National initiatives like No Child Left Behind and Race to the Top illustrate Tyler's linking of objectives and assessment with accountability. Instrumental schooling thus perpetuates the sequestering function of schools by which teachers and children form the "fabric of habits" necessary to produce a docile subjectivity (Foucault, 1977/1995, 2015). Tyler's (1949) regime of truth, predicated on the following four questions he posed (p. 1), persists in the present. We re-present Tyler's protocol, encapsulated in the four questions around which it is based through a Foucauldian analytical lens and suggest that Tyler's systemic understanding of curriculum has proven a durable technology of power for decades.

1 What Educational Purposes Should the School Seek to Attain?

Tyler (1949) links "all aspects of an educational program" to objectives, which "become the criteria" for material selection, content, instructional procedures, and assessment (p. 3). The emphasis on objectives and characterization education as "means to accomplish basic educational purposes" (Tyler, 1949, p. 1) configure education as "a process of changing the behavior patterns of people." Tyler's (1949) association of objectives with the "difference or gap" between a child's thoughts and behaviors "compared with some desirable standards, some conception of acceptable norms" (p. 6) is a normalizing process imbricated with deficit ideology and overt and subtle disciplinary power.

2 What Educational Experiences Can Be Provided That Are Likely to Attain These Purposes?

Tyler (1949) places responsibility for demonstrable, measurable student learning – defined in explicitly behaviorist terms as normative learning objectives that address children's behavioral and intellectual deficiencies – on teachers and their ability to create commensurable "educational experiences." Tyler's (1949) linkage between objectives and the teacher's responsibility to create and sequence educational experiences to meet those objectives reflects the standardizing principle of curricular alignment. That linkage also has become institutionalized in Michelle Rhee's maxim, "teachers are everything" (Ravitch, 2010, p. 172) and the corollary scapegoating of teachers who ostensibly require punitive accountability systems to ensure their effectiveness (Kumashiro, 2008, 2012; Pinar, 2006, 2012). Glossing over the "Pavlovian overtones" of his "rationale" (Kliebard, 1970, p. 268), Tyler's (1949) systematic program supports habituating students and teachers to behavioral norms that supersede both academic content and the subjective lived experiences of children and teachers alike. Tyler (1949) used language about schooling similar to that used by Foucault (1977/1995) in his analysis of disciplinary tactics of the prison, which form "the art of constructing, with located bodies, coded activities and trained aptitudes" (p. 167). Tyler (1949) recommends five "general principles in selecting learning experiences": opportunities to practice desired behaviors; student satisfaction; adjusting experiences to students' "present attainments"; using a variety of experiences; and efficient use of time (pp. 65–68). Learning experiences anchored to objectives formulate a regimen through which individuals develop the normalizing habits of compliant, useful, governable subjects.

3 How Can These Educational Experiences Be Effectively Organized?

The organization of educational experiences maximizes their cumulative effect through disciplinary techniques. Tyler's (1949) protocol consists of the development of objectives based on the need to habituate children to embody desirable behavioral norms, which in neoliberal audit culture are policed through constant observation and intrusive technologies of data collection, assessment, and measurement. Tyler (1949) thus completes his systematic curriculum and instruction program based on the articulation of objectives and the creation and organization of educational experiences aligned with those objectives by subsuming it under assessment, which has configured education as an "apparatus of uninterrupted examination" (Foucault, 1977/1995, p. 186).

4 How Can We Determine Whether These Purposes Are Being Attained?

Evaluation for Tyler (1949) provides the evidence for the systematic judgment of the effectiveness of any school's curriculum and instruction program, and in contemporary accountability discourses, the effectiveness of teachers and even teacher education programs. Currently, the persistent "rituals of verification" (Shore & Wright, 2000, p. 84) illustrated by the "Tyler Rationale" have institutionalized an "age of infinite examination and of compulsory objectification" (Foucault, 1977/1995, p. 189). Yet Tyler's (1949) curricular protocol of objectives linked to the summative evaluation of the effectiveness of learning experiences has created an incommensurable system, which Kliebard (1970) critiques through Dewey's argument that ends arise and function within action:

> If ends arise only *within* activity it is not clear how one can state objectives before the activity (learning experience) begins. Dewey's position, then, has important consequences not just for Tyler's process of evaluation but for the rationale as a whole. . . . The most significant dimensions of an educational activity or any activity may be those that are completely unplanned and wholly unanticipated. An evaluation procedure that ignores this fact is plainly unsatisfactory.
>
> *(pp. 268–269)*

If, as Dewey suggested, ends emerge only within activity, then Tyler's (1949) predetermination of ends before learning experiences begin forecloses children's learning possibilities inherent in the unknowabilities of teaching and learning and eliminate the subjective agency of children and teachers alike (Pinar, 2012). The role of assessment in Tyler's (1949) protocol links the formation of institutional knowledge with the exercise of power in four ways. First, examination transforms an "economy of visibility into the exercise of power" (Foucault, 1977/1995, p. 187). Rationalizing carceral institutions, including schools, effect disciplinary power through rendering those who inhabit those spaces constantly visible:

> It is the fact of constantly being seen, of being able always to be seen, that maintains the disciplined individual in his [sic] subjection. And the examination is the technique by which power, instead of emitting the signs of its potency, instead of imposing its mark on its subjects, holds them in a mechanism of objectification. . . . The examination is, as it were, the ceremony of this objectification.
>
> *(p. 187)*

Second, examination "introduces individuality into the field of documentation," which habituates submission to authority by creating a cumulative, detailed, system of written records that fix children and teachers within institutions:

> The examination leaves behind it a whole meticulous archive constituted in terms of bodies and days. The examination that places individuals in a field of surveillance also situates them in a network of writing; it engages them in a whole mass of documents that capture and fix them. The procedures of examination were accompanied at the same time by a system of intense registration and of documentary accumulation. A "power of writing" was constituted as an essential part in the mechanisms of discipline.
>
> *(Foucault, 1977/1995, p. 189)*

Third, constant examination and documentary technologies make "each individual a 'case'" that can be "described, judged, measured, compared with others in his [sic] very individuality; and it is also the individual who has to be trained or corrected, classified, normalized, excluded, etc." (Foucault, 1977/1995, p. 191). Examination comprises a technology of power that confers individuality to children, teachers, and education professors by linking their individuality to the characteristics that constitute them as individual cases.

Fourth, examination constitutes individuals as the "effect and object of power, as effect and object of knowledge" (Foucault, 1977/1995, p. 192). Examination combines "hierarchical surveillance and normalizing judgment" to assure the "disciplinary functions of distribution and classification" designed to maximize the forces of civil society, and in systems of classificatory power "individual difference is relevant" (Foucault, 1977/1995, p. 192). The normalizing power to create and make even the smallest individual differences visible is essential in systems of governmentality because the chief concern of governmental rationalization is the building and distribution of the bodies that comprised the state's forces – in neoliberal terminology, its human capital – to assure social order and contribute to prevailing modes of economic production.

The "Tyler Rationale" became accepted as canonical by the 1970s, and remains so today, except among curriculum theorists and historians (Pinar, 2011). Tyler's (1949) "small book" has persisted precisely because of its very rationality (Kliebard, 1970), which has deified Tyler to some and contributes to the ongoing tragedy of American education:

> Establishing objectives disguises the political content of the curriculum by creating the illusion of a rational professional practice independent of ideological investment. . . . The 1949 Tyler was evidently blind to the ways his emphasis upon objectives devalued academic knowledge by reducing it to a means. . . to an external end, even a laudable one like "social sensitivity." Such instrumentality effaces experimentation by determining the destination before the journey has begun. . . . The specification of objectives – then linking evaluation to these – forecloses the unknown future as it recapitulates the present.
>
> *(Pinar, 2011, pp. 84–85)*

Currently, popular curriculum design protocols, notably Understanding by Design (UbD) or "backward design," are ubiquitous in schools and teacher education programs. UbD restates the "Tyler Rationale" nearly verbatim: "An essential act of our profession is the crafting of curriculum and learning experiences to meet specified purposes" (Wiggins & McTighe, 2005, p. 13). UbD's three stages of backward design have distilled Tyler's (1949) four fundamental questions into a pithy three-step protocol (Wiggins & McTighe, 2005, pp. 17–18):

1 Identify desired results
2 Determine acceptable evidence
3 Plan learning experiences and instruction

UbD's identification of desired results corresponds with Tyler's (1949) statement of desired objectives, and Wiggins and McTighe (2005, p. 18) reformulate and move Tyler's (1949) fourth question ("How can we determine whether these purposes are being attained?") to Stage 2 of backward design and ask, again restating the "Tyler Rationale" nearly verbatim: "How will we know if students have achieved the desired results?" UbD moves the planning of learning experiences to the final stage of backward design because the "specifics of instructional planning," including the sequencing of learning experiences, rely on prior identification of "desired results and assessments" (Wiggins & McTighe, 2005, p. 19), a move that further reduces curriculum to a means to attain assessable "desired results" (p. 18). We view systems like UbD as further retrenchment toward teaching to the test, which actually supports punitive accountability discourses that place responsibility for student learning solely on the teacher.

Wiggins and McTighe (2005), in homage to Tyler (1949), present their backward design model as scientifically proven educational common sense: "This view of focusing intently on the desired learning is hardly radical or new. Tyler (1949) described the logic of backward design clearly and succinctly more than 50 years ago." UbD ultimately reifies a framework that reduces curriculum to an assemblage of assessable performance tasks:

> Thus, the local assessment plan has to involve more high-quality, application-focused performance tasks. . . . Yet most curriculum frameworks ignore or give short shrift to assessments, even though specificity about the curriculum requires clarity about the performance targets that embody its goals – the assessments and rubrics.
>
> *(p. 282)*

UbD restates the Tyler Rationale's conflation of curriculum, teaching, and evaluation, its link between behaviorist predetermined objectives and assessment, and its focus on transferable performance tasks. Wiggins and McTighe (2005) characterize Tyler (1949) as the "dean of modern student assessment" whose "seminal book on design" forefronts "the need to think about curricular matters from the perspective of desired outcomes and the learner's needs," which "laid out the basic principles of backward design" (p. 298).

Tyler (1949) and his progeny have institutionalized among far too many in teaching and teacher education an oppressive rationalizing definition of curriculum as a noun, a commodity, a means to some predefined practical end. That conceptualization of curriculum has institutionalized a regime of veridiction through which the truths of learning and teaching are continuously extracted from children and teachers through subtle disciplinary tactics. Curriculum as protocol is one example of the insidiousness of the carceral society of which Foucault (1977/1995) wrote. We reject that view of curriculum and devote the remainder of this chapter to wondering new ways of curriculum as a verb, of *currere* – the running of the course (Pinar, 2004, 2012) as ways of being with each other and in solitary moments of study and self and social reconstruction.

Gazing toward the Horizon: Re-understanding Curriculum

The organizing principle of the curriculum studies field is a complicated conversation, of encounter with many interlocutors, including ourselves, from the past and the present, of subjective risk, of self and social reconstruction (Pinar et al., 1995). To the detriment of curriculum as complicated conversation and the reflexivity of lived experience, many schools of education have responded to contemporary punitive accountability regimes – school deform (Pinar, 2012) – through an intensive research focus on instruction that prioritizes teaching effectiveness to facilitate quicker student learning as measured by standardized assessments (Pinar, 2004). Curriculum theorists invite more emphasis on curriculum, although not in the prevailing sense of curriculum as bureaucratized protocols (Pinar, 2004). Indeed, the imposition of order by schools and their current rationalizing curriculum development templates circumvents the very intellectual and affective disorder that is necessary to continuously reconstruct one's understanding of the self and the social world. The labor of reconstructing our understanding of curriculum as complicated conversation involves excavating knowledges and ways of being that have been institutionally subjugated to effect normalizing power over teachers, children, and increasingly teacher education programs.

Just as Gadamer's (2004) concept of horizon envisages a voyage of continuous reinterpretation of self and world, Ricoeur's (1981) hermeneutic notion of distanciation, or distancing, introduces a "paradox of otherness, a tension between proximity and distance, which is essential to historical consciousness" (p. 61). The curricular method of *currere* intentionally cultivates the "temporality of subjectivity, insisting on the distinctiveness *and* simultaneity of past, present, and future, a temporal complexity in which difference does not dissolve onto a flattened never-ending 'now'" (Pinar, 2012, p. 227, emphasis in original). The concept of horizon acknowledges the limitations inherent in the present and requires the "person who is trying to understand... to look beyond what is close at hand – not in order to look away from it but to see it better, within a larger whole and in truer proportion" (Gadamer, 2004, p. 304). Re-understanding curriculum thus moves away from education as delivering information, and toward a hermeneutic imbricated with subjective agency, complex intersubjective inquiry. This occurs within spaces imbued with Ricoeur's (1981) paradox of otherness, the humility to put our deepest-held beliefs and assumptions to self and social scrutiny, and the courage to reconstruct our partial knowledges as we work toward the reconstruction of the social world.

Curriculum as we conceive of it is not a corpus of official knowledge (Apple, 2001) delivered or banked (Freire, 1970) through effective teaching strategies and best practices (Taubman, 2009). Rather, we are re-understanding curriculum as the creation of spaces both inside and outside classrooms where we, and our students, share our lived experiences, interests, and desires. Those non-instrumental curricular spaces, unshackled from the conformity of a script and the replication of predetermined measurable learning outcomes (Pinar, 2012), might cultivate the affective and intellectual capacities of children, and ourselves as teachers and teacher educators. The intellectual disposition of a deep desire to know and to understand the self and the social world is an aspect of curriculum design that is deeply lacking in schools and teacher education programs. It is that nascent intellectual tradition, historically denigrated in the American psyche as extraneous to the practical effects of instrumental schooling as disciplinary power (Hofstadter, 1962), that might help us resuscitate the nearly moribund democratic project. It is toward those possibilities that we now turn.

Possibilities

Curriculum, on one level, is everything that goes on in the life of the classroom or school – the unanticipated and unintended as well as the planned, the hidden as well as the overt, the experienced as well as the stated. It also is both the intentional and unintentional efforts to develop the social, intellectual, physical, emotional, creative, and ethical capacities of each child and to build a safe, caring, and respectful curricular and pedagogical community. In our practice, we have understood curriculum to be every attempt we make continuously to create possibilities for the emergence of authentic relationships between and among children, teachers, parents, and other members of the learning community we call the classroom. Like Pinar (2004), we have also come to understand that a singular focus on the classroom or the school can divert our attention from the rich, unstructured, and unanticipated curricular possibilities that exist in myriad other social and subjective spaces.

A recent example of the formation of just such a public complicated curricular conversation lies in the public actions of many of the students who survived the February 14, 2018, massacre perpetrated by a former student at Marjorie Stoneman High School in Parkland, Florida. Those young people rallied around the possibility of creating a safer and more just and humane world by acting on their rights as citizens in a democratic society. They confronted state and national political leaders and organized a series of student-led walkouts and strikes across the country to demand that elected leaders act to address the existential threat posed by the unmitigated proliferation of military weapons among the population. Students like Emma Gonzalez and David Hogg, who faced harassment that ranged from taunting on right-wing media to numerous death threats, opened a national and international curricular space on a curricular topic of grave importance – masculinized violence perpetrated in school and society. This, while certainly informed by their academic study in their classrooms, also embodied an ethics of social reconstruction predicated on their abiding concerns for a more just and peaceful world. The curricular ethics demonstrated by these students, and others like them, invited the world to engage in a difficult, necessary dialogue about healing, inclusivity, and a badly needed reconciliation between and among individuals and groups who are suffering tremendous emotional pain in a fractured country filled with animus and rage. They publicly embodied an ethic of reconstruction of the public sphere through curricular discourse, which Pinar (2006) characterized as a public practice to teach, rather than to impose one's viewpoints on others:

> Explaining one's point of view while working to understand others' in dialogical encounters enacts a pedagogical model of the public sphere wherein social relationships become less combative, manipulative, and self-serving and, instead, more educational.
>
> *(Pinar, 2006, p. 8)*

While we understand that this volume focuses on early childhood curriculum, our critique and the possibilities we ask readers to consider are applicable across all levels of education. The essentialized audit culture has denigrated a humanizing and whole child education and led to a myopic view of the child's journey in the process of becoming. We envision, alternatively, a curriculum that would allow us to focus on what was, what is, and what is to come and to effect continuities. It would allow opportunities to explore other ways of seeing and being and emphasize the human freedom to surpass the given and look at things as if they could be otherwise (Dewey, 1902, 1960; Greene, 1988; Rinaldi, 2004). Curriculum thus imagined would enable children at any age to ask their own questions and create their own educational experience as an effort to compose and make meaning of their lives, interpret their pasts, and imagine possibilities.

A look at Dewey's view of the child and the curriculum helps to clarify this point. In the now classic book *The Child and the Curriculum*, John Dewey (1902) stated,

> The child's present experience is in no way self-explanatory. It is not final, but transitional. It is nothing complete in itself, but just a sign or index of certain growth-tendencies. As long as we confine our gaze to what the child here and now puts forth, we are confused and misled. We cannot read its meaning. Extreme depreciations of the child morally and intellectually, and sentimental idealizations of him, have their root in a common fallacy. Both spring from taking stages of growth or movement as something cut off and fixed.
>
> *(p. 191)*

What Dewey (1902) suggests, is that the child is always in transition. Some of what we observe, if we observe carefully at all, are the child's waning tendencies.

Other activities are signs of culminating ability and interest (the place where curriculum, teaching, and learning should intersect). Moreover, under the right conditions we see behaviors and feelings and insights that are prophetic of what might or will be, or as Dewey (1902) states so eloquently, "the dawning of a flickering light that will shine steadily in the future" (p. 192). In essence, when we observe the child we see what is, what was, and what could be, the development of new strategies, new ways of thinking, new ways of problem-solving, and new ways of being.

If the child is in transition, then confining our gaze to what the child puts forth here and now might limit our understanding of who the child is. An essentialized educational view promotes the idea of the child as a statistical profile (i.e., a test score, an age, a gender stereotype, a commodity). Test scores and grades often are the rationale for preparing children for what comes next in the curriculum, what and how we teach. They are not fair measures of intelligence, achievement, or worth.

An understanding of how to educate, a theory of teaching and learning, must begin with the child (Rinaldi, 2004), which implies considerable faith and confidence in the potential and capabilities of the child. While this should be a self-evident reality, it is a reality often lost in the current audit culture. It also suggests that education happens in relationships and that excellent teaching can be demonstrated only in the encounter of togetherness between adult and child (Rinaldi, 2004; van Manen, 1991). Curriculum focused on hope and possibility invites children to become somehow more capable, more thoughtful and powerful in their choices, more engaged in a culture and a community. How do we warrant that invitation?

What Does a Curriculum of Possibilities Look Like?

What kind of curriculum, then, would we develop that would support both a view of the child as active, competent, communicative, and social and the view of learning as the development of personal meaning, hope, understanding of self and others, caring, social justice, and possibility? Our aim is to invite the reader to re-understand curriculum as a complex conversation around the inexhaustible question: "What knowledge and experience is of most value?" (Ayers, 1993; Pinar, 2006; Schubert, 2012). We suggest that curriculum engages children and immerses them as fully as possible into every aspect of the life of the community. This is a curriculum where children learn by doing, thinking, and problem solving. Children's questions and interests are honored and built upon as they move naturally to what draws them. Children act as apprentices, observing and participating with others at first, as they develop greater skills and more independence with experience (Vygotsky, 1978).

There is a word used among the Igbu people of Nigeria that beautifully expresses the respect for children that is the hallmark of any curriculum designed to honor the interests and curiosities of children. It is the word *ginekanwa*, which means, "What is greater than a child?", and the implicit response is, "Nothing is greater than a child." A strong and positive understanding of the child is critical to the way teachers interact with and support the becoming of every child. From birth, infants begin to navigate and understand their world. Their eyes and gestures show their intentions to communicate, establish a relationship, and express a feeling, a thought, or a question. Children investigate, explore, and search for meaning and understanding in everything they do. Thus, the image of children as strong, competent, filled with curiosity and potential, is the one that we invite all educators to remain mindful of if we are to support children in their process of becoming and not treat them as objects to be taught subjects (Ayers, 2016; Rinaldi, 2004).

A humanizing curriculum focused on possibilities would begin with the question: "How do we acknowledge children's competence and ability to make sense of their worlds and contribute to their own learning and understanding and to be agents of change?" Addressing this question would involve a deliberate action to restore children's agency and re-claim their voice in the classroom (Ayers, 2016; Zinn & Rodgers, 2012). From the earliest days of life, children ask their own questions and then attempt to figure out their answers. As children interact with their world, their minds are continuously active trying to make sense of things – they question, develop hunches, test ideas, carefully observe, make inferences and then accept, modify, or reject their conclusions based on experience. Thus, curriculum designed to foster children's natural curiosity and desire to know and question would be the heart of everything that happens in an early childhood classroom. What if the classroom was viewed as a laboratory for inquiry and experimentation, a place where every kind of dramatic, verbal, social, literary, and cultural idea could be played out (Ayers, 2016; Paley, 2013)? This might be a place where the real problems that children encounter could be addressed through interactions with others who may have different ideas and perspectives, and where children's own stories could be brought to life in the classroom. From a pedagogical standpoint, the most important question a teacher would ask is "How does the child experience this situation, relationship, or event?" From a perspective of an ethic of caring, the children themselves become the central concern.

The essentialized curriculum is about providing adult answers, imposing content or subject matter from the outside. Yet, to develop the curriculum by objectives to be achieved assumes that knowledge can be predicted in advance of an educational experience and may set limits on human agency and development (Dewey, 1960; Stenhouse, 1975). "What if learning, not teaching or performing to meet specific objectives, was our primary focus?" Then, education would be about living now and curriculum would involve learning real content while children engage in worthwhile pursuits. Children learn what they live.

John Holt (1990) suggested that children do not think of themselves as learning; they think of themselves as doing. He reminds us that children do not choose to learn things in order to do them in the future. They choose to do right now what matters to them in the moment – real things, whole meaningful activities like problem solving and figuring things out. Furthermore, Hatch (2010, 2012) has argued that learning provides the framework upon which early childhood curriculum should be built. Citing Vygotsky (1978), Hatch suggested that learning happens in exchanges with adults and peers who are more competent in tasks and activities that are personally and culturally meaningful. He further adds that children should be learning real content, focusing on children's natural tendencies to learn, question, and figure out. We believe this content should, in some way, include a goal of problem solving, whether it is trying to understand something that is puzzling; finding a practical solution to a vexing situation; designing or creating something new and testing and evaluating it; or using prediction, reasoning, and analysis to make a decision, an interpretation, or draw a conclusion.

Schools are civic institutions that should contribute to (and reflect) a democratic society.

Children are citizens of their communities and should participate in meaningful ways in the activities and dilemmas of their communities (Rinaldi, 2004). "What if curriculum encouraged democratic living, where each child had the right to be heard and listened to, and could pursue real problems and preferences without fear of judgement?" This curriculum would promote dialogue; problem-solving; collaboration; perspective taking; appreciation for diverse views; and listening within a community of living and learning. Children would not be isolated in classrooms, but engaged in authentic and meaningful community activities with audacity and vision. Projects and investigations that enable children to participate in their communities and engage in meaningful problems would constitute curriculum. Authentic projects such as fixing broken things; repairing neighborhood houses; creating neighborhood gardens; solving community problems related to food production and transportation; or providing food and clothing for the homeless would foster community pride and citizenship. Children's questions (inquiry) into real problems within their school or local communities would tap into the deep well of human values (e.g., cooperation and collaboration, helping others, sharing knowledge, understandings, feelings and perspectives) that give life shape and meaning (Ayers, 2016; Zinn & Rodgers, 2012).

Summary

The classroom of the twenty-first century is a place of highly prescribed and enforced learning and legislatively prescribed standards. The act of re-understanding curriculum began with an analysis of what has contributed to the legacy of essentialized curriculum followed by an imagining of possibilities for what a humanizing curriculum might look like. In whatever way curriculum is imagined, we suggest that it enable children to ask their own questions, pursue their passions, and create their own educational experience as an effort to compose and make meaning of their lives, interpret their pasts, and imagine their own futures. A curriculum focused on the child and learning is about hope and possibility, about relationships and the process of becoming. Rather than a group of subjects to be taught or learned, curriculum is something to be lived. It should allow children and teachers together to live their questions with one another rather than answer them. It should enable the endless pursuit of the inexhaustible question of what matters, what knowledge and experiences are of most worth (Ayers, 1993, 2016; Pinar, 2006; Schubert, 2012). The response is always tentative and contingent, always uncertain and insufficient, yet always dynamic and complex. What should matter is how education relates to human life.

References

Apple, M.W. (2001). *Educating the "right" way: Markets, standards, God, and inequality*. New York: Routledge Falmer.
Ayers, W. (1993). *To teach: The journey of a teacher*. New York: Teacher College Press.
Ayers, W. (2016). *Teaching with conscience in an imperfect world*. New York: Teacher College Press.
Christakis, E. (2016). *The importance of being little: What young children really need from grownups*. New York: Penguin Books.
Dewey, J. (1902). The child and the curriculum. In *The School and Society and the Child and the Curriculum*, (Centennial Publications of The University of Chicago Press) 1st Edition. Chicago, IL: University of Chicago Press, 1991.
Dewey, J. (1960). *On experience, nature, and freedom*. New York: The Liberal Arts Press.
Foucault, M. (1977/1995). *Discipline & punish: The birth of the prison* (A. Sheridan, Trans.). New York: Vintage. (Original work published 1977).
Foucault, M. (2007). *Security, territory, population: Lectures at the Collège de France 1977–1978*. M. Senellart (Ed.), (G. Burchell, Trans.). New York: Picador.
Foucault, M. (2008). *The birth of biopolitics: Lectures at the Collège de France 1977–1978*. M. Senellart (Ed.), (G. Burchell, Trans.). New York: Picador.
Foucault, M. (2015). *The punitive society: Lectures at the Collège de France 1972–1973*. B.E. Harcourt (Ed.), (G. Burchell, Trans.). New York: Palgrave Macmillan.
Freire, P. (1970). *Pedagogy of the oppressed*. New York: Herder and Herder.
Gadamer, H.G. (2004). *Truth and method*. New York: Continuum.
Giroux, H.A. (2012). *Education and the crisis of public values: Challenging the assault on teachers, students, & public education*. New York: Peter Lang.
Greene, M. (1988). *The dialectic of freedom*. New York: Teacher College Press.
Grumet, M. (1988). *Bitter milk: Women and teaching*. Amherst, MA: University of Massachusetts Press.
Hatch, J.A. (2010). Rethinking the relationship between learning and development: Teaching for learning in early childhood classrooms. *The Educational Forum*, 74(3), 258–268.
Hatch, J.A. (2012). From theory to curriculum: Developmental theory and its relationship to curriculum and instruction in early childhood education. In N. File, J.J. Mueller, & D.R. Wisneski (Eds.), *Curriculum in early childhood education: Re-examined, rediscovered, renewed*. New York: Routledge.
Hofstadter, R. (1962). *Anti-intellectualism in American life*. New York: Vintage Books.
Holt, J. (1990). *A life worth living: The selected letters of John Holt*. S. Sheffer (Ed.). Columbus, OH: Ohio State University Press.

Kliebard, H. (1970). Reappraisal: The Tyler rationale. *The School Review*, 78(2), 259–272.

Kliebard, H. (2004). *The struggle for the American curriculum: 1893–1958* (3rd ed.). New York: Routledge.

Kumashiro, K.K. (2008). *The seduction of common sense: How the right has framed the debate on America's schools*. New York: Teachers College Press.

Kumashiro, K.K. (2012). *Bad teacher! How blaming teachers distorts the bigger picture*. New York: Teachers College Press.

Paley, V. (2013). Getting back on track: The importance of play and storytelling in young children's development. *Learning Landscapes*, 7(1), 43–49.

Palmer, P. (1998). *The courage to teach: Exploring the inner landscape of a teacher's life*. San Francisco, CA: Jossey-Bass.

Pinar, W. (2004). *What is curriculum theory?* Mahwah, NJ: Lawrence Erlbaum Associates, Publishers.

Pinar, W. (2006). *The synoptic text today and other essays: Curriculum development after the reconceptualization*. New York: Peter Lang.

Pinar, W. (2011). *The character of curriculum studies: Bildung, currere, and the recurring question of the subject*. New York: Palgrave Macmillan.

Pinar, W. (2012). *What is curriculum theory?* (2nd ed.). New York: Routledge.

Pinar, W., Reynolds, W., Slattery, P., & Taubman, P. (1995). *Understanding curriculum*. New York: Peter Lang.

Ravitch, D. (2010). *The death and life of the great American school system: How testing and choice are undermining education*. New York: Basic Books.

Ricoeur, P. (1981). *Hermeneutics & the human sciences*. J.B. Thompson (Ed. & Trans.). New York: Cambridge University Press.

Rinaldi, C. (2004). *In dialogue with Reggio Emilia*. New York: Routledge.

Schubert, W. (2012). Reverence for what? A teacher's quest. In A.G. Rud & J. Garrison (Eds.), *Teaching with reverence: Reviving an ancient virtue for today's schools* (pp. 113–128). New York: Palgrave Macmillan.

Shore, C., & Wright, S. (1999). Audit culture and anthropology: Neo-liberalism in British higher education. *The Journal of the Royal Anthropological Institute*, 5(4), 557–575.

Shore, C., & Wright, S. (2000). Coercive accountability: The rise of audit culture in higher education. In M. Strathern (Ed.), *Audit cultures: Anthropological studies in accountability, ethics, and the academy* (pp. 57–89). New York: Routledge.

Stenhouse, L. (1975). *An introduction to curriculum research and development*. London: Heinemann.

Stremmel, A.J., Burns, J., Nganga, C., & Bertolini, K. (2015). Countering the essentialized discourse of teacher education. *Journal of Early Childhood Teacher Education*, 36(2), 156–174.

Taubman, P.M. (2009). *Teaching by numbers: Deconstructing the discourse of standards and accountability in education*. New York: Routledge.

Tyler, R.W. (1949). *Basic principles of curriculum and instruction*. Chicago, IL: The University of Chicago Press.

Vaidhyanathan, S. (2018). *Anti-social media: How Facebook disconnects us and undermines democracy*. New York: Oxford University Press.

van Manen, M. (1991). *The tact of teaching: The meaning of pedagogical thoughtfulness*. London, Ontario, Canada: The Althouse Press.

Vygotsky, L.S. (1978). *Mind in society*. Cambridge, MA: Harvard University Press.

Wiggins, G., & McTighe, J. (2005). *Understanding by design* (2nd ed.). Alexandria, VA: ASCD.

Zinn, D., & Rodgers, C. (2012). A humanizing pedagogy: Getting beneath the rhetoric. *Perspectives in Education*, 30(4), 76–87.

13

A VISION OF EARLY CHILDHOOD CURRICULUM BUILT ON STRONG FOUNDATIONS

Katherine K. Delaney, Kristin L. Whyte, and M. Elizabeth Graue

As the bell rings, the children in Mrs. Narje's third grade classroom begin to settle down on the carpet. Mrs. Narje climbs over several reclining children and joins them on the carpet. She opens the meeting by asking the children to share anything interesting from their evening and early morning outside of school. Several children share that there was a rowdy game of HORSE happening at the basketball courts prior to the start of school. "These third graders keep stealing our ball!" one boy shouts, his face stormy. "Wow, that's really frustrating. Anyone have an idea for how we might deal with this issue?" Mrs. Narje asks. Several children shout out ideas, talking over each other. "So many strong feelings about this! Maybe we need to spend some of our math time this morning coming up with ideas. Then we could share those out and vote on the top ideas." Many children nod and agree. "Ok, great. Then we can write up our ideas and share them with the other third and fourth grade classrooms," Mrs. Narje continues. The boy who had shouted about the ball speaks up again, "They could vote too and then we might know what the top solution could be?" "We could graph it!" a girl pipes up. "Great idea!" Mrs. Narje smiles, "I love how you are connecting this with the graphing we have been doing in math. Let's make time for this today! We need to solve this problem."

Misha, almost 4 months old, is lying on her belly on a soft mat, carefully lifting and turning her head. A soft, grapefruit-sized ball is next to her body, and her left hand brushes against it as she lays her head down. The ball makes a crackling noise as her hand hits it. This pattern repeats several times with Misha batting at the ball as she lifts her chest from the ground. Her teacher, Ms. Leesa, sits nearby, holding another baby who is finishing a bottle. "You are reaching, Misha. Did you touch the ball? I heard it crackle when you touched it with your hand. Your touch made a reaction. You caused the reaction," Ms. Leesa tells her. Misha, responding to the warm, encouraging voice, squeals and smiles. She lifts her head again, this time pushing on the ground with her legs as well as her arms. Then, frustration seems to overwhelm her and she begins to whimper. "Is that enough? Do you need to move your body? Are you stuck on your belly? I am going to help you roll over," Ms. Leesa tells her, gently repositioning Misha. Ms. Leesa then hands the ball to Misha, who holds it on her chest. "I hear it crinkle when you squeeze it with your hands!" she tells Misha, who squeals again and bites down on the soft ball.

Free play is in full effect in the Head Start classroom – all centers in the classroom are occupied and children are busily engaged. One child walks up to Ms. Marcia, who is at the writing center working with several children on an ongoing letter writing project, and says, "I want to write a letter to my Mama." "Ok, Jayden, let's do it together. How do letters start?" Ms. Marcia asks him. "I dunno. Just tell me!" says Jayden, stomping a foot and looking unhappy. "Hmmm. . . Do you remember that book we read yesterday – the one that Jeremy brought from home?" asks Ms. Marcia. "Yeah, but just tell me how!" Jayden insists, stomping again. "That book was about a girl who wrote letters to her teacher," Ms. Marcia persists. Jayden thinks for a minute. "It was called 'Dear Mr. Blueberry!' So 'Dear Mama'!" Ms. Marica smiles and nods, "Yes! Dear Mama. . . That's a great way to start a letter." "Can you write it for me?" Jayden asks. "I can, but I what if we did it together?" Jayden considers this, momentarily looking like he is going to refuse, but then he scratches his head and says, "Ok. . . I know 'Dear' starts with 'D.' " "Wow – yes!" says Ms. Marcia. "Dear starts with D because D says 'd.' What other sounds do you hear? Let's stretch it out." Jayden picks up a pencil from the writing table and a sheet of lined paper. Ms. Marcia, motioning to some examples on the wall behind the writing table, says, "Here are some letters that the first graders wrote to us when we told them we were doing a project about letter writing. Maybe these examples can help us too!" Jayden nods, carefully beginning to write his "D."

Introduction

The previous vignettes, in third grade, infant, and preschool classrooms, all share multiple characteristics. What are they? They show teachers responding to, and building on, the interests of children. The teachers work to match their responses to children's bids for interaction; to make connections just beyond the moment at hand – to math, to letter sounds, to attempts, efforts and effects; to use knowledge of the children's developmental and individual needs; and to scaffold and support learning. The teachers also build from their knowledge of each child, making this central in planning how to address children's interests and engage them in learning. All of these characteristics are connected within an early childhood (EC) approach to pedagogy, curriculum, and practice.

However, it is also important to recognize how these vignettes reflect a variety of instructional practices and goals. For example, in the third grade classroom, Mrs. Narje is helping the children to connect problem-solving and mathematical practices within an everyday experience, as well as problem-solving their social interactions with peers. This connection brings together mathematical expectations (uses of graphing) framed by the district curriculum benchmarks, with opportunities for real-life problem-solving and application of these skills. In the preschool example, the teacher is bringing in skills (letter-sounds recognition and decoding) to support a child's emerging literacy practices. In this instance, this teacher is aware of both the skills he will need in kindergarten, skills that are foregrounded in programs like Head Start and state pre-kindergarten programs, as well as how to integrate and support these skills in ways that are child-centered and based on the child's interests. The third grade and preschool teachers are striking careful balances between responsive, child-centered engagements and knowledge of grade-level expectations. Even in the infant classroom example, the teacher's language reflects recent training on a classroom quality measure of infant/toddler classrooms. The teacher is carefully choosing language to help expand both her interaction with the child and practicing notions of high quality language as framed by this measure (e.g., "reaction," "cause").

These three vignettes, drawn from real classrooms,[1] provide examples of foundational elements of high quality EC practice: knowledge of individual children, of general developmental patterns, and of responsive, scaffolding practices to build on this knowledge. And these examples highlight an ongoing conundrum in educating young children – this foundational knowledge, so important for responsive caregiving and teaching, is not equally distributed in all EC settings. For example, while teachers in infant and toddler programs are expected to rely on developmental knowledge to respond to children, in early elementary settings the focus is on meeting grade level targets. In the next section, we explore the forces shaping EC curriculum, for good and ill, and what this means for how we advocate for EC practices in birth to grade 3 classrooms. We then imagine how we can sustain practices based on EC theory to inform decision-making, to create a counter-balance to the current academic push down that we see impacting pre-K, K, and possibly soon, toddler classrooms.

Current Early Childhood Context

The opening vignettes painted a picture of the expansive range of EC settings. This birth to age 8 range is not simply a historic construct of our field, but a unique developmental period where children's skills and abilities show much greater variability by age and domain than in any other period (Phillips & Shonkoff, 2000). The unique nature of this period is reflected in developmental research and indicates that EC teachers need special skills, knowledge, and dispositions to best support and guide young children's learning. In EC classrooms, the role of developmental knowledge and responsive practices in teachers' work is paramount.

The perceptions of EC teachers also lend credence to the validity of conceptualizing this age range as unique in terms of approaches to practice and pedagogy. A recent report published by the National Association for the Education of Young Children (NAEYC, 2017) found that 66 percent of the K-3 teachers surveyed identified as EC teachers, with the highest proportion at kindergarten (93 percent) and declining percentages to third grade. In addition, the NAEYC report revealed that 76 percent of K-3 teachers support the idea of a unified professional educational experience for teachers working in the birth to age 8 range, citing unique developmental knowledge and education in responsive practices as needed to be successful in this age range. While this belief in our unique and united nature is heartening, we are concerned about how we can think of EC practices, experiences, and expectations as "united" when the auspices for care for children ages 0 to 5 continue to be so incredibly varied in both type and quality. These settings include privately funded, and locally, state-, and federally funded programs. Each of these settings and their curricula have strengths and weaknesses, relevant to child and family needs, local understandings of EC education, and policies that impact practice. Within these greatly variable auspices for care and early learning, constructing a shared notion of curriculum, pedagogy, and practice continues to be a challenge we strive to meet. In addition, the number of voices engaged in determining what EC curriculum means has grown in recent years.

Investment and Early Childhood Contexts

Much of what happens within EC classrooms is now determined by outside forces, driven by policymakers, politicians, celebrities, economists, and researchers who view the purposes and practices of EC very differently from EC educators (Whitehurst, 2018). These influencers often see EC education as an investment and focus on proximal and distal outcomes that reflect the possibility of bringing EC programs to scale. The idea that EC pays a dividend academically and financially (Heckman, 2006; 2011) seemed to validate what we had known for so long – EC education can really matter in the lives of young children. Using findings from studies like Perry Preschool and the Chicago Parent Centers, programs that were highly funded and supported families in ways that go well beyond current levels of provision of care in the United States, Heckman and others argued for the power of EC. While EC educators welcomed attention on young children and their care, this attention has come with increased scrutiny and oversight. Discussions have (for the most part) moved from "Is daycare bad for children?" to "Is EC a good investment for closing achievement gaps?" This question of value as return on investment (ROI) will continue to haunt the birth–age 5 sector until funding for education and care mirrors the funding for K-12 education. In other words, if the only value of EC is measurable outcomes, the model is investment/return-driven rather than rights-oriented.

Accounting for Early Childhood Investments

Making EC programs responsible for driving children's long-term success places a great deal of pressure on the EC community to actualize these expectations. Conceptualizing EC as an inoculation against poverty and/or risk factors began with Head Start (Lubeck, DeVries, Nicholson, & Post, 1997) and continues as we design EC programs that focus on achieving particular kinds of academic outcomes. It continues as public pre-K grows and policymakers want to see that the investments made pay off in terms of later achievement. Public preschool continues to be touted as a key means for improving children's long-term outcomes.

Much of this investment in publicly funded EC programs is at the state level, and these investments in EC are being monitored. For each penny placed into EC programs, there typically is a way of accounting it. For example, as of 2017, 49 of 50 states have implemented Quality Rating Improvement Systems (QRIS) linked to childcare licensing to drive quality in publicly funded childcare programs (Cannon, Zellman, Karoly, & Schwartz, 2017). Program reimbursement is tied to how well these systems are implemented, driving how programs meet definitions of what matters in professional development, teacher education levels and choosing curriculum.

At the federal level, explicit accountability requirements have included the 2012 Head Start Designation Renewal System (HS-DRS) which codified a system of program evaluation that ties continued Head Start funding to scores on a single measure of classroom quality. Programs failing to meet these and other requirements cannot compete to keep their funds, linking investment in these EC programs back to measurable aspects of the program that have been defined as consistent with quality in order to validate Head Start funding. Even Early Head Start programs, serving children prenatally through age 3, are required to evaluate classroom quality.

The datafication of the early years now covers infancy to grade 3, linking decisions at every level of publicly funded EC to the investments and outcomes model (Roberts-Holmes & Bradbury, 2016). In this investment model, the value of EC education is defined by measurable outcomes that represent return on investment. No return, no value. Missing from this ROI approach are questions of the responsibilities of society to provide high quality care and learning contexts and caregivers and as well as the rights of children and families to access regardless of socioeconomic status. In the next section we zoom in on the impacts of the "EC as Investment" model more closely through the example of readiness.

Readiness in the Early Years

As demand for returns on EC investment have grown and merged with the K-12 accountability movement, notions of readiness have evolved to fit. Historically, kindergarten was envisioned as a year in which children would be supported in their transition to the academic challenges ahead, framing readiness as composed of many developmental domains and skills. In the current context, readiness is informed by expectations for student achievement, first in the high stakes No Child Left Behind context, and now with the broad adoption of the Common Core standards. As a result, the work of early years teachers has evolved. In states like Ohio and Michigan, where state legislatures require children to read on grade level by grade 3 or be retained, the work of teaching children to read starts long before the first day of kindergarten. With these emerging expectations for readiness, pre-K has been pulled into the K-12 orbit (Graue, Ryan, Nocera, Northey, & Wilinski, 2017) just as kindergarten was.

As states have made greater investments in pre-K, expectations too have grown for how this experience will make children "ready" for a kindergarten with increased rigors. With high levels of reading proficiency expected and tested by the end of 3rd grade, the curriculum is back-mapped to grades 2, 1, and kindergarten, leaving early educators in the shadow of rigid expectations. Children who do not enter kindergarten ready to begin to read (with letter, phoneme and blend identification knowledge) or do math (counting with one to one correspondence and identifying numbers 1 to 10, subitizing up to 4) are labeled as behind and put on improvement plans that often include summer school – *before* kindergarten. This directly conflicts with the belief that young children's development is highly variable and episodic from birth to age 8; EC programs are increasingly tied to age and grade benchmarks that serve as powerful learning targets.

As a result, EC programs are increasingly focused on very specific readiness skills and engage in practices that support a narrow band of skills that now comprise the notion of readiness. This trend ignores the myriad of other strengths and needs children bring to school (Jenkins et al., 2018). Despite readiness-focused interventions, however, evaluation studies of EC intervention and public pre-K programs indicate that participating children often experience a fadeout of positive effects (Bailey et al., 2017). Research efforts now focus on understanding the mechanisms underlying fadeout, and some suggest that fadeout may result from a tight focus on narrowly defined teacher directed instruction in the early years (Farran, 2016). The short-term gains made in readiness-focused programs may not result in the skills necessary to be active, engaged agents of their own learning (Whitehurst, 2018). In other words, when EC programming is focused on discrete academic skills in a didactic, teacher-directed format beginning at ages 3 and 4, children may not develop robust capacities as learners (Farran, 2016). They may also learn to resist both instructional and assessment-oriented learning experiences in the future. We recognize the importance of early academic skills, but worry that programming that only addresses the "testable" skills that can be acquired in EC settings conceals the importance of developmentally responsive pedagogical experiences that address all aspects of development.

Given these challenges, how can we advocate for the EC practices that we value? In the next section we describe the elements of our approach to pedagogy that make it uniquely EC, and then we address ways to support this knowledge.

Envisioning the Pasts/Currents/Futures of Early Childhood Curriculum

EC and elementary pedagogy are frequently contrasted in terms of where they begin. It is often argued that EC pedagogy begins with a sense of where children are, using observation over time to plan rich experiences that support multiple domains of development. In contrast more formal elementary programming starts with a content domain, estimating the path between a child's current status and some benchmark (Katz, 2015). We are concerned that strict adherence to either approach is limited and argue that curriculum design is most responsive and therefore strongest when teachers consider both the children with whom they are working and where they hope the learning journey will take them. EC approaches to curriculum have been traditionally good at recognizing that children will, can, and should travel different pathways along common points of development. These pathways will reflect their lived experiences, their community/cultural/linguistic backgrounds, and the opportunities that they access as they grow and learn. Patterns of development and trajectories of learning, both abstract and currently popular constructs, are key, but we wonder if we have lost a focus on the child who sits at their intersection and who grows through responsive curriculum.

While historically teachers of the youngest children have focused less on content-focused instruction than teachers of older children in the birth–age 8 band (Hatch, 2010; Goldstein, 1997; Katz, 1995), we advocate for instructional practices that balance developmental and content-based knowledge and practices. This balance in curriculum and practice builds the foundational capacities that children gain from play-based experiences. Within play-based experiences children engage with both teachers and peers to support their knowledge and development. These foundational capacities reflect the notion that children are agentic actors in their learning, seeking more knowledge and, when engaged with new content knowledge, new vocabulary, and new concepts with teachers and peers, can make connections in and through play (Hatch, 2010; Hedges, 2000).

From this perspective, we cannot set false boundaries for what children "can" or "should" be learning, or not, in EC settings. For example, the idea that letter charts and number lines, or letter-sound instruction are developmentally inappropriate for preschool classrooms are premised on the idea that preschool children have much more important things to learn through play in which these types of learning (and the teachers who use them) are considered to be interfering in the real work of children. This stance, however, runs contrary to a commitment to responding to and supporting children. If children express interest in numbers or letters, if they are looking for supports that will help them produce written language for their own reasons, we should be willing to use these tools to support their interests. Instead of framing this kind of instruction or joint-learning as interfering, or domineering children's play, we must consider how we as teachers can create access and support to all sort of learning tools, materials, ways of engaging.

Similarly, when children express interest in scientific phenomena and the natural world around them or mathematical concepts like addition or grouping, we should support this learning, even if we feel like we have limited knowledge about a topic, or that the ideas we are introducing are too challenging. Here we should follow the children's leads and allow their engagement and interest to inform our decision-making about what to teach them and when, rather than drawing tight lines around teaching and learning roles for teachers and children in EC settings. We must think of the ways in which different approaches to teaching can support young children as they roll/crawl/walk the often uneven path of learning and development. How we teach in EC must reflect the rich knowledge of each child in our care, not a list of practices, materials, and/or approaches that are or are not appropriate. This dance and balancing act of giving and supporting children's knowledge and understanding of the world, while responding to their needs, interests, and development, is at the heart of improvisational early childhood teaching (Graue, Karabon, & Delaney, 2012).

Yes, we want children to have access to skills and knowledge that will support their later learning. However, in EC curriculum we also want content-focused learning to reflect opportunities to engage with new knowledge, to access and understand rich vocabulary or the mathematical processes that solve *real child* problems. This kind of engagement with content is unique to EC.

Marrying Responsiveness with Content

EC practices are marked by teachers' use of developmental knowledge, knowledge of individual children and their culture, and their capacity to marry these with key content. This responsive approach starts with the child, building from their experiences and interests to provide access to rich learning experiences. This approach to curriculum design is seen in Reggio Emilia, the Project Approach, emergent curriculum, and HighScope, for example. However, in each of these approaches, rich learning is not inevitable, and it is not scripted in advance. Highly skilled EC teachers are the active ingredient that make these curricular approaches responsive to young children and foment strong engagement and opportunities for learning. Some argue, however, that without an explicit path or content-related instruction (e.g., pacing guides, daily and weekly plans provided by curriculum authors, etc.), and measurable, discrete outcomes, these are not curricula.

Rather than scripts that promote a strict path of teaching and learning, the kind of responsive work at the heart of great EC pedagogy is improvisational, based on teachers' deep knowledge of pedagogy while taking up the bids for learning in their classroom (Graue, Whyte, & Delaney, 2014; Graue, Whyte, & Karabon, 2015). It is both fixed and open, reflecting goals for teaching through responsive pedagogy for a particular group of children in a specific time and place. A natural approach is to build EC curriculum based on a Funds of Knowledge approach

(Moll & Gonzalez, 2004), taking up developmental and individual child knowledge, as well as learning about and responding to community and cultural practices for supporting children's learning. For example, Tobin, Arzubiaga, and Adair (2013) found that for diverse communities, the Eurocentric, developmentally appropriate practices of EC practitioners rarely considered the goals of families and communities. In this research, Tobin et al. found that Latino families valued some of the pre-academic skill development (letter and letter-sound identification, rote counting) that the EC teachers in the program devalued or saw as developmentally inappropriate. This is an example where traditional EC pedagogy was in fact not culturally responsive (Hedges, 2011).

In both project-based and emergent curricula in EC, teachers are the facilitators as well as co-learners. They hold the process knowledge – how to design a knowledge web, keep track of the many questions that need to be answered through the project work, and where to go in the library or on the internet to access necessary information. As facilitators, teachers can set the goal posts, define sub-projects, determine endpoints, and provide counterfactuals and question reasoning that doesn't quite work. But children get to manage the questioning and the wanting to know.

One of our favorite examples of this is in a project on the Boston Marathon that one Boston area preschool conducted several years ago (Mardell, 2011). In this project, children wanted to know more about many elements of the race that went past their school and shut down and impacted much of the city that they lived in. While beginning their investigations, nearly all of the children were convinced that running a marathon wasn't that hard. Instead of challenging this thinking with words, the teachers took the children out to a track and told them how many times they would need to run around the track to complete a marathon, and then told them to start running. The children realized quickly, without an adult directly challenging their reasoning or assertions, that running a marathon was quite a lot of work. They learned this through the natural experience of testing an assumption, rather than an adult simply telling them that it was so. Through this project, the children also learned important content knowledge, some of which included how many steps are in a mile, how to estimate/measure, and the different roles and responsibilities of race planners, safety workers, and the runners themselves in preparing for and executing a marathon run. However, examples such as this of rich, inquiry-driven, project-based learning in diverse socioeconomic, ethnic, linguistic, and cultural settings are less visible and accessible, and this is a real issue (Smith, 2015). Too often this type of learning is the purview of white, affluent children, while children identified as having "risk factors" (non-white, low-income, non-primary English speaking, or developmentally delayed/disabled, to name only a few) are targeted for intervention, and specific outcomes; their EC experiences are focused on structured paths toward readiness rather than, possibly, learning.

As the Boston Marathon experience exemplifies, when teachers build on children's knowledge, lived experience, and interests to enact content-infused curriculum, rich, engaged learning can take place, and we believe should take place in all EC settings as a recognition of the rights of all children to learn in this way. We argue that when teachers place children, cultural/community knowledge, and developmental knowledge at the center of their planning and decision-making, rich and valuable learning takes place – and we define this as a curricular experience. This is the foundational knowledge of EC teaching and practice for which we must advocate.

For communities whose practices are not tightly aligned with formalized schooling, children are forced to figure out how to fit within the narrow space that schools allow for students. Concepts like Funds of Knowledge can help teachers see that schools can be culturally responsive spaces and that there are many ways they could approach teaching. This starts by thinking about learning that support students who are coming from historically marginalized communities. Scholars have expanded the original Funds of Knowledge concept in a variety of ways, building on what children bring to the process of learning. Helen Hedges has done a series of projects that explore how teachers can build on children's knowledge of pop culture. While Funds of Knowledge focuses on utilizing cultural knowledge as capital to inform curriculum, Hedges (2011) notes that popular knowledge can also be utilized to engage children in project work oriented toward critical thinking and learning. In other words, even SpongeBob deserves the status of cultural knowledge if it helps children and teachers create learning opportunities. In this study, teachers used the example of children's interest in SpongeBob as a way to leverage into content knowledge. This work is an interesting counterpoint to many US EC programs that explicitly forbid inclusion of commercial content in the curriculum. Here again is an excellent example of teachers working to find topics that their children are deeply engaged with and using those as opportunities for rich, meaningful content learning.

Emergent and/or open approaches to EC curricula present us with many ways of enacting the central tenets that we value in the EC. The richness of any curriculum is directly in proportion to the teacher's ability and willingness to respond to children, taking up their knowledge and experience to improvise new, contingent ways of teaching. While these are some examples of ways to enact EC curricula there are many, many more. What we are trying to impart in this chapter is that it is not so much the structure of the curricula that makes it successful, but rather the ways in which teachers can connect various kinds of knowledge (individual child, developmental, cultural, content) and embed them in responsive learning opportunities for children.

If we hope to enact responsive approaches to curricula that support children's success, the EC community should commit to integrating content knowledge into learning experiences for *all* children, in learning contexts informed by the EC knowledge base of developmental and responsive practices. This means foregrounding children's rights to learn and engage in meaningful, inquiry-driven ways, and finding approaches that integrate multiple goals and outcomes. This is an amendment to the investment model that currently drives EC, framing the value added by early education in terms of children's right to high quality, engaging, and intellectually rich learning environments while recognizing the importance of child outcomes in the economy of education policy. We must acknowledge the right of young children to early years education, rather than framing it as a vehicle for other goals. And we must do this even in the face of increasing standardization of EC programs driven by goals for improved child outcomes and readiness is enacted both explicitly (required curricula, program quality evaluations, program ratings) and implicitly (expectations of the next year's teacher, concerns about a state-wide third grade reading guarantee). Across the EC span, efforts continue to link children's earliest care experiences with later outcomes (Bailey, Duncan, Odgers, & Yu, 2017; Bloom & Weiland, 2015; Lipsey, Farran, & Durkin, 2018; Weiland & Yoshikawa, 2013; Yoshikawa et al., 2013). This framing of EC education as a lever to reduce achievement gaps and produce later economic payouts has not been without consequences, and we must speak out for a vision of EC that values and foregrounds the rights of young children. We recognize that this is not an easy task and that EC professionals could use support in what is effectively a culture shift. How should we ask early educators to engage in this work and how do we promote "sharing up"?

Ways to Support and Advocate for Rich EC Practice

In this section, we make suggestions about what may matter most if we are going to "share up" the rich knowledge of EC practice. To do this we see our future work as needing to be focused on preparing EC teachers, including connecting birth to grade 3 teachers in professional communities and advocating for what we want to see in terms of EC curriculum, practice, and professionalism.

While we strongly argue that EC curriculum should utilize responsiveness and improvisation to support (and sometimes lead) young children's learning, the reality is that this kind of work requires a great deal of professional skill and knowledge. To promote children's development of foundational skills in literacy, mathematics, social studies, and science, EC teachers need to understand how children can engage with this new knowledge, drawing on both content knowledge and their developmental and individual knowledge of each child. Knowing what comes next to help children continue to build onto their foundational knowledge means understanding what benchmarks matter in these processes. As a field, we must find a way to balance responding to children with scaffolds and guidance so they develop the skills that will support their engagement and critical thinking. This means that EC teachers must have key professional skills and knowledge, as well as dispositions, to successfully implement EC curriculum.

EC teachers need knowledge of typical child development and culturally responsive practices to engage children in learning that is designed to reach beyond a generic understanding of children at a certain age and engage a specific child's experiences, resources, and goals. This knowledge/practice builds on children's experiences and recognizes likely learning in the future, but is fully engaged in the present child. This knowledge informs improvisational practice, weaving content knowledge into topics children are interested in, following those interests to build knowledge along the way. It recognizes that we learn important things in the context of topics that engage us. This requires linking understandings of child development, responsivity, and content standards/benchmarks in our teacher education coursework and professional development experiences.

Second, EC teachers need the dispositional attitude that their work is as an expert learner *with* students as well as an expert teacher. In these roles, EC teachers respond to students' queries with "I don't know either, but let's find out!" and then take the steps to build that inquiry into pedagogy. When teachers position themselves as co-learners, the content knowledge that responds to a query is jointly held and creates magical opportunities for children to see adults as vulnerable and open to continued learning. The value of the all-knowing teacher is drastically overrated. In fact, it could stand in the way of interesting and socially engaged learning. Engaged learning happens when a teacher says, "I don't know either! How could we find out?" and then scaffolds, supports, and guides a joint but child-driven learning experience.

Third, EC teachers need to know how to balance different "agendas" at play in their daily work with young children. These include accountability-driven requirements, the focus on readiness, and the rights of young children to have access to developmentally appropriate, play-based learning experience. These competing demands call for early educators who are knowledgeable enough about the needs of their students and professionally secure enough to have the power to advocate for these rights and needs. Currently, many EC teachers believe that they do not have the professional standing or agency to push for the needs of young children in the face of larger, more powerful mandates and accountability (Brown, 2009; Brown, Weber, & Yoon, 2016; Delaney, 2018; Graue, Wilinski, & Nocera, 2016). While this is not a new phenomenon (File & Gullo, 2002), it has a growing urgency today.

In the current context, instructional practices are increasingly shaped by educational leaders (state and local superintendents, principals, and program directors) who work to align curricula and build coherence within and across systems (Graue, et al., 2017). As accountability requirements rise, so too do the reforms and/or strategies developed by these leaders, many of whom have little knowledge or experience in early childhood settings. As a result, early educators find themselves subject to decisions that may not align with EC practice, and with limited power to advocate to those in the administrative hierarchy. Rather than accepting this as a function of EC being pulled into the K-12 orbit, we need to take advantage of the opportunity to provide professional development for these leaders (Rieg, 2007). Educational leaders have the ability to be particularly impactful on classroom practices (Coburn, 2005; Spillane, Halverson, &

Diamond, 2001). Knowing this, we should be working to reach out to childcare and elementary school leaders to share and build relationships that create opportunities for joint understanding and engagement (Graue, et al., 2012).

There are currently trends afoot to bring practices that are an everyday part of many EC classrooms into elementary settings. For example, in elementary schools, there is an emerging emphasis on the need for children in elementary school contexts to engage with "problem-based learning" that develop critical thinking skills (Daugherty, Carter, & Swagerty, 2014). However, these experiences are usually discrete and separated from the rest of the curriculum – an hour or two every week over several weeks (Chiu, Price, & Ovrahim, 2015). While these experiences allow children to engage with these critical thinking, project-based approaches, they are not integrated in to the larger curriculum. Once completed, the children return to more teacher-directed, skills-focused work that is aligned to grade level benchmarks. Interestingly, the growing and concerted effort to shift elementary school learning towards a more responsive, integrated approach that foregrounds joint problem-solving as a key way to engage learners (Daugherty et al., 2014) is something that we, in EC, are already familiar with.

This example provides a glimmer of hope that EC pedagogy might be "shared up" into the broader educational system. Finding ways to engage both child interest and content through active teaching and learning should be valued in all classrooms. We wonder if engaging upper elementary teachers in responsive practices could benefit all teachers working with children between birth and third grade. Building relationships, knowledge, and understanding of the motivations and goals for curriculum in early care and elementary settings, as well as unique pressures and expectations, could prevent disconnects between these teaching communities that are both a part of the larger EC period.

Earlier in this chapter we referenced a recent report by NAEYC detailing how birth to grade 3 teachers envision their professional identities and connectedness. One of the findings of this report was that as teachers move up the EC age band, they are less likely to identify as EC teachers (NAEYC, 2017). Creating opportunities to connect teachers along the birth to age 8 range will help to support shared identities as EC teachers, as well as to help all teachers to learn about and recognize the varied needs and developmental pathways that children travel during this period. More research in this area is also warranted to better understand what supporting relationships among EC teachers might mean for our field.

We have important work to do in reframing what we mean by EC education in ways that foregrounds our responsive practices, beliefs in the rights of children, and the broad community of teachers who do the work of this field. While building relationships across educational communities is something we may need to stretch to do, we have a shared experience as teachers – in infant/toddler classrooms, preschools and Head Start, and early elementary classrooms. We have a shared language for talking about the idiosyncrasies of development, children, and practice during this period. While strengthening these connections within

EC, particularly across childcare and elementary settings, is fundamental and important, we also need to reach beyond these connections, toward policymakers and economists, politicians and media representatives, community stake-holders and activists, all of whom inform how we think about early years education, and what it can and/or should be. We must figure out how to sustain the knowledge that grounds our work, and we must all find a way to be a part of this process.

Conclusion

In the chapter that Delaney and Graue (2012) wrote for the first edition of this book, we focused on how EC curriculum is like a palimpsest, in which elements from prior practices and knowledges seep into current pedagogical approaches, often in ways that we do not easily recognize. Despite this palimpsest of knowledge about how to support young children's development, their learning environments are growing increasingly non-responsive to their needs. In this chapter, we argue that we must unearth this EC knowledge, as this is our leverage to build a foundation for future action and advocacy. Our palimpsest, these layers of knowledge embedded within our EC curriculum decision-making, gives our community a strong base for action for the rights and needs of children and teachers. But the field also has work to do, to knit together the developmental practices that are the hallmark of the field with a commitment to responsive practice and content-rich teaching, without shutting doors and drawing lines about how we will or won't teach young children. We are convinced that these are not just compatible knowledges and practices but that they are synergistic, potentially creating something greater than their simple sum. Our vision is that we must believe in our shared, foundational knowledge enough to sustain it with all those who teach, lead, design, and implement policy, in ways that benefit young children, families, communities, and teachers.

Note

1 All names have been changed to pseudonyms to protect the identities of research participants, who consented to IRB approved research.

References

Bailey, D., Duncan, G.J., Odgers, C.L., & Yu, W. (2017). Persistence and fadeout in the impacts of child and adolescent interventions. *Journal of Research on Educational Effectiveness*, 10(1), 7–39.

Bloom, H., & Weiland, C. (2015). *Quantifying variation in Head Start effects on young children's cognitive and socio-emotional skills using data from the National Head Start Impact Study*. MDRC Report.

Brown, C.P. (2009). Being accountable for one's own governing: A case study of early educators responding to standards-based early childhood education reform. *Contemporary Issues in Early Childhood*, 10(1), 3–23.

Brown, C.P., Weber, N.B., & Yoon, Y. (2016). Reluctantly governed: The struggles of early educators in a professional development course that challenged their teaching in a high-stakes neo-liberal early education context. *Contemporary Issues in Early Childhood*, 17(2), 210–234.

Cannon, J., Zellman, G.L., Karoly, L.A., & Schwartz, H.L. (2017). *Quality rating and improvement systems for early care and education programs: Making the second generation better.* Retrieved from www.rand.org/pubs/perspectives/PE235.html

Chiu, A., Price, C.A., & Ovrahim, E. (2015, April). Supporting elementary and middle school STEM education at the whole school level: A review of the literature. In NARST 2015 Annual Conference, Chicago, IL.

Coburn, C.E. (2005). Shaping teacher sensemaking: School leaders and the enactment of reading policy. *Educational Policy*, 19(3), 476–509.

Daugherty, M.K., Carter, V., & Swagerty, L. (2014). Elementary STEM education: The future for technology and engineering education? *Journal of STEM Teacher Education*, 49(1), 7.

Delaney, K.K. (2018). Looking away: An analysis of early childhood teaching and learning experiences framed through a quality metric. *Contemporary Issues in Early Childhood*, https://doi.org/10.1177/1463949118778023

Delaney, K., & Graue, E. (2012). Early childhood curriculum as palimpsest. In N. File, J.J. Mueller, & D.B. Wisneski (Eds.), *Curriculum in early childhood education: Re-examined, rediscovered, renewed* (pp. 188–199). New York: Routledge.

Farran, D.C. (2016). We need more evidence in order to create effective pre-K programs. *Evidence Speaks Reports*, 1(11). Center on Children and Families at Brookings.

File, N., & Gullo, D.F. (2002). A comparison of early childhood and elementary education students' beliefs about primary classroom teaching practices. *Early Childhood Research Quarterly*, 17(1), 126–137.

Goldstein, L.S. (1997). Between a rock and a hard place in the primary grades: The challenge of providing developmentally appropriate early childhood education in an elementary school setting. *Early Childhood Research Quarterly*, 12(1), 3–27.

Graue, M.E., Karabon, A., & Delaney, K. (2012). Learning to love your noisy neighbor: A principal's guide to the education of young children. In G. Theoharris & J.S. Brooks (Eds.), *What every principal needs to know to create excellent and equitable schools* (pp. 110–129). New York: Teachers College Press.

Graue, M.E., Whyte, K., & Delaney, K.K. (2014). Fostering culturally and developmentally responsive teaching through improvisational practice. *Journal of Early Childhood Teacher Education*, 35(4), 37–41. https://doi.org/10.1080/10901027.2014.968296

Graue, M.E., Whyte, K.L., & Karabon, A.E. (2015). The power of improvisational teaching. *Teaching and Teacher Education*, 48(May 2015), 13–21.

Graue, M.E., Wilinski, B., & Nocera, A. (2016). Local control in the era of accountability: A case study of Wisconsin preK. *Education Policy Analysis Archives/Archivos Analíticos de Políticas Educativas*, 24(60). Retrieved from https://epaa.asu.edu/ojs/article/viewFile/2366/1784

Graue, M.E., Ryan, S., Nocera, A., Northey, K., & Wilinski, B. (2017). Pulling preK into a K-12 orbit: the evolution of preK in the age of standards. *Early Years*, 37(1), 108–122.

Hatch, J.A. (2010). Rethinking the relationship between learning and development: Teaching for learning in early childhood classrooms. *The Educational Forum*, 74(3), 258–268.

Heckman, J.J. (2006). Skill formation and the economics of investing in disadvantaged children. *Science*, 312(5782), 1900–1902.

Heckman, J.J. (2011). The economics of inequality: The value of early childhood education. *American Educator*, 35(1), 31.

Hedges, H. (2000). Teaching in early childhood: Time to merge constructivist views so learning through play equals teaching through play. *Australian Journal of Early Childhood*, 25(4), 16–16.

Hedges, H. (2011). Rethinking Sponge Bob and Ninja Turtles: Popular culture as funds of knowledge for curriculum co-construction. *Australasian Journal of Early Childhood*, 36(1), 25.

Jenkins, J.M., Duncan, G.J., Auger, A., Bitler, M., Domina, T., & Burchinal, M. (2018). Boosting school readiness: Should preschool teachers target skills or the whole child? *Economics of Education Review*.

Katz, L.G. (1995). *Talks with teachers of young children: A collection*. Newark: Ablex Publishing Corporation.

Katz, L. (2015). *Lively minds: Distinctions between academic versus intellectual goals for young children*. Retrieved from http://deyproject.org/2015/04/09/lively-minds-distinctionsbetween-academic-versus-intellectual-goals-for-youngchildren/

Lipsey, M.W., Farran, D.C., & Durkin, K. (2018). Effects of the Tennessee prekindergarten program on children's achievement and behavior through third grade. *Early Childhood Research Quarterly*, 45(4), 155–176.

Lubeck, S., DeVries, M., Nicholson, J., & Post, J. (1997). Head Start in transition. *Early Education and Development*, 8(3), 219–244.

Mardell, B. (2011). *Learning as a team sport: Kindergartners study the Boston Marathon*. Documentary Film. www.pz.harvard.edu/resources/learning-is-a-team-sport-kindergartners-study-the-boston-marathon

Moll, L.C., & González, N. (2004). Engaging life: A funds of knowledge approach to multicultural education. In J.A. Banks & C.M. Banks (Eds.), *Handbook of Research on Multicultural Education*, (pp. 699–715). New York: Macmillan.

NAEYC (2017). *K-3 market research: Executive summary*. Downloaded from www.naeyc.org/sites/default/files/wysiwyg/user-74/k-3_executive_summary_final.pdf on June 1, 2018.

Rieg, S.A. (2007). Principals and young children: A dozen recommendations for building positive relationships. *Early Childhood Education Journal*, 35(3), 209–213.

Roberts-Holmes, G., & Bradbury, A. (2016). The datafication of early years education and its impact upon pedagogy. *Improving Schools*, 19(2), 119–128.

Phillips, D.A., & Shonkoff, J.P. (Eds.). (2000). *From neurons to neighborhoods: The science of early childhood development*. Washington, DC: National Academies Press.

Smith, S. (2015). *Against race- and class-based pedagogy in early childhood education*. New York: Palgrave Macmillan.

Spillane, J.P., Halverson, R., & Diamond, J.B. (2001). Investigating school leadership practice: A distributed perspective. *Educational Researcher*, 30(3), 23–28.

Tobin, J., Arzubiaga, A.E., & Adair, J.K. (2013). *Children crossing borders: Immigrant parents and teacher perspectives on preschools*. New York: Russell Sage Foundation.

Weiland, C., & Yoshikawa, H. (2013). Impacts of a prekindergarten program on children's mathematics, language, literacy, executive function, and emotional skills. *Child Development*, 84(6), 2112–2130.

Whitehurst, G.J. (2018). The positive impacts of public pre-K fade quickly, and sometimes reverse: What does this portend for future research and policy? *Early Childhood Research Quarterly*, 45(4), 183–187.

Yoshikawa, H., Weiland, C., Brooks-Gunn, J., Burchinal, M., Espinosa, L.M., Gormley, W.T., . . . & Zaslow, M.J. (2013). *Investing in our future: The evidence base on preschool education*. New York: Foundation for Child Development.

14

RECLAIMING AND REDISCOVERING IN EARLY CHILDHOOD CURRICULUM

Possibility and Promise

Nancy File and Jennifer J. Mueller

Given the discussions across these amazing chapters, we want to once again acknowledge the efforts and diligence of teachers and teacher educators in the field of early childhood. As we think, write, and talk about their work it is they who engage in the day-to-day labor of sorting out and making sense of all of the components of classroom life in real time. We know that while it is a labor of love, it is not easy work and the urgency of and responsibility inherent in ensuring that our youngest are well-served must be recognized. And as we consider the idea of reclaiming in the field, we must always center that consideration on the children who set the stage and context for all of our theorizing, examining, considering, planning, and acting. We thank them for being just who they are, for challenging us to act with integrity and care, and to be our best selves for them and with them.

We believe this work to be an important dialogue, and engaging with these authors and these chapters has been a journey and a joy for us. While we set the stage with suggestions for each chapter, we were continually astonished at the new directions and ideas that were brought forth. And, we were also affirmed that we have co-travelers in this journey who are willing to face the uncertainty and ambiguity of our times – and to face that with hope, resilience, dedication, and possibility.

A central theme that emerged for us – and the one that prompted us to change the title of the volume – was the idea that now is the time for us as a field to reclaim our work, and thus reclaim the field. As we look at the history of the field, it has often (though not always) seemed the case that outside forces have defined who we are, what is important to know, and what our role is as early childhood educators and researchers in the larger educational landscape. We acknowledge, as well, that colleagues at other levels in the educational system would resonate with this concern. As we mentioned in the preface, it is a time where we no longer need to focus on establishing our importance as a field of study, justify our rigor in our research, or stake our place in the educational trajectory. The benefits of early childhood education are firmly understood and our capacity for scientific rigor in our research is well-established and respected.

That we did not enter into the project with reclaiming as a theme, but rather that this emerged as a strong message across the chapters is key. Each of the authors offered important ways for us to think about this reclamation process. Connecting across epistemological paradigms in our research has long been a call in early childhood, and File's chapter helped us to think about how centering our research on important questions, noting the importance of what we don't know, and intentionally bringing needed methodological diversity to those questions (avoiding the trap of the single story), will be a key endeavor. In describing the differences in policy impacting early childhood in both the pre- and post-eras of No Child Left Behind, Brown and Barry outlined how those in the field can reclaim their work within this recent context. Mueller and File demonstrated the degree to which we have moved away from the agentic teacher in packaged curricula for ever-younger children, providing food for thought about what is being lost in attempts to guarantee children's performances, even in a context in which much attention has been given to developing ideas for what we see as the desired outcomes in early childhood.

In the chapters focusing on particular theoretical frameworks, the authors looked historically at how these have shaped early childhood curriculum, but all offered new ideas and innovative ways that these theories could support our progress. We found a reclamation to our work in the field in the latter half of each of these chapters, as the authors focused on illustrating the possible. Thus, Hatch offered examples of practice within the classroom, Mueller and Whyte claimed the space of democratic participation for reimagining the curriculum, and Blaise and Ryan called for ongoing work in developing critical theorizing.

A frankness and openness to consideration, critique, and learning lessons from the ways that current curricular approaches are being enacted has opened spaces for us to take what is helpful and build forward in new ways that perhaps would not be available as possibility without the trials of the past. Horm, Kwon, and Laurin remind us of the inclusion of infants/toddlers in the early childhood field while noting that this is an area of high need in regard to understanding, conceptualizing, and developing what we mean by "curriculum." While overall the authors in this volume are in favor of greater teacher agency in planning and enacting a responsive and authentic curriculum, Michael-Luna, Heimer, and Grey remind us of how complex this work is and how it needs to be supported for teachers to be able to implement differently. In continuing to claim play for the field, Sutterby and Kharod provide ideas about newer venues for supporting play, which can be applied to reclaiming that mode of learning for our children. Finally, Quintero, working from her qualitative inquiry with multilingual children and their teachers, claims the space of story for notions of how children can learn – a reclamation of a central human experience as an orienting point for curriculum.

In the latter part of the volume we have authors with the courage and foresight to bring theories into the early childhood context not typically included in the conversation to show us new possibilities, but perhaps more importantly illuminate the path of reclaiming. Buzzelli asks how the field would be impacted if there was a focus on children's abilities being considered as capabilities that would enable them to live lives that they value, a move away from education as a commodity in the economic structures within which we live. Working from the starting point of the prescriptive curriculum approach, Stremmel, Burns, Nganga, and Bertolini present us with a dialogue about reclaiming a child-centered approach. Lastly, Delaney, Whyte, and Graue envision a place in which curriculum is less dictated by often-unexamined norms and refocuses on practices that support the vitality and engagement of young children making meaning in their worlds.

It was evident to us that chapter authors mirrored each other in their advocacy for the early childhood field to put the *child* back at the center of early childhood. While it seems like this is a foundational tenet of our field, and should go without saying, the work in these chapters makes it clear that competition, accountability, standardization, alignment, curriculum as a product and a commodity, early childhood as a business enterprise, and children and families as part of a current and future economy, have come to rule the day. While all of these elements may have their place, it is clear that we have lost our focus at times on what children need in their lives both now and in the future. The "now" is being encapsulated within the plethora of standards and benchmarks. While not a negative in and of itself, we believe there is much for the field to grapple with regarding the proliferation of standards coming from different directions, the frequent lack of clarity regarding "why these, why now," and most concerning, the impact of the accountability and alignment movements continuing to push the practices of teachers.

Children's experiences are being transformed by the movement toward *more, more, earlier, earlier* (Bassok, Latham, & Rorem, 2016). The approach operates to fit what children are experiencing to these shifting expectations. The future is defined by ensuring that children are "ready" for that next step, which then ensures readiness for the step after, and so on and so on. But rarely do we see questions such as, "Who should our children be as adults? What abilities will they need and will our society need from them? How can we ensure that ALL children have the possibility to follow a path toward those goals? And, what is important for children, right now, when they are toddlers, or four, or five?" The answer must be more than competency on the Common Core State Standards or high standardized test scores, backmapped step by step to the early childhood period. The questions we have framed are both complex and sure to lead in multiple directions without a common endpoint. And, our chapter authors provide fodder for rethinking about what it might mean to listen to children and have them help guide us in where curriculum can and should take them – to have *children* be a central part of the "complicated conversations." What became clear to us through this volume is that it is the time now to pause and really, *really* re-examine where we place children in the process of reclaiming our work. It also is clear that we will continue to have this work defined for us unless we reclaim the space to define curriculum and engage with others in this work.

Bhabha's (2004) work related to "third space" is not new, nor new to early childhood, and we thank Betsy Quintero for bringing it into the conversation in this volume. The notion of third space is that of the possibility of hybrid thinking. It is something more than collaboration or integration. It is the space and allowance of ways of thinking to converge and because of that very convergence new concepts, ideas, or ways of acting are born – ways that could not have been conceived of without the convergence. And, then these new ideas and concepts become the jumping off point for progress forward. Without the convergence, the new cannot emerge. And this does not advocate disregarding of previous thoughts or ideas, but rather the seeds planted are evident in new ways of moving forward.

In consideration of reclaiming our field, it is clear that we will not (and should not) be able to maintain status quo, business as usual approaches. This time in history has created the need for the third space in education. Teachers are under fire and we see past factional loyalties being laid aside in order that we can come together to accomplish common goals for the common good – a convergence of which we should take full advantage. Too many children are not visible in the mass standardization project – too many voices unheard and ways of knowing and being untapped. We are educating all of our children for a quickly shifting society, much of which we cannot even imagine. We suggest (with the support of our authors) that it will be by engaging in the third space that we will imagine and define our future. And it will take faith, trust, and courage to do so. This is not easy work for educators, and many of our authors point out that there is often little support for them to engage in the third space.

One third space we envision from these chapters is a broad definition of education, as an act that is not neutral. Our authors help us to see curriculum is an intervention, an act intended toward change. In practice, however, it must be defined as not just practices determined by the rigor of scientific evidence buttressed by developmental theory. Our authors point us toward a space influenced by a moral stance, curriculum and critical theorizing, democratic participation, and the very essence of what it means to be human, in both little and big bodies.

Another third space involves considering the notion of what curriculum is, the definition that we admittedly avoided for this volume. As noted by Mueller and Whyte in Chapter 5, from the curriculum theory field Pinar (2004) declared that curriculum can be viewed as a stand-in for the experience of school in its totality. There is something of this perspective in the traditional practice of early childhood. For example, days were planned around child-time and child interests – the need for frequent food breaks, chatty conversation, and the daily nap or rest; the respect for the teachable moment, or perhaps just the interest of the moment (for example, the afternoon that all stopped in Nancy's preschool classroom to watch the window washer do his job); the need for experiences that allowed for the exploration of making friends and negotiating conflict; the sense that being in school was also living. In the new curriculum approach, we find that every moment has a purpose toward learning, play is invariably set up for particular learning goals, and that not a moment is *wasted*, yet unfortunately not planned in response to children's lives in their context in the moment. In this space we need to consider both children's learning and children's lives.

Yet another third space emerges when we push ourselves to consider developmentally appropriate practice in convergence with disciplinary based content teaching and learning. When the DAP document was published in 2009, we were at a different period of needing to reclaim the field. It was essential to establish that early childhood had a necessarily specified and unique knowledge base, skill-set, and set of dispositional approaches that needed to be considered in the education and care of young children. And, this was during the time of the proliferation of content standards, standardization of curriculum, and the ongoing "push-down" of related curriculum into the early childhood years. As several authors here have pointed out, this set of ideals served as an important basis and foundation for the field. However, as Mueller and File pointed out in Chapter 3, most of the work on content standards and learning largely ignored early learning contexts. In practice this has often meant an assumption that disciplinary-based content learning could be "watered down" for use with young children, or that young children were simply not capable of this content-steeped learning. And, we would argue, this has supported early childhood curricula that are superficial and do not actually support foundational disciplinary teaching and learning.

What we believe our authors advocate in this volume is that by engaging a focus on the child, we can bring a convergence of that which is developmentally appropriate into our understandings of rich content-based teaching and learning – and something that is different from simply pushing down what older children are expected to know and do. Certainly in some fields (mathematics and early literacy in particular) scholars and educators have delved in and examined how young children learn in these areas, though this has not always appropriately impacted curriculum. By supporting young children, in developmentally appropriate ways, to engage in learning opportunities steeped in rich and authentic content-based concepts, ideas, and ways of knowing – centered on their desires, needs, and assets – we will create third space contexts where the children can guide us to new understandings. Of course, this will require us to support and engage our educators in the spaces to be able to enact these types of teaching and learning.

When we speak of reclaiming, we are not proposing a move backward to earlier practices. Grieshaber (2008) critiqued the early childhood field's traditional reliance on development theory: "Developmental theories, particularly Piagetian stage theories, have become weapons of mass seduction in ECE across the globe, valorizing Piagetian developmental perspectives and, by default, mitigating against overt teaching and instruction" (p. 508). The field must continue to grapple with the notions of teaching and learning in order to create new spaces for the agency of both children and teachers to function. Our authors have provided much to spur those discussions. Even in a standards-based context, we must question whether standards are the tail that wags the curriculum dog or whether standards can provide some goalposts toward which we can still define where and how children are learning and adults are teaching. All of this volume's authors are teachers themselves, working with the upcoming generations of early childhood teachers. We don't believe that any of us has conceded that in a standards-based context that our own decisions about content and pedagogy in our teacher preparation classes are, and should be, pre-determined and constrained. We are entrusted to develop a curriculum toward defined endpoints, but it most likely never occurs twice in the exact same way. None of us is measured on the concept of fidelity. Yes, we need to continue pressing to ensure that standards are based upon rich learning and responsive teaching. But in the meantime, we also need to advocate within the field for curricula that reclaim the space of responsive decision-making by teachers, a focus on the agentic and multi-dimensional child, rich engagement with content that is meaningful to children, and a strong rationale for "why this, why now?"

Another important part of the mission is ensuring that the field has teachers, at all levels of early childhood, who are professionally equipped to make decisions, understand their children and families and local context, draw upon professional and content-based knowledge, and respond to the current moment. It is not an easy lift to provide professionals who do not need the "teacher-proofed" curriculum. Yet, authentic professional development for early childhood teachers that would allow third space thinking is an important topic for another volume.

We never approach a writing task – or perhaps most parts of our professional lives – with the assumption that the end point consists of ideas that form answers. For us, the search continues to engender questions. With that perspective, we propose the following questions that arise for us from this volume.

How do we finally remove ourselves from the demand that early childhood prove its worth? For instance, there is much more research about the existence of a program (formerly Head Start, then child care, now pre-kindergarten) and its worth, or return on investment, compared to research about how *what in particular we are doing in the classroom matters*.

What do we need to do to promote the use of less-limited outcome measures for children's learning? The use of a restricted set of outcome measures has fostered certain kinds of learning (e.g., constrained literacy-related skills) and may even come to work against our ability to maintain those whole-child curricula with broad goals traditionally believed to be important for young children.

How do we define learning? We contend that for a long period of time the maturationist approach was the closeted component of early childhood. Never acknowledged, not mentioned in textbooks, the idea that development would occur with little to no intervention still drove much of the practice. Now, we contend that what is lurking in the closet is the unacknowledged input-output model built from behaviorist theory. Every teacher works within the tenets of behaviorism, particularly for behavioral issues. But the degree to which curriculum is pre-scripted, with a scope, sequence, and detailed lesson plans, is much more indicative of this theoretical approach than constructivism in its various forms.

How can we reframe the conversations about the purpose of learning in early childhood? Curriculum is being defined by policy-makers, by researchers, and by publishers; even with the involvement of early childhood professionals in these arenas, we have lost many voices to the conversations. Teachers and children have lost agency in the classroom.

How can we build curriculum around the notion of what *all* children need? Currently the notion that some children are not ready for school-based learning is a stronger driver of these efforts. We acknowledge the importance, and the ultimate devastation for individuals, of achievement gaps in children's learning. Yet, there is much we can do to ensure that our approach to this problem is equitable and promises that the same rich learning opportunities are available to all. This means getting beyond the notion of curriculum as fixing certain children.

Finally, how do we start conversations around the notion of the rights of children? This approach is almost absent in the United States compared to other countries. A rights-based approach would reframe curriculum to something done *with* children; they would become more than the recipients of experiences planned according to the scope and sequence model built around the universal, but nonexistent, child.

With this rights-of-children approach, we draw our conclusions back around to our discussions from the preface of the need for rich, deliberative, democratic participation (Apple, 2018) in work of reclaiming curriculum for early childhood. It is here where we can see classrooms and other learning spaces as the sites of this process – the sites of third space, generative progress; the spaces where we carefully consider what knowledge all children have the right to access; what all of their ways of knowing and being can tell us about teaching, learning, and curriculum.

Apple (2018) reminds us that "lasting critically democratic education requires us to understand that doing so will at times be filled with tensions and contradictions. The politics of this will be complicated. It will involve a combination of joy and sometimes sorrow" (p. 3).

This volume gives us the hope and collaborative strength that there is a will to move us toward these lofty goals that perhaps have yet to be thought!

References

Apple, M. (2018). *The struggle for democracy in education: Lessons from social realities.* New York: Routledge.
Bassok, D., Latham, S., & Rorem, A. (2016). Is kindergarten the new first grade? *AERA Open,* 1(4), 1–31.
Bhabha, H. (2004). *The location of culture.* New York: Routledge.
Grieshaber, S.J. (2008). Interrupting stereotypes: Teaching and the education of young children. *Early Education and Development,* 19(3), 505–518.
Pinar, W. (2004). *What is curriculum theory?* Mahwah, NJ: Lawrence Earlbaum Associates.

CONTRIBUTOR BIOGRAPHIES

David P. Barry is a doctoral student at the University of Texas at Austin studying Early Childhood Education within the Department of Curriculum and Instruction. Before pursuing his PhD, David taught Kindergarten in the Boston Public Schools for ten years and was a Teaching Fellow at the Harvard Graduate School of Education for five years. His research interests include early childhood teacher education, early childhood teacher self-care, and the incorporation of trauma-informed teaching practices in early childhood learning spaces.

Katherine Bertolini is the Superintendent of Maple Valley Schools in Vermontville, MI. Her research interests have been in the areas of professional development for teachers, social justice, and deconstruction of educational silos across the PK-20 system. Her research has appeared in the *Journal of Early Childhood Teacher Education, Journal of Research in Childhood Education, Multicultural Education, Kappa Delta Pi Record*, and the *International Journal of Choice Theory and Reality Therapy*.

Mindy Blaise is a Vice-Chancellor's Professorial Research Fellow in the School of Education at Edith Cowan University, Western Australia. She is a co-founder (with Veronica Pacini-Ketchabaw and Affrica Taylor) of the Common Worlds Research Collective (www.commonworlds.net), and with Emily Gray and Linda Knight she co-founded #FEAS Feminist Educators Against Sexism (www.feministeducatorsagainstsexism.com). Mindy's research is grounded in a feminist ethic, and she is currently conducting a multisensory and affect-focused inquiry on children's relations with the more-than-human.

Christopher P. Brown is a Professor of Early Childhood Education in the Department of Curriculum and Instruction at the University of Texas at Austin. His research centers on how early childhood stakeholders across a range of political and educational contexts make sense of and respond to policymakers' reforms. He has looked at this issue across a range of contexts using multiple theoretical and practitioner-based perspectives that span the fields of early childhood education, curriculum and instruction, teacher education, and policy analysis. Through this work, his goal is to advocate for early learning environments that foster, sustain, and extend the complex educational, cultural, and individual goals and aspirations of teachers, children, and their families.

James P. Burns is an Assistant Professor of Curriculum Studies in the Department of Teaching and Learning at Florida International University. His research is situated in curriculum theory, specifically in masculinities studies and the genealogies of institutional power and violence. His research has been published in journals including *Peace Review*, *Education Policy Analysis Archives*, *The Journal for Critical Education Policy Studies*, *The Journal of the American Association for the Advancement of Curriculum Studies*, and *The Journal of Curriculum Theorizing*. He is the author of *Power, Curriculum, and Embodiment: Re-thinking Curriculum as Counter-Conduct and Counter-Politics* (Palgrave Macmillan).

Cary A. Buzzelli is Professor Emeritus of Early Childhood Education at Indiana University. He was a preschool teacher in the Child Development Laboratory Preschool at Purdue University and a faculty member in the School of Education at the University of Alabama at Birmingham. He co-authored with Bill Johnston a number of articles and the book *The Moral Dimensions of Teaching* (Routledge/Falmer, 2002). His recent publications examine the implications of the Capability Approach for curriculum development, teaching practices, and assessment and evaluation methods in early childhood education.

Katherine K. Delaney is an Assistant Professor of Early Childhood Education at the University of Toledo. Kate's research focuses on how teachers, children, and families experience the impacts of federal, state, and/or local policies in their daily lives in early childhood settings. Kate's recent work has been focused in Head Start and Title 1 preschool classrooms in Ohio. Long ago, Kate was a preschool teacher in New York City and Milwaukee, Wisconsin.

Nancy File is Kellner Professor of Early Childhood at the University of Wisconsin-Milwaukee. She earned her PhD from Purdue University. She began her career teaching children from ages 2 to 5. Her research interests revolve around children's experiences in classrooms as teachers shape their learning experiences. This has led to an interest in the topic of curriculum, particularly for children from infancy through 4 years of age. File has participated in two multi-site longitudinal studies of children's early childhood experiences. Her work has been disseminated in journals for both scholarly and practitioner audiences.

M. Elizabeth Graue is the Sorenson Professor of Early Childhood Education and Director of the Center for Research on Early Childhood Education at the University of Wisconsin Madison. A fellow of the American Educational Research Association, Graue has studied implementation of class size reduction programs, home school relations, kindergarten readiness, policy enactment in pre-K, and culturally and developmentally responsive early mathematics professional development. She is currently exploring how pre-K and kindergarten teachers develop rich play-based teaching contexts and improving instructional practices in pre-K programs.

Leslee Grey is an Associate Professor of Educational Foundations in the Department of Secondary Education and Youth Services at Queens College – CUNY. Grey earned a doctorate from Georgia State University, where she studied cultural and philosophical foundations of education, with concentrations in educational policy studies and qualitative research methodology, as well as women's and gender studies. She teaches historical, social, and philosophical foundations of education from a critical cultural theory perspective at both the undergraduate and graduate levels. Her scholarship offers several interrelated strands including privatization and education, gender studies and education, adolescent and youth culture, and teaching for social change. Grey's current work includes: critical investigation of school-business partnerships and corporate-sponsored educational reform movements; exploration of young adult literature relating to the schooling experiences of young people; and ethnographic study of the ways in which young people learn and negotiate multiple identities.

J. Amos Hatch is Professor Emeritus at the University of Tennessee. During his career in higher education, he published seven books and over 130 articles. He was executive editor of two highly regarded academic journals and served in numerous leadership roles in early childhood professional organizations, including a four-year term on the governing board of the National Association for the Education of Young Children.

Lucinda G. Heimer is Associate Professor and Program Coordinator of the Early Childhood/Special Education dual licensure program at University of Wisconsin-Whitewater. Dr. Heimer has published on topics including interdisciplinary curriculum and collaboration in the *Journal of Early Childhood Teacher Education, Global Studies of Childhood*, and *Early Years*, as well as chapters in multiple edited texts. Presentations include the use of critical theory, duoethnography, and decolonizing methodologies to illuminate future teacher perspectives regarding identity, race, and social justice in early education specifically working with Indigenous communities.

Diane M. Horm is the George Kaiser Family Foundation Endowed Chair of Early Childhood Education and Founding Director of the Early Childhood Education Institute (ECEI) at the University of Oklahoma-Tulsa. Prior to her 2006 OU appointment, she held faculty and administrative positions at the University of Rhode Island, including the Director of the URI Child Development Centers. Through the ECEI, Horm is currently leading several applied research initiatives including program evaluation research in collaboration with Tulsa's Educare and CAP Head Start Programs and a multi-year study with colleagues from Georgetown University to investigate children's development from pre-K through grade 4.

Deepti Kharod is an Assistant Professor at University of the Incarnate Word in San Antonio, Texas. She teaches preservice teachers in the Dreeben School of Education and enjoys sharing her research about young children, play, and early childhood environmental education.

Kyong-Ah Kwon is originally from Seoul, South Korea. Dr. Kwon is an Associate Professor at the University of Oklahoma-Tulsa. She received her doctoral degree in Developmental Studies from Purdue University. She has worked with children from birth through kindergarten in Korea and the US as a teacher for nine years. She is a dedicated researcher and teacher educator who is interested in children's early experiences at school and home and their relation to children's social emotional development and learning. She has received several internal and external grants to support her research on child development and early childhood education.

Deborah E. Laurin is an Assistant Professor at Eastern Michigan University with the Department of Early Childhood Education and the Research Chair for Pikler® USA, a nonprofit organization for the global well-being of children. Her research examines the care routines, specifically diapering, in infant and toddler group childcare. Deborah is interested in caregiver interactions that promote child well-being and involvement through bidirectional responsiveness. Deborah recently published articles about diapering practices in *ZERO-TO-THREE* and *Young Children*. She presented at the 2018 World Association for Infant Mental Health (WAIMH) and at the 2018 European Early Childhood Education Research conference (EECERA).

Sara Michael-Luna received her PhD in Curriculum and Instruction from the University of Wisconsin-Madison. She is an Associate Professor of Early Childhood Education at the University of Central Florida in the College of Community Innovation and Education, School of Teacher Education. She has published work in Pre-Kindergarten Curriculum, Literacy, and Academic Language.

Jennifer J. Mueller is currently serving as the Dean of the School of Education at St. Cloud State University in St. Cloud, Minnesota. After teaching young children for several years, she earned her PhD from the University of Michigan in teacher education, and then served as the Chair of the Early Childhood Education program at the University of Wisconsin-Milwaukee. Mueller's teaching and research has focused on effective preparation of teachers toward social justice and equity. She has examined how indices of identity shape and influence how teachers "take up" issues of diversity and multicultural education.

Christine Nganga is an Assistant Professor of Educational Leadership at the George Washington University. Her research interests include leadership for equity and social justice, pedagogical orientations of teaching for social justice, narrative inquiry, and mentoring theory and practice. Her work has been published in journals including *Educational Leadership Review*, *International Journal of Critical Pedagogy*, *Mentoring and Tutoring Journal*, and *Journal of Early Childhood Teacher Education*.

Elizabeth P. Quintero has been involved with early childhood and family education programs and as a teacher educator for many years in many different states and countries as teacher, program developer, curriculum specialist, and guiding supervisor. Her passion is programs serving families in multilingual communities that represent a variety of cultural and historical backgrounds. She is Professor and Chair of Early Childhood Studies at CSU Channel Islands.

Sharon Ryan is Professor of Early Childhood Education at Rutgers, the State University of New Jersey. Dr. Ryan uses a range of qualitative and mixed methods designs to research early childhood teacher education and professional development, curriculum, policy enactment, and the potential of critical theories for rethinking early childhood practices. She has published a number of articles, book chapters, and reports in these areas.

Andrew J. Stremmel is Professor of Early Childhood Education in the Department of Teaching, Learning, and Leadership at South Dakota State University. His research is in the areas of early childhood teacher research and Reggio Emilia-inspired, inquiry-based approaches to early childhood curriculum. He has co-edited or co-authored four books including *Teaching as Inquiry: Rethinking Curriculum in Early Childhood Education* (co-edited with Victoria Fu and Lynn Hill). Dr. Stremmel is executive editor of *Voices of Practitioners: Teacher Research in Early Childhood Education,* the National Association for the Education of Young Children's peer-reviewed, professional online journal for early childhood teacher researchers.

John A. Sutterby is an Associate Professor at the University of Texas San Antonio. His teaching focuses on action research methodology and play. His research focus has been on children's play and play environments, social justice and play and popular culture.

Kristin L. Whyte is an Assistant Professor at Mount Mary University. She began her career as an early childhood and public elementary school teacher in Milwaukee, WI. She received her PhD from the University of Madison in curriculum and instruction and completed post-graduate work at Northwestern University, conducting educational policy research. Kristin's teaching and research primarily focuses on early childhood teaching and learning, relationships between home and school, educational policies' impacts on schools, and the construction of socially just educational practices.

INDEX

Abecedarian Early Childhood Intervention Project 118
Abecedarian Study 116
academic achievement 23, 25, 26–7
academic failure 20
academic performance 22, 23
accountability 23, 72, 204; deprofessionalization of work 45; impact on early childhood curriculum 34; issues 20–1; narrowed learning experiences due to 45–6; and play 131–2; pressure on teachers 45; problems with 44–6; QRIS 24; results in devaluing individuals 46; shovedown 22–3, 54
accountability regime: curriculum packages, for early childhood Pre-K classrooms 43–7; English and Language Arts (ELA) 39; examining early childhood curriculum 34–48; National Association for the Education of Young Children (NAEYC) 39–40; National Council for Teachers of Mathematics (NCTM) 36–7; National Council of the Social Studies (NCSS) 38–9; Next Generation Science Standards (NGSS) 37; sources of standards 35; state-level early learning standards 40–2
ACEI *see* Association for Childhood Education International (ACEI)
ACF *see* Administration for Children and Families (ACF)

achievement gaps 70, 71, 73, 121–2, 158, 196, 203, 215
achievement test scores 3
Adair, J.K. 11, 26, 171, 173, 201
adequate yearly progress (AYP) 22
Administration for Children and Families (ACF) 98, 99
adult(s): child interaction 117; and children's play 134–5
advocacy 68, 211
African American children 3, 6, 26, 117, 118
age span, of early childhood 12, 35
agency 91, 161, 166, 170, 171–2, 182; teacher 118–19
Alarcón, Francisco X. 147
Alford, B.L. 25
alignment 35, 42, 47, 105–6, 120–1, 181, 211
Alkire, S. 163
alphabetic knowledge 6, 12
American Academy of Pediatrics 135
anti-racism 27, 134
Anzaldúa, Gloria 152, 155
Apple, M. 65, 76, 215
Areas of Interest 118
Arnold, D.H. 10
Arzubiaga, A.E. 201
assessments 185; boundaries 37; and curriculum 105; and evaluation changes 171; of individual

children's learning 117; practices 171–2; standardized 12
Association for Childhood Education International (ACEI) 21, 129
attentiveness 166, 196
audit culture 178–9, 181, 187, 188; essentialized 178, 187
Auger, A. 4
AYP *see* adequate yearly progress (AYP)

backward design 183–4
Bailey (teacher) 171–2
Baker, C.N. 10
Baker, D. 77
Ballenger, C. 6
Ballet, J. 163
Barad, K. 90
Barbarin, O.A. 6
Barry, David P. 17, 210
Bassok, D. 8–9
Becker, Gary 163
behavioral objectives 67, 69
behaviorist theory 214
behaviors 137; and emotions 120; and feelings 188; gap between child's thoughts and 180; learning 34; practicing desired 181
benchmark scores 11, 171
Berke, K. 104, 120
Bertolini, Katherine 177, 211
Bhabha, H. 212
bi-nationality 147, 149
Bickart, T. 120
Big Day for Pre-K 43
Biggeri, M. 163
bilingualism/biliteracy 123, 124, 153; summer programs 139
binary thinking 88–91
Bitler, M. 4
Bizzell, R.P. 3
Blaise, Mindy 80, 85, 210
Bloch, M. 67–8, 69
Blow, Susan 18
Bobbit, J.F. 66–7
Bojczyk, K.E. 10
Book Conversation Cards 105
Booker, B.M. 59
Boston Marathon 201–2
Brayko, K. 76
Bredekamp, S. 40, 47, 70–2
broadening, strategy of 134–5
Brown, Christopher P. 17, 27, 210
Bruner, J. 155

Bugbee, M.R. 11
Bullough, R.V. Jr. 25–6
Burchinal, M. 4
Burns, James P. 177, 211
Burts, D. 120
Bush Administration 23, 41
Butera, G. 10
Butler, J. 85
Buzzelli, Cary A. 161, 211
Byrnes, J.P. 4

C3 Framework 38
CA *see* Capability Approach (CA)
Cannella, G. 69
Cannon, J. 58
Capability Approach (CA) 162–3; changing discourse in ECE 165–73; children's abilities 168–70; and education 163–5; implications and speculations 166–8, 169–70; moral framework for curriculum development 171–3; moral language of 167–8; normative language for early childhood education 165–6
caregiver-child interactions 97–100, 101, 109
"carrying our roots" idea 147, 150, 152, 155
Cedillo, S. 27
Charters, W.W. 66–7
Chazan-Cohen, R.C. 99–100, 106
Chen, R 133
Chicago Parent Centers 196
The Child and the Curriculum (Dewey) 187
child-based decision-making 45
child care centers 104, 136
child-centered curricula 52, 87
child development 67; DAP *see* developmentally appropriate practice (DAP); and early childhood education 51–61; learning and development 55–6; math and science learning 57–60; moral approach to 165–6; and occupational therapists 101; PITC and developmental theory 103–4; promoting 203; suggestions from psychologists 116; theories 146, 156; understanding 13, 19
Child Observation Record (COR) assessment 121
children: abilities as capabilities 168–9, 211; autonomy of 119; child-guided activities 53; child-initiated activity 52; considerations, of play 133–4; museums 138–9; performances 210; risk factors for

201; role in curriculum 9–11; teacher-assigned activities 6; teaching alphabet knowledge in 6; threat of pressure on 44
Children's Bureau 18
civil rights 162
"clarification" statements 37
Cleaver, J. 138
Clements, D.H. 8
Clinton Administration 21
cognition/general knowledge domain 41
cognitive development 55, 57–8, 120, 130; for preschoolers 40
cognitive scientists 57–8
Colegrove, K.S. 11, 26, 171, 173
The College, Career, and Civic Life (C3) Framework for Social Studies State Standards see C3 Framework
colonialism 85–6, 87; de-colonialism 27; see also postcolonialism
Comim, F. 163
commercialization, of popular media 135–6
Common Core State Standards 24, 114–15, 120–1, 198, 211
complicated conversations 146, 148, 150, 211; curricula as 178; spaces for 177–91
Comprehensive Child Development Act of 1971 29
Conocimiento Theory 146, 152, 154, 155
Consortium for Longitudinal Studies 2, 3
constrained skills 12; literacy-related 214
content: knowledge based on 201–2, 214; learning focused on 200; learning steeped in 213; Creative Curriculum 105; developmental theory and 53, 54, 55; infant-toddler curriculum 105, 108; responsiveness with 200–3
contexts, and stories 149–50
continuity of care 98, 102
continuum, of teaching strategies 54
conversion factors 167, 172; examining 173
Copple, C. 40, 47, 70–2
COR assessment *see* Child Observation Record (COR) assessment
Cordero, M.I. 58
Cornbleth, C. 66, 73
correlation matrices 35, 48
Crawford, G.M. 6
Creative Curriculum 43, 45; development 105–6, 117–18; education policy on 120–2; English learners 122–4; and High/Scope 4–5, 115–16; implications and opportunities 118–19; for Infants & Toddlers 104–6; standards and assessment 120–2
critical theory 64, 69, 73, 146; engaging with 80–92; gender 83–4; importance, to early childhood curriculum 91–2; post-structuralism 82–3; race and ethnicity 85–7; review of 81; sexuality 84–5; troubling Western logic 88–91
critical thinking skills 12, 163, 202, 205
Cross, C.T. 58
cultural deficiencies 122
cultural wealth 27
currere method 185
curriculum: and assessment 105; bureaucratic rationalization of 177; as complicated conversation 178; defined 7–9, 65; in early childhood 52; ECE curriculum *see* early childhood education (ECE) curriculum; episodes 66; evidence based 70; examination of 6; focal points 36; focused on hope and possibility 188; history of 65–72; importance of 7–9; outcomes of 12–13; packages for early childhood Pre-K classrooms 43–7; and possibilities 188–90; prescriptive 211; re-understanding 185–6, 188, 190; and research 1–14; studies 65–6; teachers and children role in 9–11; working of 2–7
curriculum theory 64–78; historical overview 65–72; impact on practice 72–4; technocratic view 66–8

Dahlberg, G. 28, 70, 145
Daily Resources 105
DAP *see* developmentally appropriate practice (DAP)
Davies, B. 83–4, 85
Davis, K. 86
Dean, A. 99–100, 106
DeBruin-Parecki, A. 41
decision making 47, 195; curricular 25–6, 45; instructional 28, 36; responsive 214
deficit perspective 11, 26, 122, 153, 158; assumptions 171
Delaney, K. 10, 193, 206, 211
Deleuze, G. 87–8, 90
DeMarie, D. 140
democratic participation 65, 68, 77, 210, 215
democratization 148
Deneulin, S. 163, 165–6, 172
deprofessionalization 45
Derrida, J. 54

224 Index

desired outcomes: in early childhood 210; in learning 34, 184
developmental constructivism 130
Developmental Foundations of School Readiness for Infants and Toddlers 98
developmental theory 51, 155; and early childhood curriculum and instruction 55–7; *see also* child development
developmentalist perspective 66, 67, 69, 115
developmentally appropriate practice (DAP) 1, 13, 21, 35, 37, 39–40, 52, 72, 80, 83, 116, 167; curriculum theory 69, 73; five domains of 120
Developmentally Appropriate Practice in Early Childhood Programs Serving Children from Birth through Age 8 see developmentally appropriate practice (DAP)
Dewey, John 182, 187–8; Laboratory School 74
Diamond, K.E. 10
digital play 136
disciplinary core 37
disciplines 26, 53, 54, 58
discrimination 26, 86, 150
DLM Early Childhood Express math software 3
Dockett, S. 132
Dodge, D. 104, 117–18, 123
Dodge, K.A. 8–9
Dombkowski, K. 18
Domina, T. 4
dominant discourses 26, 74, 158, 178
dual language: classrooms 124; learners 122, 125, 157
Duijkers, D. 134
Duncan, G.J. 4, 5
Duschl, R.A. 59

early childhood education (ECE) curriculum 1, 52–4, 193–206, 209–15; and Capability Approach (CA) 161–73; context 195–6; current policies 24–5; and developmental theory 55–7; evolution of 18, 65; future of 28–9; impact of curricular policies 27–8; policy impact on teachers' curricular decision-making 25–6; investment and 196–7; responsiveness and content in 200–3; pedagogy 198–9; policymakers' reforms 26–7; post-NCLB *see* post-NCLB; pre-NCLB *see* pre-NCLB; play in 129–40 *see also* play; readiness in 197–8; supporting and advocating for practice 203–6; *see also* accountability regime; critical theory; preschool curriculum
Early Childhood Environment Rating Scale 4, 170
Early Childhood Longitudinal Study (ECLS) 25
Early, D.M. 6
Early Head Start programs 42, 97, 105, 197
Early Learning Outcomes Framework 25, 42, 44, 105
early learning standards (ELS) 23, 25, 34, 121; state-level 35, 40–2, 105
ECE curriculum *see* early childhood education (ECE) curriculum
ECLS *see* Early Childhood Longitudinal Study (ECLS)
economic freedom 162
Economic Opportunity Act 20
education: and Capability Approach (CA) 163–5; framing of 203; inequalities of opportunity 169; instrumental and intrinsic value of 168, 169; pursuit of reform initiatives 21
educational experiences 45, 177, 180–1, 187, 189, 196
educational purpose 180–5
Edwards, S. 135
effectiveness 119, 169; of curriculum 3, 181; of ECE 1; educational 109; of PITC 103–4; of research 2; of RIE 102; of teachers 23
Eisenband, J.G. 58
ELA *see* English and Language Arts (ELA)Elementary and Secondary Education Act (ESEA) 20
elementary schools 67; post-NCLB 22–3; and standards-based accountability reform 21–2
Eliason, C. 60
Elicker, J. 99–100, 106
ELS *see* early learning standards (ELS)
Emmi Pikler Day Care 101
emotions 130, 187; and behaviors 120–1; *see also* social–emotional development
engaged learning 204
English and Language Arts (ELA) 39, 121; curricula 114–25_
English language: children with home languages other than 71, 153–4, 201; learners of 44, 122–4, 145, 149, 156, 157, 171;

environments 117; infant-toddler curriculum and 103; learning 202–3; for play 134
Epstein, A.S. 53, 124
"Equality of What?" (Sen) 172
ESEA *see* Elementary and Secondary Education Act (ESEA)
essentialized curriculum 178–9, 189, 190
ethnicity/race 3, 6, 81, 85–7
Every Students Succeeds Act 24
executive function 12, 131
experimentation 89–90, 91
expertise knowledge 35, 144

"fabric of habits", formation of 177, 180
facilitation, of learning 98, 179
family history, and multilingual children 145, 146–8, 149, 150–7
Farquhar, S. 72
Farran, D.C. 7, 8, 11, 12
Fátima (student teacher) 152
Federal Emergency Relief Administration (FERA) 19
fidelity 8, 10, 47, 73, 104, 107, 214
File, Nancy 1, 34, 209, 210, 213
Firmender, J.M. 4
Fish, L.E. 102
Fitzsimons, P. 72
Foucault, M. 81–2, 181
The Foundation (Creative Curriculum) 105, 118
Framework for K-12 Science Education 37
Frankfurt school 81
free play 45, 58, 101, 131, 194
freedom 161, 166, 170; of movement 100; political 162; social freedoms 162; substantive 167
Freire, P. 54, 146
Friesen, A. 10
Froebel, F. 18
Frog Street Pre-K 43, 46
Frost, J. 136
"functionings" (Sen) 162, 173
Funds of Knowledge concept 27, 75, 200–1, 202

Gadamer, H.G. 185
Gainer, J. 134, 139
Galanter, M. 58
Gallas, K. 6
GDP *see* gross domestic product (GDP)gender: critical theory 83–4, 85; issues of 81
Georgia, Pre-K programs in 43
Gerber, M. 101
Gerde, H.K. 10
Gibbons, A. 131–2
ginekanwa ("What is greater than a child?") 188
Ginsburg, H.P. 58
Giroux, H.A. 179
Giugni (teacher-researcher) 83
Global North/South 147, 150, 152, 155
Goals 2000 legislation 21
Goffin, S. 68
Gold Assessment System (Creative Curriculum) 105, 106
Gonzalez, Emma 186
Good Start, Grow Smart (GSGS) initiative 23, 41
Gordon, K. 102
Goulet, D. 166, 169
Graue, E. 10, 193, 206, 211
Great Depression 19, 68
Grey, L. 114, 119, 210
Grieshaber, S.J. 213
Groark, C.J. 102
Gronlund, G. 46–7
Grumet, M. 178
GSGS initiative *see* Good Start, Grow Smart (GSGS) initiative
Guattari, F. 87–8, 90
The Guide 105
Gupta, A. 85
Guss, S. 98

Habermas, J. 81
Hall, G. Stanley 19, 67
Hall-Kenyon, K.M. 25–6
hands-off approach, to play 130, 131, 134–5
Harkins, D. 102
Hart, B. 26
Haskins, R. 8–9
Hatch, J.A. 22, 43, 44–7, 51, 190, 210
Head Start Designation Renewal System (HS-DRS) 197
Head Start project 4, 5, 20–1, 105, 114, 117, 136, 169; Early Learning Outcomes Framework 25, 42, 44, 105; and publicly funded preschool 23
Heckman, J. 20, 196
Hedges, Helen 202
Heimer, Lucinda G. 114, 210
Heroman, C. 120

heteronormativity 85
(hetero)sexuality 81, 83, 84–5
"high-stakes" assessments 22
Highlights Hello 105
High/Scope curriculum 115–16, 200; education policy on 120–2; English learners 122–4; implications and opportunities 118–19; standards and assessment 120–2
Hogg, David 186
Holt, John 189
homeschooling 136–7
horizon, concept of 185
Horm, D. 96, 98, 210
Hu, G. 27
Huerta, M. 139
human capital model 163–4, 168
human capital theory 20, 163–5, 168, 169
human rights discourse 163, 164, 165
humanizing curriculum 189
Hybertson, D.W. 11

IASA *see* Improving American Schools Act (IASA)
identity *see* ethnicity/race; gender; sexuality
IELS *see* International Early Learning and Child Well-being Study (IELS)
Igbu people 188
Ilia (student teacher) 152
immigrants 18, 26, 124, 133, 149, 171
Improving American Schools Act (IASA) 21
Including Relationship-Based Care Practices in Infant-Toddler Care 98
inclusion 54, 103, 108, 210
Indigenous ontology 86
individuality 182–3
individualization, of curriculum 46, 48
infant-toddler curriculum 96–109; comparison of three curricula 106–8; Creative Curriculum 104–6; development 99; future directions 106–9; Program for Infant/Toddler Care (PITC) 102–4; programs 195; Resources for Infant Educarers (RIE) 100–2; review of research on 97–100
Inhelder, B. 59
Institute of Medicine (IOM) 99
instrumental freedoms 162
instrumental schooling 179–80, 186
integrated curriculum 145–7; contexts and stories 149–50; family history and theoretical musings 150–7; "Matters of Concern" theory 157–8; third space through 147–9; *see also* project approach
The Intentional Teacher (Epstein) 53
Intentional Teaching Cards 105
Interest Areas (Creative Curriculum) 118
International Early Learning and Child Well-being Study (IELS) 168, 170
intra-active pedagogy 90
investment, EC education as 20, 24, 85, 196–8, 203, 214
IOM *see* Institute of Medicine (IOM)
Iruka, I.U. 6

Jarrett, O. 132, 140
Jenkins, J.M. 4, 5
Jenkins, L. 60
Johnson Administration 20
Jones, C. 120
Justice, L.M. 10

K-3 schools 40, 196
K-12 education 38, 41, 120, 196
Kaefer, T. 12
Kagan, S.L. 41
Kamii, C. 59
Kane, N. 133
Kaplan, R.G. 58
Key Developmental Indicators, for language 124
Kharod, Deepti 129, 210
Kinard, T. 134, 139
Kind, S. 91
kindergarten 3, 7, 21, 25, 35, 37, 39,42–4, 46–7, 54, 58–60, 72, 131,132, 137, 153, 169, 195, 196, 197–8: post-NCLB 22–3; pre-NCLB 18–19; *see also* pre-kindergarten
Kliebard, H. 66, 67–8, 74, 182
knowledge: acquisition of 125; content-based 214; multiple sources of 146; and power 69–70, 82–3, 92
Kocher, L.M. 91
Kriener-Althen, K. 99–100, 106
Kruse, T. 124
Kuhl, P. 148
Kupersmidt, J.B. 10
Kwon, Kyong-Ah 96, 210

Laboratory School (Dewey) 74

Lan, Y. 27
language 82; acquisition of 123, 149, 154; communication domain 41; and discourse, examination of 88
language arts *see* English and Language Arts (ELA)
Lanham Act 18
Larremore, A. 85
Latino/a/x 150, 151, 153; children 6, 26, 102; families 201; immigrants 171
Latour, B. 157–8
Laurin, Deborah E. 96, 98, 210
Lea (student teacher) 152
Learn Every Day 43, 45
learning 48, 214; appropriate 10; behaviors 34; children's 8; development and 55–6; engaged 204; environments 202–3; experiences 181; facilitation of 179; knowledge and 200; math and science 57–60; objectives 120; play and 130–1, 199; student 180; time 132; of vocabulary words 12
Learning Games 105
Lee, J.E. 26
Lee, S. 135
Lenz Taguchi, H. 73, 90
Lewis, B.A. 59
lines of flight 89
Lionni, Leo 6
Lipman, M. 54
Lipman, P. 122
Lipsey, M.W. 8–9
Literacy (Creative Curriculum) 118, 121
literacy 4, 40, 41, 121, 162; activities 6, 8; assessments 12; bilingual 123–4, 149; curricula focused on 4; in integrated curricula 145; neoliberal 27; practices 195; through stories 155, 156, 157
locally developed curricula 4
Loczy Institute, Budapest 101
Loh, J. 27

MacKay, K.L. 25–6
MacNaughton, G. 53–4, 83, 86
Malewski, E. 68, 77
Mantilla, A. 135
Mardell, B. 6
Marjorie Stoneman High School (Parkland, Florida) 186
Marshall, E.E. 25–6
Marx, K. 81
material feminism 90

mathematics 193, 195, 200; curricula 3–4, 5, 8–9; learning 36, 57–60; literacy and 41; NTCM standards 36–7; practices 195; science learning and 57–60
Mathematics (Creative Curriculum) 118
"Matters of Concern" theory 146, 157–8
Matthews, T.J. 12
McCall, R. 102
McManus, M.E. 26
McTighe, J. 184
meaning-making 146, 148, 150–1, 155
media and technology, in play 135–6
Meier, D. 27
Michael-Luna, S. 114, 119, 210
Might Minutes 105
Mihai, A. 10
Miller, L.B. 3, 11
missing addends 59
Mixtec community 149, 152, 153–4, 157
Morgenlander, M. 58
Moss, P. 28, 70, 72, 77, 145
Mueller, Jennifer J. 34, 64, 209, 210, 212, 213
multilingualism 124; children 144–59, 210
Muñoz (student teacher) 154–5

NACCRRA *see* National Association of Childcare Resource & Referral Agencies (NACCRRA)
NAEYC *see* National Association for the Education of Young Children (NAEYC)
A Nation at Risk (NCEE) 21
National Association for the Education of Young Children (NAEYC) 21, 35, 39–40, 42, 52, 116, 121, 129, 196; Code of Ethical Conduct 167; DAP *see* developmentally appropriate practice (DAP); technology in classroom 135
National Association of Childcare Resource & Referral Agencies (NACCRRA) 102
National Commission on Excellence in Education (NCEE) 21
National Council for Teachers of Mathematics (NCTM) 36–7
National Council of Teachers of English and the International Reading Association (NCTE/IRA) 39
National Council of the Social Studies (NCSS) 38–9
National Education Goals Panel (NEGP) 98

National Institute of Education 20
National Research Council (NRC) 58, 99
National Science Teachers Association 37
nature preschools 136, 137–8
NCEE *see* National Commission on Excellence in Education (NCEE)
NCLB *see* No Child Left Behind (NCLB) Act
NCSS *see* National Council of the Social Studies (NCSS)
NCTM *see* National Council for Teachers of Mathematics (NCTM)
NEGP *see* National Education Goals Panel (NEGP)
Nelson, K. 145, 150, 155–7
neoliberalism 24, 27
Neuman, S.B. 12
Next Generation and Common Core State Standards 120
Next Generation Science Standards (NGSS) 37, 114
Nganga, Christine 177, 211
NGSS *see* Next Generation Science Standards (NGSS)
Nguyen, T. 4, 5
Nixon administration 20
No Child Left Behind (NCLB) Act 17, 72, 180, 198, 210
non-traditional schools, homeschooling and 136–7
normative language 165–6, 170
NRC *see* National Research Council (NRC)
nursery schools 19
Nussbaum, M. 163, 165
Nuttall, J. 135
Nxumalo, F. 27, 87

Obama Administration 23
Objectives for Development and Learning (Creative Curriculum) 118, 120
Oklahoma State Pilot Program to Expand and Enhance Infant/Toddler Services 109
Olsson, L.M. 89
open-ended curricula, teacher agency in 115, 118–19, 124–5
Opening the World of Learning (OWL) 43, 46
OPRE study 114
orienting, strategy of 134
othering/otherness 85–6, 185
OWL *see* Opening the World of Learning (OWL)

Pacini-Ketchabaw, V. 86, 91
Padrón, Y.N. 25
Paley, V. 6
parent attitudes, and play 133
Parent-Infant Guidance Classes 101
Patte, M. 132
Paulsell, D. 99–100, 106
Payne, K. 76
PCER Consortium *see* Preschool Curriculum Evaluation Research (PCER) Consortium
Peabody Picture-Vocabulary Test 12
pedagogistas (consulting teachers) 75
pedagogy 67, 73, 74, 80, 124–5, 196, 198–9 200–1; intra-active 90; story as 147, 147, 148; study of 67
Pence, A. 28, 145
Pence, K.L. 10
performance expectations 37
Perry Preschool 116, 196
Phillips, D.A. 8–9
Piaget, J. 40, 51, 55–7, 59, 116, 130, 213; developmental theory compared with Vygotsky's 55–6; notion of reversibility 59; science and math learning 57–8
Pianta, R.C. 6
Pikler, E. 100–1; Pikler approach 100–2
Pinar, W. 65, 68, 80, 148, 186
Pinkham, A. 12
PITC *see* Program for Infant/Toddler Care (PITC)
Plan-Do-Review cycle of learning 117
play 210, 213; and accountability 131–2; adults setting stage for 134–5; alternative places for 136–40; areas for growth 140; challenges to 131; children's considerations 133–4; children's museums 138–9; in early childhood curriculum 129–40; and learning 130–1; media and technology in 135–6; nature preschools 137–8; parent attitudes 133; summer school programs 139; teacher attitudes 132–3; unschooling movement 136–7
positive outcomes 44, 70, 103, 134
possibilities, curricular 186–8
post-NCLB: current ECE policy and curriculum 24–5; Head Start and publicly funded preschool 23; kindergarten and elementary school 22–3; Pre-K reform 23; Quality Rating

Improvement Systems (QRIS) 24; RTT-ELC 23–4
post-structuralism 81, 82–3, 88; feminist 83, 84
postcolonialism 85–7
posthumanism 87–8; philosophers 87
postmodernism 69, 81, 87–8
poverty: children in 71, 97; effects of 169; overcoming through education 116–17; war on 20, 69, 116
Powell, D.R. 2, 7, 10
power: critical theory 82–5, 92; knowledge and 82–3, 92
Power, J.R. 4
practitioners 76
pre-kindergarten (pre-K) programs 4, 23, 25, 35, 43, 98, 198; research about 8–9; standards 120–1; state-/public-funded 47, 197; universal 114–15, 119, 129, 169
pre-NCLB: elementary school and SBA reform 21–2; Head Start project 20–1; kindergarten 18–19; nursery schools 19
pre/in-service teachers 28, 59–60, 76, 133
preschool curriculum 2–3; creative curriculum 117–18; early childhood curriculum as policy 115–16; education policy on Creative Curriculum and High/Scope enactment 120–2; English learners 122–4; high/scope 116–17; historical development and description 116; teacher agency in open-ended curricula 118–19
Preschool Curriculum Evaluation Research (PCER) Consortium 2–3, 4
preschools 2–4, 6, 40, 83–4, 91, 99, 106, 107–9, 136, 149, 194–5, 196–7, 199; curricula, open-ended 114–25; nature 137–8; publicly funded 23
prescriptive curriculum 211
primary care 98, 103
The Principles to Action: Ensuring Mathematical Success for All 36
"probable destination" 67
problem-solving 195; spaces 38
professional development 76, 105–6, 107–8, 109, 204; teachers in 10, 17, 75, 214
Program for Infant/Toddler Care (PITC): new developments 103; overview 102–3; PITC-Program Assessment Rating System (PITC-PARS) 103; recent research 103–4
project approach 75, 167, 200

Project Follow Through 5
psychology 67–8, 80; cultural 58; developmental 70, 131
public policy, and early childhood curriculum, in US 17–29
publicly funded ECE programs 20, 22, 23
push down curriculum 125, 132

QRIS *see* Quality Rating and Improvement Systems (QRIS)
qualitative research 7, 9–10, 218
Quality Rating and Improvement Systems (QRIS) 24, 97, 109, 197
quantitative research 7, 10–11, 13
queer theory 84–5
Quintero, Elizabeth P. 6, 144, 210, 212

Race to the Top initiative 23–4, 180
race/ethnicity 3, 6, 81, 85–7
Raikes, H.H. 99–100, 106
readiness 7, 11, 76–7, 114, 197–8
Reading First initiative 18, 22
reconceptualization 64, 69–74, 178, 179
reflecting, strategy of 135
Reggio Emilia approach 75, 167, 200
Reifel, S. 131, 133
research: and curriculum 1–14; and ECE 1; effectiveness of 2; knowledge 2; language acquisition 123
Resource Organizer 105
Resources for Infant Educarers (RIE): new developments 101–2; overview 100–1; recent research 102
return on investment (ROI) approach 20, 196
Reynolds, W. 68, 80
Rhee, Michelle 181
rhizomatic logic 90
"rhythm of the heart" project 89
Ricoeur, P. 185
RIE *see* Resources for Infant Educarers (RIE)
Risley, T.R. 26
Ritchie, S. 6
Robeyns, I. 161, 163
Rockefeller Memorial Foundation 19
ROI approach *see* return on investment (ROI) approach
Rollins, K.B. 25

routines 6, 102, 105, 106, 117; caregiving 98, 100
Rudick, S. 104
Ryan, Sharon 80, 210

Santi, M. 163
Sarama, J. 8
SBA reform *see* standards-based accountability (SBA) reform
scholarly rationale 38
school readiness 17, 20, 22, 23, 26–7, 98, 98–9, 103, 105, 108, 131, 133
Schultz, Theodore 163
Schurz, Margarethe Meyer 18
Schweingruber, H. 58, 59
science 48n1, 48n3, 66, 67–8, 90; content, genuine 59; learning 37, 57–60; in nursery schools 19; standards 37; teaching 6
Scott, D. 66–7
Scott-Little, C. 41
secure attachment 104
Segal, G. 59
self-efficacy 10
self-realization 148
Sen, A. 161–73
Serrano, G. 102
sexuality 84–5
Shahani, L. 163
Shaw, Pauline 19
Sherwood, S.A.S. 133
Shouse, A.W. 59
skills: constrained/unconstrained 12; testable 198
Slattery, P. 68, 80
Slutzky, C. 41
small groups 5, 86, 103, 132, 135
Snow, C.E. 12
social efficiency 66, 179
social–emotional development 41, 104, 119social justice 134; and play 139, 140
Social Learning and Piklerian Observation 101social meliorists 66, 68, 69
social policy 131, 134
social studies education 38–9
socio-dramatic play 130–1
Spanish laguage 46, 103, 123, 149, 153, 156special education 154, 156: placement in 3, 118
Spelman, Laura 19
Spock, Michael 138
Srinivasan, P. 86

Stallings, J. 5–6
standardization 12, 27, 72, 114, 120, 124; of assessments 179, 185; sources of 35
standards-based accountability (SBA) reform 21–2, 23, 25, 27
standards-based context 214
standards-based instruction, threats resulting from 43
Standards for English and the Language Arts (ELA) 39
standards overload 40, 45
state-level early learning standards 35, 40–2, 105
Stebbins-Frelow, V. 41
STEM fields (science, technology, engineering and mathematics) 57
Stenhouse, V. 140
stories: and integrated curriculum 144–59; as pedagogy 146
Stremmel, Andrew J. 177, 211
structuring and deepening, strategy of 134
subjectivity 82–3, 84
summer school programs 136, 139, 198
superheroes, children's interest in 151
surveillance, system of 179, 182, 183
Sutterby, J. 11, 129, 140, 210

Taft, W.H. 18
Taubman, P. 68, 80
Taylor, A. 86
Te Whariki 167
Teacher Interactions with Infants and Toddlers 98
teachers: agency in open-ended curricula 118–19; as agents of democracy 27; attitudes, and play 132–3; child interactions 98; as co-learners 204; curriculum fidelity, variation in 10; education programs 27–8; educators 76–7; implications and opportunities 118–24; policy impact on curricular decision-making 25–6; pre-service 76; professional development 108; responses to children 194; role in curriculum 9–11, 105; self-efficacy 10
teaching: hands-off 134; responsive 214; strategies 53–4, 67
Teaching Strategies 104–6, 117–18; GOLD® 120
technocratic view, of curriculum 66–8, 71, 72

technology, in play 135–6
test scores 170, 188, 211
theory/practice divide 73
thick democracy 65, 75, 76
third spaces 145, 147–9, 212–13
Tobin, J. 201
transformative actions 146, 150
Transforming the Workforce for Children Birth Through Age 8: A Unifying Foundation 99
Tyler, R. 66–7, 177, 179–82, 183–4
Tyler Rationale 179–80, 183–4

UbD *see* Understanding by Design (UbD)
"underlife", of children's play 133
Understanding by Design (UbD) 183–4
United States: Department of Education 3; public policy and ECE in 17–29
Universal Pre-Kindergarten (UPK) policy 114, 119
unschooling movement 136–7, 140
Unterhalter, E. 163
UPK *see* Universal Pre-Kindergarten (UPK) policy

Van Oers, B. 134
Viruru, R. 85
vocabulary development, proactive 70
Voegler-Lee, M.E. 10
Vygotsky, L. 51, 116, 129, 130, 190; developmental theory, compared with Piaget's 55–6; zone of proximal development 56

Walker, M. 163
Waller, T. 136
Wang, A.H. 4
war on poverty 20, 69, 116
Waxman, H.C. 25
We Can Early Learning Curriculum 43
Weikart, David 116
Weiland, C. 8–9
well-being 161, 166, 167

WestEd Program for Infant Toddler Care 102
Western logic, critical theory and 88–91
Westinghouse Learning Corporation 20
"What Works Clearinghouse" initiative 3
"what works" approach 1, 3, 5, 11, 27
Whitaker, A. A 4, 5
whiteness, discourses of 86
"whole child" approach 4, 5, 9, 18, 108, 187, 214
Whyte, K. 10, 64, 193, 210, 211, 212
Wiggins, A.K. 10
Wiggins, G. 184
Williams, G. 53–4
Willoughby, M.T. 10
Winn, D.C. 6
Wisconsin Model Early Learning Standards (WMELS) 121
Wisneski, D. 131
WMELS *see* Wisconsin Model Early Learning Standards (WMELS)
Wood, E. 133, 135
Woodcock-Johnson battery 12
Woods, T.A. 58
word gap 26
Works Progress Administration (WPA) 19

Yahya, R. 133
Yosso, T.J. 27

Zaslow, M. 99–100, 106
Zeanah, C. 102
Zeichner, K. 76
zeitgeist 97, 99, 108
Zero to Three 42
zone of proximal development 56, 129

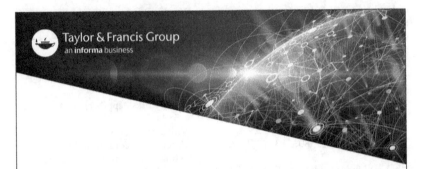